The Quest

Haywood Hansell and American Strategic Bombing in World War II

CHARLES GRIFFITH

Air University Press
Maxwell Air Force Base, Alabama

September 1999

Library of Congress Cataloging-in-Publication Data

Griffith, Charles, 1957–
   The quest : Haywood Hansell and American strategic bombing in World War II /
Charles Griffith.
     p.   cm.
   Includes bibliographical references and index.
   1. World War, 1939–1945—Aerial operations, American. 2. Bombing, Aerial—History.
3. Strategy. 4. Hansell, Haywood S. 5. Generals—United States Biography. 6. United
States. Army Air Forces Biography. I. Title.
   D790.G732 1999
   940.54'4973—dc21   99-43324
                                                             CIP
   ISBN 1-58566-069-8

Disclaimer

This book is dedicated
to my son, Alexander Griffith,
and to the memory of
Lt Col Theodore B. Brydges, USAF.

Contents

Photographs

Foreword

Maj Gen Haywood "Possum" Hansell Jr. was the first legendary airman from the interwar years and World War II I had the opportunity to meet on a personal basis. This happened in 1972 when I was on the faculty of the history department at the Air Force Academy. From that experience I became a lifelong admirer of General Hansell and his gracious wife, Dotta. He was a gentleman of great intellect who continued throughout his life to be an active student of history, a lecturer, and a spokesman who articulated the advantages of airpower.

I first heard of Hansell 12 years earlier when I was a cadet studying the history of airpower. The Air Force had been an independent service for less than 15 years. Much of the history being taught focused on the contributions of a few airmen who were visionary thinkers with an almost zealous belief in the potential of airpower to change the nature of warfare. The key to achieving the promise was the ability to conduct air operations independent of ground forces with an objective of taking the war directly to the enemy heartland in daylight precision attacks against key industrial and military targets. The theory held that such attacks conducted against a strategic target array would destroy an enemy's ability to field and support military forces by destroying his capacity to manufacture and transport war materials.

In his book *The Quest: Haywood Hansell and American Strategic Bombing in World War II*, Charles Griffith makes a major contribution in detailing the role played by General Hansell from his early days as an instructor at the Air Corps Tactical School to the heady days and nights as a young war planner developing the air war plan used by the United States during World War II to his triumphs and disappointments as a commander in the field. While the book tells this story well, it does more than just relate the life and times of Possum Hansell. The book goes a long way toward explaining the origins of many of the arguments about the utility of airpower in the closing decade of the twentieth century.

The bottom line is Hansell had it right—technology and time have made his vision a reality as evidenced by Desert Storm in 1991, Bosnia in 1995, and most recently in Kosovo. At the heart of his vision was the idea of airpower as a tool for precision engagement, not an indiscriminate weapon of mass destruction. A tool that, if properly understood and employed, would allow the United States to prevail while greatly reducing the price of victory.

RONALD R. FOGLEMAN
General, USAF, Retired

CHARLES GRIFFITH

About the Author

Charles Griffith received a bachelor's and master's degree in history from East Tennessee State University and earned his doctorate in military history from the University of Tennessee. He teaches advance placement American history and serves as chairman of the social studies department at Science Hill High School in Johnson City, Tennessee. Dr. Griffith also serves as adjunct professor of history at East Tennessee State University.

Introduction

On the night of 24 November 1944, B-29 Superfortresses landed in the darkness of Saipan with only smudge pots alongside the runway to light their path. Inside the control tower an anxious Brig Gen Haywood Hansell awaited their return. The bombers were returning from the first bombing mission over Tokyo since Jimmy Doolittle's famous raid in 1942. This time the raid consisted of 111 heavy bombers. Their target was the Nakajima-Musashino aircraft factory complex, not token targets to boost American morale. Hansell had been warned by the chief of the Army Air Forces, Gen Henry H. "Hap" Arnold, that experts had predicted that the raid as Hansell had planned it was almost certainly doomed to fail, and Arnold had placed full responsibility for the raid on Hansell's shoulders. In addition to this ominous warning, Brig Gen Emmett "Rosie" O'Donnell, commander of the 73d Bombardment Wing, which was executing the mission, had written a letter to Hansell in which he advocated abandoning the planned daylight mission in favor of a safer night mission. Since the very idea of a night bombing mission ran counter to all that Hansell believed about strategic bombing, Hansell rejected the idea. Now, after hours of "sweating out" the mission, Hansell's decision was vindicated. Of the 111 bombers that had launched early that morning, 88 had attacked targets in Japan and only two B-29s failed to return; Hansell had proved that American heavy bombers could conduct daylight operations over the Japanese home islands without prohibitive losses. This was Hansell's moment of triumph. This triumph would all too soon be followed by the tragedy of his dismissal, the end of his career, and the temporary end of the strategic bombing doctrine he had done so much to formulate and execute.

Haywood Hansell is arguably the most important proponent and practitioner of high-altitude, daylight precision bombing in the United States Army Air Forces in World War II. Even though his name is not as immediately recognized as the names of Chennault, Spaatz, Doolittle, LeMay, Eaker, or

Arnold, Hansell's accomplishments are significant and impressive. He flew as a stunt pilot in the barnstorming days with Claire Chennault. He later attended and taught at the Air Corps Tactical School, where he helped formulate America's prewar air doctrine. He then took a leading role in preparing the three great air war plans (AWPD-1, AWPD-42, and the plan for the Combined Bomber Offensive) for the strategic bombing campaign against Nazi Germany. He commanded the only operational B-17 wing in England from January to June 1943 and had thus directed the first American bombing missions over Germany. Then, at the request of General Arnold, he returned to Washington to create the world's first global striking force, the Twentieth Air Force. As chief of staff of the Twentieth Air Force, Hansell was given virtually a free hand to oversee the early missions of the XX Bomber Command in distant China. Then as commander of the XXI Bomber Command in the Marianas, Hansell overcame many operational difficulties to direct the first B-29 raids over Tokyo and successfully established the basis for the sustained strategic bombing campaign against Japan, which ultimately contributed greatly to the collapse of the Japanese Empire.

Hansell was ahead of his time. In view of recent operations carried out against Iraq and Serbia, it is clear that Hansell's vision for American strategic air doctrine was ultimately made possible by advances in technology. In the classrooms of the Air Corps Tactical School in Alabama and in the old munitions building in Washington, Hansell and his colleagues Harold George, Kenneth Walker, and Laurence Kuter had literally sweated out the details of what would become America's unique doctrine of bombing predetermined, specific economic/military targets using heavy bombers operating in broad daylight. This doctrine came to life in Europe when the United States Eighth Air Force began its legendary campaign against Hitler's war machine. Kenneth Walker was killed in action in a bombing raid over New Britain, and Harold George and Laurence Kuter were both assigned to duties in the States during most of the war. It was up to Hansell, the only one of the original planners to have the opportunity to influence actual operations, to see that their doctrine of daylight precision bombardment was carried out during World War II.

In Europe the frictions of war meant that Hansell would see his vision of strategic air war altered by the needs of ground operations in the Mediterranean and in Operation Overlord, the fierce resistance of the Luftwaffe and German antiaircraft defenses, and by other factors such as weather and an ever-changing target list. Once Hansell's B-29s were operational in the Pacific, he believed that he would have a free hand to finally conduct the kind of strategic air war for which he had prepared all his professional life. But frictions arose in the Pacific as well. New, unproven aircraft, lack of supplies and maintenance facilities, and unpredictable weather all contributed to a less than auspicious start of Hansell's air offensive against Japan. The results of his high-altitude, daylight bombing campaign did not meet Hansell's own expectations, much less those of General Arnold. Hansell resisted suggestions that he switch to night area bombing tactics using incendiary bombs against Japanese cities, and as a result he was abruptly relieved of command in January 1945. Maj Gen Curtis LeMay picked up operations where Hansell left off. He too failed to achieve the expected results, but Tokyo and many other Japanese cities burned.

Hansell has been criticized as being one of the leaders in the "Bomber Mafia" and for being inflexible concerning his belief in the war-winning capability of strategic bombing. It is perhaps true that Hansell failed to distinguish the difference between doctrine and dogma and that this cost him his career. Yet, it is important to note that today's American strategic air forces have the technology to carry out the doctrine Hansell had espoused with the zeal of an apostle. Perhaps too, Hansell was overzealous in his quest, but he was no Don Quixote and he was not jousting windmills. If today the United States has a reputation for "pinpoint" accuracy in its bombing campaigns that yield swift and easily discernable results and for avoiding civilian casualties, Hansell's efforts are at least in part responsible. Hansell did not "lose" or squander his career as some suppose; he sacrificed his career for a principle.

Chapter 1

The Problems of Airpower

In September 1987 Maj Gen Haywood S. Hansell Jr. and his son, Col Haywood S. Hansell III, spoke before the Nuclear Strategy Symposium given by the Center for Aerospace Doctrine, Research, and Education at Maxwell Air Force Base (AFB), Alabama. The speech, "Air Power in National Strategy," proposed a thesis that must have taken the audience by surprise. The Hansells assumed that the Strategic Defense Initiative (SDI or "Star Wars") would be possible and operational thus ending the ominous threat of mutual assured destruction, and for that reason conventional airpower would emerge as the most important deterrent. The proposed dethronement of nuclear weapons as the cornerstone of United States military strategy after more than four decades required careful planning and a willingness to stand in the face of current professional opinion.[1]

The speech was divided into two parts: "Then," delivered by General Hansell, and "Now," delivered by Colonel Hansell. General Hansell minced no words in extolling the virtues of the daylight precision bombing campaign of the United States against Germany during World War II. This campaign, which lasted from August 1942 to April 1945, called for "undermining the enemy military capability to fight as well as the enemy national 'will' by destroying the physical elements which support the military forces and the societal will to wage war."[2] General Hansell acknowledged the fact that the campaign failed to accomplish the goals of the operational strategy as planned. However, he concluded that if airpower had not been diverted to the Mediterranean and had been concentrated on essential economic targets, the strategic air campaign could have been successfully completed before the Normandy invasion in June 1944. Had this been the case, Germany would have collapsed much earlier because Hitler would have been unable to sustain the war materially.[3]

Colonel Hansell, building upon his father's thesis, maintained that a constant force of 200 modern bombers (B-1 and

B-2) using conventional, unguided bomb weapons could reasonably replicate the entire destructive effect of strategic bombing (area bombing included) of Germany in World War II in just 21 operational days. Moreover, a force of 230 such bombers using conventional weapons could fatally weaken the Soviet Union's ability to make war. This was predicated on the assumption that SDI would have been successfully deployed and that the bomber force suffered no more than a two percent attrition rate per day for 21 days. SDI would theoretically protect the United States from missile attacks while the Air Force would deploy the B-1B with its low radar profile, which would protect it from being detected and shot down, and the B-2, which has almost no radar profile. In addition to the stealth aircraft, the Air Force would attack Soviet ground-based and air-based radar capabilities, thus suppressing Soviet air defenses, which were heavily dependent upon radar direction.[4]

It is appropriate that General Hansell's last public appearance was at the site of his first real Air Corps assignment

B-1 Bomber

where he had taught the concepts of strategic air war to future commanders attending the Air Corps Tactical School (ACTS) at Maxwell Field, Alabama. He died in November 1988 as he was packing to deliver a variation of his speech to the Canadian War College. His life had been devoted to the theory and practice of strategic airpower—the single most controversial military debate of the twentieth century. Since his death, the world has witnessed the highly successful air campaign in the Persian Gulf War and the demise of the Soviet Union. These events have caused a radical reduction in the American nuclear triad and presented the world with a wide variety of potential military scenarios. Yet the debate over the proper use of strategic air war continues. It is a debate as old as the airplane itself.[5]

Unlike theorists of surface warfare both on land and sea, there could be no Clausewitz, Jomini, or Mahan to form a theory of air war based on historical precedent. At the beginning of the First World War the concept of air war was still novel and existed, if at all, in the realm of the fantastic, best exemplified by H. G. Wells's *The War in the Air*, first published in 1908. Wells described a German air attack on New York City, an attack that caused the city to become "a furnace of crimson flames."[6] Such fantasies dominated the popular conception of airpower and brought with them efforts to prevent the unleashing of such a destructive force upon mankind. The 1907 Hague Convention included a prohibition on the bombardment of "towns and villages, dwellings, or buildings that are not defended."[7] The fear of aerial bombardment opened an entirely new debate concerning morality and warfare.

The nineteenth century was a century of technological progress. Industrial facilities were mass producing everything from sewing needles to machine-gun bullets; advances in transportation had made the world a much smaller place; and political advances had given rise to massive "people's armies." Novelties such as heavier-than-air flight certainly fit into the pattern of unlimited progress. Even after the terrible American Civil War with its mass-produced weapons and large-scale killing, Americans did not automatically equate new technology with increased deadliness in warfare. Gen William T. Sherman's famed march to the sea did not have the killing of

3

women and children as its object, yet Sherman was aiming at economic targets that would indirectly affect civilians. As the historian Michael Sherry observed, "In America, airplanes were seen as instruments of progress, not terrible weapons of destruction."[8] The use of airplanes to kill civilians indiscriminately, including women and children, was beyond the Americans' concept of morality in warfare. There was still a distinction between combatant and noncombatant, and even though Americans agreed with Sherman that "war is hell," it should be so only in an ancillary way—not in the direct targeting of civilians for military purposes.

The Europeans took a much more martial view of the uses of the airplane. To them preparedness was an important prerequisite to peace or war, and they viewed with favor any weapon that could either deter aggression or win a quick, decisive victory. In 1911 the Italians sent nine airplanes and two dirigibles to Libya for service in their war against the Turks. The aircraft participated in reconnaissance and crude bombing missions, but without decisive effect. Aircraft also played a minor role in the Balkan wars of 1912–13. Even though these early efforts proved somewhat less effective than expected, the major European powers took notice. In 1910 the combined air strength of Germany, Austria-Hungary, France, Russia, and Great Britain was around 50 airplanes. By 1914 their combined air fleets had reached the 700 mark.[9]

The European vision of air war was revealed in 1913 by French aviator Pol Timonier in his book, *How We Are Going to Torpedo Berlin with Our Squadron of Airplanes as Soon as the War Begins.* In this scenario the Germans would attack Paris with upwards of 132,000 pounds of explosives, which would decimate the population "amidst indescribable horrors," after which the French would retaliate with a massive attack against Berlin, unleashing 1,360 "torpedoes," thus bringing the war to a successful and rapid conclusion. The Europeans not only saw fit to prepare air fleets, some were willing (in theory at least) to unleash that power on civilians in order to win wars in the shortest, most decisive manner. Referring to Europe, Sherry concluded, "War itself was not unthinkable, only endless and meaningless war."[10]

In the popular imagination, the destructive power of the airplane before the First World War was formidable. In spite of rulings by the Hague Convention, it was conceivable that undefended cities and their inhabitants could be targeted. The armies and navies that would have to deploy the air forces had not yet formulated practical ways of using the airplane nor had they decided how the airplane would fit into existing military strategy. Air war doctrine would emerge from the experience of war and the further development of the airplane's technical capabilities.

Air war exists in many forms, but has been most simply broken down into two segments—tactical and strategic. Tactical air warfare, simply defined, is combat support given to ground or naval units either in actual attack on opposing surface forces or in defending friendly surface forces from air attacks. Tactical air forces are subservient to and serve the interests and needs of the surface forces. Strategic air war, on the other hand, consists of independent air attacks against the enemy's infrastructure with the intent of effecting the enemy's surrender or, that failing, of weakening the enemy to the point that he cannot carry out effective military operations. Strategic air war is in keeping with Clausewitz's definition of war: "War therefore is an act of violence intended to compel our opponent to fulfill our will." Clausewitz, however, saw only the dispersion of an enemy's army, the capture of his capital, or the elimination of his principal ally as a means of bringing about the enemy's overthrow. Strategic air war offers a more direct and, in some ways, more simple means of overthrowing an enemy. But, as Clausewitz pointed out, "Everything is very simple in war, but the simplest thing is difficult."[11]

The First World War offered the first chance to use aircraft on a large scale for military purposes, and the fears and fantasies were proven to be incorrect or incomplete. No cities were set ablaze in the opening phases of the war. In fact it was only through much trial and error that the airplane finally took its place among the weapons of war. None of the prewar predictions took into account such factors as weather, navigation, bombing accuracy, or the impact the bombs would have if and when they actually struck their intended targets. Strategic bombing existed as an interesting possibility in the Great War, but was used only sparingly. Aircraft were used as tactical instruments in this conflict, first for reconnaissance purposes, then for air superiority roles, and finally for ground attack and interdiction. Even though many historians have branded the use of military aircraft a failure in the First World War, historian Lee Kennett holds another view. He maintains that the air war itself failed to make a real difference in the outcome of the war, but that reconnaissance aircraft directed the awesome firepower of the artillery, and bombing aircraft added to the bombardments, which in turn helped perpetuate the stalemate.[12]

Strategic bombing in the First World War was first practiced in 1915 by Imperial Germany with the zeppelin raids on England. The raids caused fear and consternation among the British, but certainly did not knock Great Britain out of the war. The second phase of German strategic bombing was begun in May 1917 and lasted until May 1918. This phase utilized what the aviation writer R. P. Hearne called "the principle of psychological influence" and saw the introduction of the new twin-engine Gotha bombers and the multiengine *Riesenflugzeug*

Z-1 Zeppelin

or R-plane. The mission of these new aircraft was to "disrupt industry and communications, destroy supply dumps, and hinder cross-Channel traffic," but the bomber crews were told that their ultimate goal was to "make war on the morale of the English people." Their orders were simply to "raid targets of military importance in Britain," and even though they carried a smaller bomb load than the zeppelins, they caused "panicky" scenes in London and actually took more British lives than had the zeppelins.[13]

As many as a third of a million Londoners were forced from their homes as a result of the bombing. This dislocation caused absenteeism to increase and war production to decrease at war factories. The war cabinet blamed the press for fanning the fires of panic by reporting the distressing scenes in London, but the effects of the bombing were real. In the final tally the Germans had dropped less than 300 tons of bombs on England, killing 1,400 people and wounding 4,800 more. The material destruction of the raids cost the British about half of one day's cost of the war in France. Since the losses suffered by the British in all the raids by the Germans were equal to only a light attack along the Western Front, the real significance of the German bombing raids lies elsewhere. Civilians had become the targets. Even though this fact did not bring about the speedy collapse of Great Britain, as the prewar predictions had assumed, the targeting of civilians did open a Pandora's box that could only bode ill for the future.[14]

Great Britain and France, two member nations of the Allies, also launched a strategic bombing campaign that attacked only military targets, at least at first. Field Marshal Horatio Herbert Kitchner (Lord Kitchner), British commander in the early years of the Great War, had argued in favor of bombing attacks on German industry as early as 1914. The Royal Naval Air Service was the first to take up the task with raids on zeppelin bases, submarine installations, marshaling yards, and, ultimately, industrial targets in western Germany. Using Sopwith 1½ Strutters and Handley Page 0/400s, they carried out a modest but methodical campaign in the summer of 1916.[15]

The French had devised a strategic bombing plan based on what they called *points sensibles* (sensitive points) or military targets that could block vital supply lines or production chains. The steel facilities of the Saar, Luxembourg, and western Germany became the focus of French attention. Since the steel mills produced fires that could be seen for miles at night, the French switched to night operations to utilize most effectively their limited supply of bombers.[16]

The British launched their attacks in the daylight, often with impunity. But on occasion their losses could be as high as 3 percent. Accuracy also suffered; the British could count only a 25 percent accuracy rate on targets as large as zeppelin sheds and only a 2 percent accuracy rate on targets such as rail junctions and rail stations. As the technology of air war improved, however, so did the size and purpose of the bombs. Incendiary bombs were constructed and used to destroy Bulgarian wheat fields and to burn grain fields inside German-occupied France. There was even consideration by the Allies of bombs containing poison gas to be dropped on German cities.[17]

Despite all the intentions of adhering to a strategic bombing policy that targeted only military targets, the absence of an able strategic bombing force and the need to retaliate against German attacks on Allied cities diverted the attention of the Allied air campaign. In the late spring of 1918 the Royal Air Force (RAF) was created as an independent branch of the British armed forces. Its commander, Air Chief Marshal Sir Hugh Montague Trenchard, had at his disposal the means for raids in force over German territory and succeeded in dropping 660 tons of bombs on German targets. But the plans for strategic bombing did not please the French because the Germans occupied Belgium and a large portion of France, thus making France more vulnerable than Germany to air attack. This fact of geography hindered the Allied hopes for a strategic air campaign against Germany. Therefore, an international strategic air force including British, French, Italian, and American bombers was never organized.[18]

The Americans did not launch a strategic air campaign against Germany even though they made a significant contribution to the air war with the services of Brig Gen William "Billy" Mitchell. Mitchell commanded the largest air effort of the war and envisioned parachuting an entire army division behind enemy lines, but these actions, both real and proposed, lay within the realm of the tactical, not the strategic. If

British Handley-Page Bomber

the war had carried over into 1919, the Allies (particularly the Americans) could have amassed a formidable air armada, but with the signing of the Armistice in November 1918, the heady plans for 1919 were never carried out.[19]

The strategic bomber turned out to be only a shadow of the threat it was believed to pose prior to the First World War. Cities were attacked, but not one of the belligerents was seriously damaged, much less induced to sue for peace because of bomber attacks. Yet the lessons of the First World War worked in favor of strategic bombing. Tens of millions had been killed or wounded on the Western Front and other battlegrounds, and victory for the Allies came only through bloody attrition after four years of unimaginable horror and sacrifice. The static stalemate of trench warfare cried out for an alternative to the terrible slaughter. Strategic bombing was to be that alternative. As Kennett observed, "Only strategic airpower seemed to offer a real alternative to the bloody, indecisive collisions along a static front: the swift, deep, surgically precise stroke at just the right objective—what Clausewitz called the enemy's center of gravity—would ensure his rapid collapse."[20]

Other lessons were learned as well. The bombing of London caused panic in the streets but also caused absenteeism and falling production in the city's war industries. Crowds stampeded, causing a number of deaths during air raids on London and Paris. These lessons seemed to teach that if the civilian population was targeted on a massive scale, war production would not be able to supply the army in the field. The population, under intense air attack, could perhaps be driven to the point of civil disobedience, thereby either causing the collapse of the government or forcing the government to sue for peace to prevent any such collapse. The lessons were apparently made more valid by the collapse of empires without invasion. Imperial Russia had been forced out of the war because of an internal revolution brought on by worsening wartime conditions. The Austrian Empire had also collapsed without a single Allied soldier coming near Vienna. Finally, Imperial Germany had accepted an armistice even though no Allied soldiers had yet reached the Rhine. All had collapsed, to one degree or another, because their people could not or would not continue the war. Therefore, if bombers could carry the war directly to the people, a war might well end before an entire generation of young men was sacrificed in the trenches.[21]

Soon after the armistice, the World War I practitioners of air war became the prophets of strategic air war, should there be a second such conflict. The British, Italians, and Americans were the most vocal in the realm of air prophecy. First, they held that another war in the trenches was unacceptable and that strategic airpower was the solution. Second, they maintained that an independent air force, exclusive of ground or naval command, was essential to establishing a strategic air force. Third, they were certain that strategic air forces would always get through enemy defenses because no effective means of stopping them then existed. Finally, they all believed that strategic air forces must hit "vital centers" well behind enemy lines. There was an intrinsic disagreement among the prophets on this last point. Should the vital centers be strictly military and economic targets, or should the population centers be included on the target lists? Indeed, should the people themselves be the targets?

Even before the First World War ended, the British had created the world's first independent air force. Gen Jan Smuts of British South Africa headed a commission to investigate air organization and home defense. In a memorandum dated August 1917, he stated, "As far as can at present be foreseen there is absolutely no limit to its [airpower's] independent war use. And the day may not be far off when aerial operations with their devastation of enemy lands and destruction of industrial and populous centers on a vast scale may become the principal operations of war, to which the older forms of military and naval operations may become secondary and subordinate."[22] This report was an important factor in the creation of the RAF and a force in its future development.[23]

Trenchard believed that the airplane could prevent the carnage and stalemate of modern war. At first he advocated attacks at the sources of an enemy's strength; but he grew more and more to favor attacks on an enemy's morale, believing that the psychological "yield" of the RAF's attacks on towns along the Rhine during the First World War was 20 times more powerful than the material damage inflicted.[24]

Count Giovanni Caproni was an early proponent of the use of airpower in the First World War. In October 1917, he and Lt Col Giulio Douhet wrote a memorandum for the United States Army Air Service in which they proposed long-range bomber attacks on German and Austrian war industries. Douhet was a staunch advocate of airpower, so much so that he spent time in an Italian prison for criticizing his superiors because of their lack of understanding of air warfare. His record was cleared, and he later rose to the rank of general. In 1921 he published *The Command of the Air,* in which he explained his belief that an independent air force could return decisiveness to war by attacking over an enemy army directly to his vital centers. These attacks would not be limited simply to traditional military objectives but would strike first at the enemy's industries and cities, including the populations of those cities.[25]

Based on the experience of the First World War, there could be no successful surface offensive, either on land or sea. If a decisive battle could be fought, it would have to be through strategic airpower. Furthermore, modern warfare, by its very nature, could no longer accept the distinction between combatant and

11

noncombatant. Civilians in the war factory were as much responsible for making war as were the soldiers in the trenches. Therefore, civilians were not only acceptable targets, they were the preferred targets. The attacks on the civilian centers would be carried out by an independent air force, which would make war without mercy upon civilians in order to end the war decisively with far fewer casualties than had been seen in the First World War.[26]

Douhet's experiences in the war had taught him that anti-aircraft artillery was mostly ineffective. He stated, "No fortifications can possibly offset these new weapons, which can strike mortal blows into the heart of the enemy with lightning speed."[27] Pursuit aircraft were of no value, according to Douhet. He maintained that firepower was far more important than speed, believing that the former could always overcome the latter. He advocated the creation of the battle plane, essentially a bombing aircraft with enough defensive armament to carry an attacker safely over enemy territory. In fact, Douhet felt that defensive armament on his battle plane was chiefly for the morale of the aircrews, not to defend them from any real threat.[28]

Target selection was very important and, according to Douhet, also very difficult. The selection of objectives and the order in which they ought to be destroyed fell under the title of *aerial strategy*. His first objective was not his opponent's air fleet. On the contrary, bombers must avoid the preliminaries of aerial combat and get on with the business of bombing strategic targets, because "the chances are not only that it [the air fleet] will fail to find the enemy air force in the air, but also that the latter is at that very moment carrying out unchallenged its operations against the home territory."[29] The only chance at air superiority lay not in dogfights high in the clouds, but in the destruction of an enemy's bases and means of production.[30]

For Douhet, *means of production* could mean only one thing—the cities. The attack must be swift, ruthless, and deadly. "Within a few minutes some 20 tons of high-explosive, incendiary, and gas bombs would rain down. First would come explosives, then fires, then deadly gases floating on the surface and preventing any approach to the stricken area."[31]

The scene is truly apocalyptic, and it was intended to be. The objective was to terrorize the survivors into capitulation through massive attacks, not only on one city but on as many as 50 in a single day. It is also important to note that from the outset poison gas would be used; Douhet's strategy did not allow for threats or posturing before his most deadly card was played.[32]

Douhet based his view of strategic air war, of course, on the experiences of the Great War. He had read newspaper accounts of the panic in London and could cite many other examples of the effects of aerial bombardment on a civilian population: "The reader who thinks I have overcolored the picture has only to recall the panic created at Brescia when, during funeral services for the victims of an earlier bombing—a negligible one compared with the one I have pictured here—one of the mourners mistook a bird for an enemy plane."[33]

Gen Billy Mitchell, the American airpower advocate, commanded the largest single air operation of the First World War when he directed nearly 1,500 combat aircraft in the Saint Mihiel offensive in 1918. This operational experience gave Mitchell a better understanding than Douhet had of the existing technology. Mitchell had more respect for antiaircraft artillery and knew that efficient pursuit aircraft patrols could indeed intercept and blunt air attacks. Mitchell would make his impact not through original ideas but through his advocacy of the ideas of others reinforced by his own experiences.[34]

During the war Mitchell had been exposed to the ideas of Trenchard, Caproni, and Douhet. It is difficult, however, to determine just how much influence each had on him. From Trenchard it is probable that Mitchell developed his advocacy for an independent air force, which could mass its power and be deployed offensively. He had a respect for the concept of striking at an enemy's vital centers, but when it came to commanding his own air units, he dealt in the realm of the tactical. As an operational commander, he was forced to deal with such mundane tasks as detailed training, unit administration, and tactical direction—all of which were essential for air operations.[35] Also, unlike Douhet, he placed emphasis upon pursuit, claiming that "the daytime use of bombardment without the cooperation of pursuit is not contemplated except in rare cases."[36]

13

With the war's end the Americans were content to abandon Europe and retire to the safety of their insular continent. This meant that advocacy of first-strike strategic bombing would have no place in postwar American doctrine. Mitchell was forced by circumstances to advocate a new, more comforting role for the bomber. He contended that the bomber could be a defensive weapon, used to protect America's sea-lanes from enemy naval attack. When the Navy discounted the ability of the bomber to sink a battleship, Mitchell took up the challenge and sank the former German battleship *Ostfriesland* at anchor off the coast of Virginia. In later tests he sank other obsolete American battleships, but he failed to convince the Navy that its ships were vulnerable to air attack. Nevertheless, with these successes in hand, he became the chief advocate of American airpower.[37]

A great deal of money would have to be spent to make the Army Air Service the chief defender of America's coasts, and the leaders in Washington had no intention of spending it. The condition of aircraft and facilities within the Army Air Service was deplorable and getting worse. Mitchell became so vocal in his criticism that in March 1925 he lost his position as assistant commander of the Army Air Services and was exiled to Fort Sam Houston, Texas. When a flight of Navy seaplanes failed to complete the trip from California to Hawaii and the Navy dirigible *Shenandoah* crashed killing 14 people all in the space of a week in the late summer of 1925, Mitchell took action. In a statement to the press he accused the War and Navy Departments of "incompetency, criminal negligence, and the almost treasonable administration of our national defense." The gauntlet was taken up by his opponents, and the ensuing battle resulted in his court-martial and forced resignation from the Army as of 1 February 1926.[38] Mitchell had welcomed his trial as a platform for publicizing his views on airpower, but the result had ended his military career.

Russell Weigley contends that there are two Billy Mitchells: the one from 1917–26, who was tied to the existing technology and existing tactical and strategic knowledge; and the post-1926 Billy Mitchell, who increasingly advocated Douhet's vital center theory. Mitchell proposed attacking the vital centers with fire, high explosives, and chemical weapons because it would be more cost-effective. Perhaps, once his official ties were severed, he could express his own views more freely or, more probably, he had lost touch with the current technology and tended to inflate existing capabilities of military aircraft. He did, however, inadvertently teach a generation of young aviators to be more circumspect in their advocacy of airpower.[39]

After Mitchell's departure from the Army Air Service, no single individual emerged to take his place as the outspoken advocate of airpower. The function of formulating air war doctrine fell to the Air Corps Tactical School. Begun as a training center for Air Corps field-grade officers, this institution served as the unofficial center for forming United States Army air policies. After resolving the conflict between pursuit and bombardment by concentrating on bombardment, ACTS questioned the idea of attacking civilians and refined the concept of attacking the enemy's vital centers to "shatter the society's economic structure." The civilians could be manipulated into forcing their nation's surrender, not by attacking them directly but by attacking the economic system that supported them.[40]

The Americans' unwillingness to target civilians was a technical as much as a public relations or moral decision. By 1935 a prototype of the Boeing B-17 Flying Fortress had taken to the air. Since it could fly faster than any existing operational pursuit aircraft of the time, it was considered to be impervious to interception. It was equipped with a precision bombsight that would allow it to attack pinpoint targets. This technology gave new life to America's strategic air war doctrine. The Army Air Corps advocated attacking specific economic targets in daylight with massive numbers of bombers flying in formation. Historian Ronald Schaffer points out that selective bombing was better for publicity in America; it fit the kind of equipment available, and it represented the best way for Air Corps officers to get the most out of a shrinking budget. This was, for the reasons stated above, a clear departure from Douhet's concept of massive, violent attacks directly against civilians.[41]

The new technology of the B-17 had been tried only in peacetime practice; it had yet to experience the realities of war. The unexpected is to be expected on the battlefield. Clausewitz explained, "Friction is the only conception which in a general way corresponds to that which distinguishes real

15

Boeing B-17 Bombers

war from war on paper."[42] It had been assumed by those who popularized strategic air war and by the serious theorists that the "bomber would always get through." Douhet had examined some of the potential problems of strategic air war, such as improved safety, better materials in aircraft construction, increased carrying capacity and radius of action, and more speed with less fuel consumption. Yet, no one addressed the real frictions of strategic air warfare.[43]

Even after the experiences of the Great War, the theorists viewed strategic bombing far too simplistically. The strategic bombing campaign itself was seen merely as a problem of targeting, but in order to select the most important targets, a complex system of specialized military intelligence must first be in place. No provisions had been made for such an intelligence network. In addition to this, the very concept of *frictions* had not been seriously considered. Before strategic bombing could commence, factors such as weather, maintenance, training, ordnance, and aircraft capabilities had to be taken into account. Yet the simplistic Douhetian concept of the self-defending battle plane reflected the firm belief by interwar theorists and the general public as well that the bomber could penetrate enemy air space, strike its target, and return safely. Only operational experience in combat would reveal many of the problems strategic bombers would face. Once World War II had begun, the strategic air war took on a dynamic driven by existing technology and actual combat conditions, not by a preconceived air war doctrine.[44]

Sherry's work illustrates the development of strategic bombing as dictated by the evolution of existing technology. Technology and friction became the masters, not the servants of strategic bombing practices. "In the case of air war, the multiplicity of motives involved, the lack of measurable criteria, and the particular remoteness of its consequences combined to give it a peculiarly unchecked momentum."[45] Schaffer has also recently examined the American strategic bombing practices during World War II and has concluded, even though virtually every figure involved in directing the American bombing campaign expressed some "views on the moral issue," that "moral considerations almost invariably bowed to what people described as military necessity."[46]

Daylight precision bombing would eventually be abandoned by the United States Army Air Forces because of the dictates of existing technology, the demands of combat, and the fact that the passions of war swept away any moral concerns involving strategic bombing. The fire raids of Tokyo and other Japanese cities in the spring and summer of 1945 were the incarnation of the Douhetian vision. This is not to say that the policy makers and commanders were simply swept up in events and had no voice in the matter. As Sherry has noted, the distances involved, the lack of measurable criteria, and the remoteness of the consequences combined with the political realities of the day served to isolate the commanders from the realities of the bombing campaigns and fostered pragmatism rather than ideology.

Only about two dozen general officers were chiefly responsible for the creation of the American air war strategy during World War II. They came from a variety of backgrounds and from all across America, yet they shared common characteristics. They were young, with an average age of 42 at the time of Pearl Harbor, and they were adventurous men who were mentally alert and physically adept. Haywood S. Hansell Jr. shared all these characteristics, although he differed in three respects:

17

he was a Southerner; he was from an Army family; and, most importantly, he was an idealist who was totally committed to the doctrine of daylight precision bombardment. Most of his fellow general officers in the Army Air Forces were pragmatists, but Hansell clearly exhibited the temperament and will to chart a particular course of action and then throw himself into the task of carrying it out. The course he charted was daylight precision bombardment, and he would risk his life and ultimately sacrifice his military career for the sake of pursuing this course in the face of the disapproval of his peers and superiors.[47]

Hansell's career serves as a microcosmic view of the course of strategic bombing policy before and during World War II. He taught his concepts of strategic air war at ACTS, influencing hundreds of future air commanders. He then pioneered target selection by setting up a one-man European air intelligence section and by gathering intelligence during his observations of the RAF in England during the summer of 1941. His efforts were instrumental in preparing the watershed document, Air War Plans Division—Plan 1 (AWPD-1) which served as the United States military's basic air war plan all through the war. In fact, his planning abilities were so important that he was the only airman involved in formulating the AWPD-1, AWPD-42, and the plan for the combined bomber offensive. As a wing commander in the Eighth Air Force from August 1942 to July 1943, he set the standards for bombing and air combat in that theater of operations. After further planning duties in England, he returned to Washington, where he planned the strategic air war against Japan and created and commanded the first independent strategic air force in history. From October 1944 to January 1945 he overcame the many frictions of aerial combat to launch the first heavy bomber raids on Japan from the Marianas. During this time he was the virtual equal of Gen Douglas MacArthur and Adm Chester W. Nimitz in the Pacific, answerable only to Gen Henry H. Arnold in Washington.

His career was meteoric until his principles came into conflict with the demands of his superiors. He insisted on deploying the XXI Bomber Command against only precision targets in daylight operations while General Arnold and others advocated incendiary raids on Japanese cities. In January 1945 he was suddenly relieved of command. American strategic bombing doctrine had always maintained that industrial and military installations would be the targets, not civilians. In 1945 this long-held doctrine was suddenly abandoned, and Hansell was the only Air Force officer who forcefully opposed area attacks on cities. This opposition cost him his career. Hansell's main contribution to air doctrine was his strong advocacy of the concept that through selective targeting and an ability to place the bombs on the target, airpower could win wars by crippling an enemy's ability to supply his forces, without wanton death and destruction among civilians. He held this belief until the day he died, defending it in three books and a number of articles.

Ronald Schaffer and Michael Sherry have examined the slide from America's insistence upon precision bombardment to the incendiary and atomic raids on Japan. According to them, there were two American strategic bombing policies in World War II: the prewar belief in precision bombardment as an almost abstract concept and the policy of all-out attacks on cities, a policy that seemed to be forced upon the Army Air Forces by necessity. Haywood Hansell represents the idealistic precision bombardment concept pursued throughout the war, while Arnold and his staff were moving to the more expedient and pragmatic policy of burning Japanese cities.

Hansell retired soon after his dismissal as commander of the XXI Bomber Command. His contemporaries such as Gen Curtis E. LeMay, Gen Lauris Norstad, and Gen Laurence S. Kuter became much more famous and each attained high rank in the new United States Air Force. Hansell passed from the scene, his achievements and ideas largely ignored. Yet Hansell clearly played a crucial role in the development of strategic air warfare. He may well have been, as Barry Watts argues, "the guiding conceptual thinker" among that small group of generals who made major contributions to America's air war doctrine during World War II and beyond.[48]

Notes

1. Col Haywood S. Hansell III to Charles Griffith, letter, 14 January 1992; and Haywood S. Hansell Jr. and Haywood S. Hansell III, "Air Power in

National Strategy," a speech delivered before the Nuclear Strategy Symposium, Maxwell AFB, Ala., 10–12 September 1987, Hansell family's private collection.

2. "Air Power in National Strategy."

3. Ibid.

4. Ibid.

5. Col Haywood S. Hansell III, interviewed by author, 16 February 1992.

6. Michael S. Sherry, *The Rise of American Air Power: The Creation of Armageddon* (New Haven: Yale University Press, 1987), 10.

7. Lee Kennett, *A History of Strategic Bombing* (New York: Charles Scribner's Sons, 1982), 10–11.

8. Sherry, 4.

9. Ibid., 5; and Kennett, 12–16.

10. Sherry, 6; and Kennett, 17.

11. Carl von Clausewitz, *On War*, ed. Anatol Rapoport (New York: Penguin Books, 1982), 23, 101, 390.

12. Lee Kennett, *The First Air War, 1914–1918* (New York: Free Press, 1991), 42, 48, 216–21.

13. Kennett, *Strategic Bombing*, 22–26.

14. Ibid., 22–26.

15. Ibid., 26.

16. Ibid., 28–29.

17. Kennett, *The First Air War*, 52; and Kennett, *Strategic Bombing*, 35–36.

18. Kennett, *Strategic Bombing*, 26–27.

19. Ibid.; and Kennett, *The First Air War*, 216.

20. Kennett, *The First Air War*, 221.

21. Kennett, *Strategic Bombing*, 26, 52–56.

22. David MacIsaac, "Voices from the Central Blue: The Air Power Theorists," in *Makers of Modern Strategy: From Machiavelli to the Nuclear Age*, ed. Peter Paret (Princeton, N.J.: Princeton University Press, 1986), 628–29.

23. Haywood S. Hansell Jr., *The Strategic Air War against Germany and Japan: A Memoir* (Washington, D.C.: Government Printing Office, 1986), 1–2.

24. Kennett, *Strategic Bombing*, 57; Hansell, *Strategic Air War*, 2; and Ronald Schaffer, *Wings of Judgment: American Bombing in World War II* (New York: Oxford University Press, 1985), 20.

25. Russell Weigley, *The American Way of War: A History of United States Military Strategy and Policy* (Bloomington, Ind.: Indiana University Press, 1981), 226.

26. Sherry, 27–28; MacIsaac, 630; and Schaffer, 21–23.

27. Giulio Douhet, *The Command of the Air* (Washington, D.C.: Office of Air Force History, 1942), 15; and Weigley, 227.

28. Douhet, 40–44.

29. Ibid., 50–60.

30. Stephen L. McFarland and Wesley P. Newton, *To Command the Sky: The Battle for Air Superiority over Germany, 1942–1944* (Washington, D.C.: Smithsonian Institution Press, 1991), 19–21.

31. Douhet, 58.

32. Ibid., 58–59.

33. Ibid.

34. Weigley, 224–27.

35. Hansell, *Strategic Air War,* 4–5; Weigley, 226; and Sherry, 18–19.

36. McFarland and Newton, 23.

37. Sherry, 29; and Weigley, 227–28.

38. Weigley, 232; and Gen James H. "Jimmy" Doolittle with Carroll V. Glines, *I Could Never Be So Lucky Again* (New York: Bantam Books, 1992), 102–3.

39. Weigley, 233, 236; and Schaffer, 26–27.

40. Schaffer, 28.

41. Ibid., 28–30; David MacIsaac, *Strategic Bombing in World War II: The Story of the United States Strategic Bombing Survey* (New York: Garland, 1976), 7; and Barry D. Watts, *The Foundations of U.S. Air Doctrine: The Problem of Friction in War* (Maxwell AFB, Ala.: Air University Press, 1984), 17–18.

42. Clausewitz, 164.

43. Douhet, 62.

44. MacIsaac, 635.

45. Sherry, 176.

46. Schaffer, xii.

47. Ibid., 7–10; and MacIsaac, 626.

48. Watts, 25.

Chapter 2

The Early Years:
Education and ACTS

Haywood Sheperd Hansell Jr. was born the son of a United States Army surgeon on 28 September 1903, Fort Monroe, Virginia. By the time he was a teenager he had acquired the nickname "Possum," which was later shortened simply to "Pos." In an effort to explain his nickname, Hansell invented the story that he selected the name himself because it is Latin for "can do." Other accounts state that he acquired the name because he "hunted the marsupial in his native Georgia" or that he napped during his morning classes at Georgia Institute of Technology. The simple truth is that his "thin, inquisitive nose and mouth and small bright eyes won him the nickname 'Possum.'" In short, he *looked* like a possum. Trivial though it may be, the nickname offers insight into the qualities of the man.[1]

Hansell was an engineer by training and possessed the stereotypical attributes of his profession. He tackled problems with a "can-do" attitude, working with an intensity that was often reflected in his "small bright eyes," and he usually accomplished what he set out to do. Once he directed his full attention to a project, he would use every means at his disposal to complete it, whether it was a formula for laying pipes or the plan for the strategic bombing of Germany. After he had gathered all the data possible and reached a decision based on his own analysis, he was determined to make his plan work simply because he believed in his own abilities.

Unlike the stereotypical engineer, however, Hansell possessed a sense of romanticism that directed him to paths that were not frequented by most technicians. He loved Gilbert and Sullivan operettas, quoted Shakespeare, wrote his own poetry and lyrics to songs, and was obsessed by Miguel de Cervantes's *Don Quixote*. Just as Don Quixote jousted with windmills, Hansell saw himself as the champion of lost causes. Even though he would later arrive at his strategic air war doctrine through an engineer's unemotional logic, he would defend that

23

Maj Gen Haywood S. Hansell Jr.

doctrine with the zeal of one committed to a romantic quest. From his days as a fledgling lieutenant to the peak of his career as commander of the XXI Bomber Command, he fought for his concept of airpower against opponents who were far more dangerous to his career than mere windmills.

Hansell displayed in his personal life and in his career an ability to determine what he wanted to accomplish and the will to accomplish it, even against great odds. In his military career he would achieve a well-earned reputation as a technological expert who was respected by his fellow officers. On the other hand, his more literary side was misunderstood by his compatriots. He was considered "nervous" and "high strung" by Gen Ira C. Eaker and was later described by Gen Barney M. Giles as a "kind of brilliant-type fellow" given to sentimentality. In short, he was fundamentally different from the other young general officers in the Army Air Forces during World War II. As one historian observed, he was set apart from the others by his southern birth and Army upbringing, yet, in addition to these obvious differences, it was his temperament more than any other factor that made him unique.[2]

Hansell's military heritage began with John Hansell, who served in the American Revolution. William Andrew Hansell had been a major in the War of 1812. Andrew Jackson Hansell served in the Confederate Army in the adjutant general's office and was briefly in charge of Atlanta's defenses. As southern gentlemen and military officers, they set the standards that guided the Hansells in their devotion to duty and country, and in their quest for family honor.[3]

Haywood Sheperd Hansell Sr. was a physician in the United States Army and was a Georgian who was devoutly southern. At the Hansell household, the evening meal was an occasion that saw Colonel Hansell arrive at the head of the table in a white linen suit and Panama hat. He believed in firm discipline and demanded nothing less than strict obedience. In later years as corps surgeon, he had prestige usually afforded a major general and received tremendous respect in accordance to his position and rank. The sense of southern aristocracy and of belonging to the officer class had a great influence on the relationship between father and son. Young Haywood was under great pressure to live up to his father's high expectations.[4]

Young Haywood's mother was also a member of the southern aristocracy. Susan Watts, like her husband, was devoutly southern, but the similarities ended there. She was a witty, intelligent woman who had a wonderful sense of humor. She loved to play practical jokes and was a talented storyteller who enthralled her children with her yarns. Young Haywood, or "Hay" as she called him, was therefore influenced strongly by two very different personalities, and as an adult he exhibited the characteristics of both parents almost equally. The self-confident, disciplined engineer was the product of his father's influence while the literate, romantic storyteller was the product of his mother's influence. Through both he received his sense of being a member of the genteel southern aristocracy.[5]

At the turn of the century, America had just acquired her empire, and the Hansell family shared in the imperial experience. Soon after young Haywood's birth in 1903, the Hansell family was stationed in Peking, China, where Lieutenant Hansell served in his capacity as an Army doctor. Mrs. Hansell kept a diary of their Chinese experiences and recorded a very memorable visit with the Dowager Empress Tz'u-hsi. Apparently Lieutenant Hansell had ingratiated himself to the imperial household by treating a royal family member who had become ill. As a reward for this act of kindness (and as an indication that the empress wanted to maintain good relations with the Westerners after the disastrous Boxer Rebellion), Mrs. Hansell was allowed to present young Haywood to the empress. The imperial court made a great deal of fuss over the child, with the empress declaring that the child was the most beautiful baby she had ever seen. Even though young Haywood would not remember the experience, living in China was an important part of his childhood. His first words were Chinese, learned from the house servants, and when the Hansells left Peking the empress gave them a chest from her palace as a gift.[6]

The family's next duty station was in the Philippines where young Haywood quickly forgot his Chinese but soon picked up Spanish from the Filipino house servants. Toward the end of their tour in the islands, young Haywood had an important experience, which he later recalled: "In 1912 I got my first glimpse of an airplane. I was standing on the fairgrounds of the annual carnival in Manila, Philippine Islands, when a bi-plane beat its slow pace across the sky. An aged Filipino standing nearby said, in astonishment, '¡Muy gran pollo!' or 'Very large chicken!' As a boy of nine I was in full agreement."[7]

Upon their return to the United States, the Hansells were fortunate to serve at Army posts in their native Georgia. First at Fort McPherson and later at Fort Benning, young Haywood got a thorough introduction to routine Army life with its monotony and red tape. Even though his father had the highest expectations for him, his school work did not measure up. Once his father was tutoring him at the dining room table and young Haywood's attention was diverted by an ant, prompting his father to strike him on the back of the head so hard that the impact on the table cut his chin. In obvious disappointment with his son's lack of discipline, Captain Hansell decided to send him away to the family's ranch along the Gila River in New Mexico to grow up as a proper Hansell should.[8]

Southwest New Mexico at the turn of the century still offered the flavor of the old West. The Hansell ranch was nothing fancy—just a couple of cowhands and a dozen horses located in scrub and desert country. Captain Hansell provided a tutor for the youngster, hoping to improve his academic performance. Young Haywood took an immediate liking to his tutor, a man living in New Mexico because he suffered from tuberculosis, and their relationship grew into a lifetime admiration. Yet he learned more than mathematics and the classics on the ranch. His lessons included roping and rounding up cattle, living in a bunkhouse, and shooting. Even though he accidentally shot himself in the foot with the pistol he wore on his hip, young Haywood thrived in this new adventurous setting, and he drifted even further away from his schoolwork. Perhaps the most important lesson he learned was horsemanship. He served as a wrangler on a surveying expedition. This experience, plus his love for horses, served him well in later Army life. The time spent in New Mexico did give the young teenager a taste of the active, adventurous life, but his father's objectives were not achieved.[9]

Young Haywood arrived at Sewanee Military Academy near Chattanooga, Tennessee, as a freshman in 1916. This private military high school was his father's answer to his poor academic standing. By 1918, however, now Colonel Hansell was in France with the American Expeditionary Force. The geographical separation of father and son did not break the strong emotional bond between the two. In a letter dated 29 May 1918, Colonel Hansell revealed that his son's progress was very much on his mind when he wrote, "Well, when Mother's letter about your school reports reached me, I decided to wait for the next report, hoping it would show improvement—and thank goodness and you, I was not disappointed." Here the father acknowledged his son's slow climb to success but went on to add, "If you do your best, remember Dad is always willing to forget the shortcomings." Young Haywood was expected to succeed and was also expected to take on the additional burdens brought on by the war: "France and the end of the war are both so far away, that you will have to assume responsibilities earlier than you would otherwise. This is hard on you, but I don't see how it could be avoided." He offered another glimmer of pride in his son by stating that if he were killed he had "a fine boy to carry on the work." He concluded by reminding his son, "Don't let Mother worry about you. You know how wrapped up she is in you and your career."[10]

Sewanee Military Academy did indeed bring out the best in young Haywood. Whether he improved because of his father's admonishments, his own maturity, or a combination of the two is difficult to say, but his academic troubles were behind him. Sewanee gave young Haywood a sense of identity that was his own. He was still high-spirited and once earned a stint at "walking the triangle" in the snow for some infraction of the rules. The punishment almost turned into tragedy when Possum developed pneumonia. He was confined to his room for two weeks with only his textbooks for company. The fortnight of isolation not only improved his health, but the self-discipline imposed by the illness improved his grades.[11]

Possum found a new home at Sewanee. His favorite teacher was his English instructor, Stuart McLean. Mr. McLean made, as Hansell later put it, "devoted Browning scholars out of us." He also encouraged the boys to read popular magazines with enthusiasm.

The cadet honor system at Sewanee was based on the assumption that a "cadet's word is as good as his bond," which meant that a cadet's word was never questioned. If any cadet were found not to have told the truth, he would have been dismissed by the cadets themselves.[12]

By his senior year in 1920, Possum had been elevated to captain of cadets. There had been a fire at Sewanee, so while the rebuilding was in progress, the cadet corps was moved to a location near Jacksonville, Florida. Hansell later recalled, "I was just a country boy and the bright lights were too much for me. I suddenly acquired an awful lot of demerits."[13] Ironically, as cadet captain he had become quite a martinet with his cadets. The combination of demerits and his harshness with the cadet corps was more than the school administration could stand. Unfortunately, Hansell's downfall came at lunchtime when a biscuit was thrown in the mess hall. Possum called the cadets to attention and ordered that no more biscuits be thrown. At that point another biscuit sailed through the air. He immediately marched the entire corps out without lunch. Then, quite by coincidence, he was handed a note informing him that he had been demoted from cadet captain to buck private. The timing of events was more than he could bear. Upon graduation a short time later, he was offered an appointment to West Point, but the humiliation and his wounded pride caused him to turn it down.[14]

There is no record of Colonel Hansell's response to his son's decision not to attend West Point, but it must have been a source of disappointment. Instead of a military education, Possum became an engineering student at the Georgia Institute of Technology in Atlanta. Upon arrival at Georgia Tech, Possum took on the role of the naive freshman and lost all his expense money in a gambling spree. Gambling was one mistake—going to his father about it would have been another.

The incident taught him the virtues of self-denial as well as the evils of gambling; he never gambled again. He joined the Sigma Nu fraternity and enjoyed the parties that went along with college life. His nickname seemed even more appropriate as he tried to stay awake in his morning classes after a night of drinking.[15]

His carefree attitude caught up with him in his differential equations class. It appeared that he would take an "F" in the class despite his belated efforts. At first he decided to escape the situation by quitting school and going to work, but Colonel Hansell refused to allow that. His next ploy was a request to transfer to another school, but again his father refused to hear of it. Finally Possum decided to tell his father the truth. Colonel Hansell's response was predictable; he indicated that he was sorry to hear the news and then asked his son where he intended to live. This made passing the class a "do-or-die" situation. Possum went to his professor with the problem, and the professor, probably hoping to give the young man enough rope to hang himself, gave him an equation that would be nearly impossible to solve. That equation became the focus of Possum's life for several weeks until, much to the professor's surprise, he solved it. Not only did he pass the course and redeem himself with his father, he did so with a good grade. Once again Colonel Hansell had provided enough incentive to ensure success.[16]

Not all incentive, however, came from his father. Possum decided that he would play football with the nationally famous Georgia Tech team. At around 125 pounds, Possum could not hope to play in many games, yet he stuck with it for four years, playing briefly only in a few games and receiving recognition from the coach only once when he dislocated his shoulder during a practice session. In addition to trying to play football, Possum also took up boxing, but he was again too small to achieve any success. He did, however, display a love of competitive sports as well as perseverance in the face of great odds. He was seldom able to joust with windmills from the bench at Georgia Tech, but he graduated in 1924 with a solid engineering degree. Once again he had an opportunity at a military career when he was offered an Army commission, but his decision to be a civilian engineer was firm.[17]

Even though the twenties have been remembered as a time of economic expansion, Haywood Hansell found it impossible to secure a position as an engineer. He had dreams of building bridges and dams in South America but was soon forced to compromise. Colonel Hansell was stationed at the Presidio in San Francisco, and his son soon joined him and Mrs. Hansell to look for employment there. The only work Possum could find was with the Steel Tank and Pipe Company of Berkeley, as a boilermaker's assistant. He worked 10 hours a day at a wage of 26 cents an hour, and he had to purchase his own tools. He used his time to study to become a journeyman boilermaker and worked part-time as a sparring partner for professional boxers. After a year of study, he was finally qualified to become a journeyman and was honored by an invitation to the boilermakers' ball. His only problem was that he did not know what to wear, so he decided it was better to be overdressed and rented a tuxedo for the occasion. Upon arrival he was shocked to see everyone else in tails; he was underdressed after all. This story became one of his favorites in later years, but despite his pride in being accepted by the boilermakers, he knew his talents were being wasted.[18]

Aviation promised America a bright future in 1928. Charles A. Lindbergh had crossed the Atlantic the year before, and aviation technology was growing at a tremendous rate. Hansell decided that his future lay in aeronautical engineering, but it was a difficult field to break into without flying experience, and the best source of such experience was the Army. The Army Air Corps was underbudgeted and flew an inventory of obsolete or obsolescent aircraft. The shortage of aviation officers was so acute that they could not replace those lost through attrition caused by accidents. It was difficult to fill the slots for commissioned pilots from West Point or even from the other branches of the Army, so each year hundreds of potential aviators enrolled as flying cadets, the successful candidates receiving reserve commissions. Hansell decided to become a flying cadet, serve in the Army for one term, and then begin his civilian career as an aeronautical engineer.[19]

Hansell began his Air Corps primary flight training at March Field, California, in March 1928. From the minute he got in the airplane his whole life turned around; he had found the direction his life had needed. By November 1928 he had completed the Primary Flying School and the Basic Flying School at March Field. In March 1929 he graduated from the Air Corps Advanced Flying School at Kelly Field near San Antonio, Texas, and was commissioned as a reserve second lieutenant. This marked a major turning point in Hansell's life. First, he had pleased his parents, his father especially, who conceded that at last young Possum was going to turn out all right. But more importantly, Hansell had finally determined his own course and had set out on the quest of his choosing.[20]

Hansell's first duty assignment was with the 2d Bombardment Group at Langley Field, Virginia. Even though he was assigned to a bombardment group, he had piloted at least 12 different types of aircraft. His main interest at Langley was in testing the capabilities of various airplanes, and in so doing he was involved in three accidents. Two accidents occurred in 1930. The first was a failed takeoff in a C-1C in six inches of snow at Uniontown, Pennsylvania. Weather conditions were blamed for the first accident, but pilot error was blamed for the second accident at Fredericksburg, Virginia, in which he suffered a ground loop upon landing a P-1F. Both accidents were considered to be minor and there were no serious injuries.[21]

In 1931 Hansell suffered a more serious accident while conducting tests that would allow a P-12 to carry a radio. He was instructed to take the P-12 on a practice run with 70 pounds of sand in the baggage compartment to check the aircraft's performance with the extra weight. While over Black River near Hampton, Virginia, the airplane went into a violent maneuver and fell into a tailspin. When he realized that he could not recover from the spin, he bailed out and parachuted into the icy river; with great difficulty he released himself and swam to a nearby duck blind. Maj George Kenney, who happened to be flying close by, saw the accident and directed the rescue boat to Hansell. After about 20 minutes the rescue boat arrived but got stuck in the mud. An oyster fisherman finally rescued him, and he was taken to Fort Monroe, Virginia, where he was treated for shock and exposure.[22]

A local newspaper quoted Hansell's fellow officers as stating that "Lieut. Hansell displayed unusual presence of mind in the difficult position in which he found himself when the ship

Boeing P-12

failed to straighten out of the spin."[23] While in the hospital at Fort Monroe, Hansell received a telegram from General Eaker welcoming him to the Caterpillar Club since he had ridden a silk parachute to safety. If his peers were impressed with his flying abilities, his superiors were not. With tight budgets every airplane counted, so the Army charged Hansell the $10,000 or so for the lost P-12. Naturally, Hansell could not afford to pay such a sum, so after the Army had made its point the issue was quietly dropped.[24]

Hansell received his regular commission as a second lieutenant in the Army on 12 June 1929, thus ensuring his future. That future was further brightened in 1930 when he met Miss Dorothy "Dotta" Rogers of Waco, Texas. She had recently graduated from Baylor University and was visiting a cousin who lived near Langley Field. On her first evening in Virginia, she passed Lieutenant Hansell, quite by accident, in the lobby of a hotel. He quickly took home the young lady he was escorting and returned to the hotel dining room where he invited himself to sit at Miss Rogers's table, much to the annoyance of her aunt. Hansell then persuaded Miss Rogers to accompany him the next day to Williamsburg, Virginia, where his niece was being christened at Bruton Parish Church. Upon returning from the outing, Miss Rogers declared the event a failure and characterized Hansell as a bore who continuously quoted poetry and sang songs for which he had written the words. Hansell's experience must have been quite different, however, because he was determined to marry Miss Rogers and made no secret of it.[25]

When she returned to Waco to accept a teaching position, she thought she was rid of this pushy young man with the curious nickname. She had underestimated the determination of her suitor. He wrote her every single day and was not deterred by the fact that she only answered two or three of his hundreds of letters. He even flew to Waco two or three times to press his suit in person. Once Possum Hansell set his goal he usually achieved it, and his courtship of Miss Rogers was no exception. Even though she was a beautiful, cultivated woman and Possum was not considered to be a catch for her, they were married in 1932.[26]

Once she had decided to become Mrs. Hansell, she seemed to be caught up in "something [she] had no control over." After the wedding in Waco, he and Dotta set out on their wedding trip, which took them first to New Orleans and then by steamer to Havana, Cuba; the Panama Canal; and California. His first act as a new husband was to get so drunk in New Orleans that he passed out at dinner, much to the embarrassment of his bride. Once at sea he caused further trouble by threatening the ship's captain because of a change in schedule. She was not at all sure what she had gotten herself into, but the die was cast.[27]

Being an officer in the United States Army in the 1930s carried with it a certain social status. Their first duty assignment was at Maxwell Field, Montgomery, Alabama. The married officers' quarters there offered grand accommodations, and even though Hansell was only a second lieutenant, he saw to it that his family had a housekeeper and a cook. Hansell also insisted on owning a pair of expensive Peal boots, which cost a month's salary; he had to look his best on the polo field for the sake of his career. Like their British counterparts, American Army officers felt it was their social prerogative to practice the equestrian arts in their off-duty hours. Even though the Hansells were able to scrape enough together to live the life of the officer class, they were often short of cash. One weekend when the cook was off, the Hansells had company and decided to go out for hamburgers, but in an age when a hamburger cost only five cents there were not three nickels to be found in the Hansell household.[28]

In Mrs. Hansell's eyes her husband's priorities were clear: the Air Corps came first, polo came second, and she ran a distant third. Soon after the birth of their first child, Hansell returned home after six weeks of temporary duty away from Maxwell Field. He brought two young lieutenants home for dinner, and Mrs. Hansell had prepared a sumptuous meal. Just as dinner began, the baby began to cry upstairs prompting Hansell to exclaim, "What in heaven's name is that?" "That," Mrs. Hansell responded, "is your son!," and she stormed away in anger. She was also expected to participate in activities she detested, such as afternoon teas, bridge games, and, worst of all, riding lessons. One afternoon she decided not to go to her riding lesson, but her husband became so angry that he punched a hole in the screen door with his fist. She went to the lesson because, like his father, Hansell demanded that every member of the family live up to his expectations.[29]

Hansell served as assistant operations officer at Maxwell Field, his first real position in the Air Corps. In addition to flying, he was involved in day-to-day base operations. He still had enough time to continue his tradition of writing ditties that turned into Air Corps songs. During this period he wrote such enduring favorites as "Eight Bucks a Day," "The Formation," "The Old Bombardment Group," and "Old 97." He also assisted Capt Harold L. George in a number of projects, including a study of the antiaircraft defenses of the Panama Canal. The working relationship and friendship between Hansell and George lasted a lifetime and was an important boost to Hansell's career later on. Up to this point Hansell had considered himself a pursuit pilot, but George dealt with bombardment. The contact between the two gave Hansell his first real exposure to the potentials of bombardment. When Hansell was transferred from this position in 1933, George wrote a letter of commendation that revealed an important aspect of Hansell's future in bombardment. The commendation read in part, "It is no exaggeration to state that the text on bombardment probabilities, as now contained in the bombardment manual, and which I consider extremely valuable, was made possible by his indefatigable work."[30]

George would later be in position to advance Hansell's career. It was, however, Hansell's association with Claire L. Chennault that first won him any degree of recognition. The Air Corps was constantly looking for ways to promote itself with the public because with public support came a better chance for a larger slice of the shrinking military budget. Lt Col John F. Curry, the commandant of the Air Corps Tactical School, noted in 1933 that the Navy had a trio of acrobatic pilots who could thrill the public with their aerial exploits, and he felt that the Air Corps needed such a team of its own. The Air Corps acrobatic team would represent Army aviation at public functions, develop tactics, and demonstrate them for students at ACTS. Captain Chennault, the Air Corps's most vocal advocate of pursuit aviation, was naturally selected to command the team.[31]

Chennault considered himself to be the best pilot in the Air Corps. He was an outspoken advocate of military aviation in general, pursuit aviation in particular, and himself above all. According to Hansell, "Chennault figured there were only two kinds of people—those who agreed with him and those who didn't."[32] Chennault selected his team as if he were auditioning for a drama production. As his biographer, Martha Byrd, explained, "Chennault chose his partners by the simple expedient of challenging any comer to stay on his wing through half an hour of head-spinning aerobatics."[33] He selected the three men he concluded were good enough to fly with him: Sgt William C. "Billy" McDonald, Sgt John H. "Luke" Williamson, and Lt Haywood "Possum" Hansell. (Both McDonald and Williamson had reserve commissions but served on active duty as enlisted men in order to fly.)[34]

The team put in many hours of practice and put on performances at Maxwell Field two or three times a week. Local schools in Montgomery would sometimes be let out just to allow the children to watch their aerial feats. They soon became known as "Three Men on a Flying Trapeze," with Chennault flying lead, Williamson flying as right wingman, Hansell flying as left wingman, and McDonald as alternate. They dazzled the public by putting on speed and precision acts at airport openings and air shows, and they represented the Air Corps at the national air races at Cleveland, Ohio. The press touted them as "daredevils who laugh at death," "exhibitionists par excellence" who "held crowds spellbound" and flew with a "perfection that seemed as if the three planes were activated by one mind."[35] Hansell's experiences on the Trapeze were an outlet for his adventurous spirit and his competitive nature; on this team he could perform with the varsity—he was no longer on the bench. The very fact that he flew with the team illustrates his dogged determination to accomplish difficult tasks because even though he was an exemplary pilot, he got airsick during the acrobatic stunts. He often grew violently ill and actually vomited in the cockpit, but he said nothing about the problem and continued with all his duties. He wanted nothing to stand between him and his chosen quest.[36]

There were several close calls but no serious accidents. Later, during a World War II interview, Hansell reflected on his service with the Trapeze, "It is sheer chance that we lived through it. If we had kept at it long enough, we certainly would have been killed."[37] Once the Trapeze put on an air show where hundreds of people had gathered near Chennault's home in Louisiana. Even though great care had been taken to prepare the field, the ceiling of about 1,500 feet was far too low to perform. Not willing to disappoint the spectators, the team decided to perform anyway. Once in the air, Chennault signaled for an Immelmann maneuver, which would take the three airplanes into the cloud cover to a near stall before hurtling back toward earth. At the apex of the maneuver nothing was visible, not even each other's aircraft. Hansell, thinking quickly, rolled and came down. The three were startled during the descent to see that they were still in formation, but Hansell and Williamson had emerged on opposite sides of Chennault. This was either evidence of superb teamwork, or as Hansell concluded, blind luck.[38]

Once, the team tied ten-foot ropes to their aircraft, but they often flew much closer than that anyway. On one occasion Hansell's P-12 blew into the tail of Chennault's, tearing up Chennault's stabilizers and elevators. Chennault proved he was indeed a superb aviator by landing safely using only the throttle to bring his airplane in to the field. Hansell left the team in 1934, and it was disbanded in 1936.[39]

Hansell took more than a thrilling experience away from his association with Chennault. In those days he was known as "Pursuit Possum" because he favored the virtues of the fighter or pursuit airplane over the bomber. The basic question in the debate was simple, "Could pursuit, operating in the defense of a target, destroy bombers at a rate high enough to make a bombing offensive impracticable?"[40] Chennault argued that bombers could be detected, intercepted, and destroyed. Even though Hansell was a loyal pursuit pilot, his position in this Air Corps debate would be turned around completely when he was accepted as a student at ACTS in 1934.[41]

Hansell's uncertainty about the future of the Army Air Service was shared by the institution itself. Billy Mitchell had been advocating an independent air force for years, but in the wake of the successful battleship tests the chief of the Air Service, Maj Gen Mason M. Patrick, rather wanted the air arm to be elevated to the status of a combat arm within the Army. He recommended the creation of a General Headquarters (GHQ) Air Force, which would operate with some degree of independence under the General Staff. In 1923 the General Staff appointed the Lassiter Board, which reached the same conclusions as had General Patrick. Naval members of the Joint Board opposed the recommendation, however, and the matter was dropped.[42]

In the wake of Mitchell's reaction to the crash of the Navy dirigible *Shenandoah* and his subsequent court-martial, President Calvin Coolidge, no friend of Mitchell, appointed Dwight W. Morrow to head a commission that Coolidge hoped would bring out "the good qualities of the Air Service." In other words, the president hoped to counter any unfavorable publicity that might come from the Mitchell court-martial and from the forthcoming report of the Lampert Committee, a joint congressional committee that had taken much testimony from

Mitchell and favored a single department of defense with equal land, naval, and air services. The report of the Morrow Board was released on 3 December 1925, 10 days before the release of the Lampert Committee report and a month before the verdict in the Mitchell court-martial. Since the board saw no threat of an air attack upon the United States, it rejected the concept of a separate air force or department of defense. In an effort to placate critics, the board recommended that the name be changed from Air Service to Air Corps, giving the Air Corps representation in the General Staff; and that assistant secretaries in charge of aviation be added to the War, Navy, and Commerce Departments.[43]

The Air Corps Act of 1926 was the direct result of the report of the Morrow Board. On 2 July 1926, the Army Air Service became the Army Air Corps, but the new name was purely cosmetic because there was no change in status; the Air Corps would still be a combat branch of the Army with less prestige than the infantry. The Air Corps Act of 1926 created the position of assistant secretary of war for aviation; took steps to regularize flying officers' pay, rating, and promotion; and instituted a five-year program that would eventually give the Air Corps 1,800 serviceable aircraft and the crews to fly them.[44]

Critics who felt that the Air Corps Act of 1926 did not go far enough were vindicated when funds to expand the Air Corps were not available, and the other reforms failed to meet expectations. From 1926 to 1931, 12 bills for the creation of a separate department of aeronautics and 17 bills for a single department of defense were introduced in Congress, but not one succeeded. Compromise was in the air, however. In 1931 Gen Douglas MacArthur, the Army chief of staff, and Adm William V. Pratt, chief of naval operations, agreed that Army aviation's role in national defense would be limited to coast defense. This agreement further clarified the mission of the Air Corps and eventually contributed to the creation of the GHQ Air Force.[45]

In 1933 Maj Gen Hugh A. Drum headed a board that explored an expanded role for the Air Corps. The Drum Board's recommendation was for the creation of a GHQ Air Force of 1,800 aircraft. This was not the independent air force desired by the advocates of airpower, but it was a more immediately achievable goal. The idea of a GHQ Air Force was further helped by the ill-fated airmail episode of the winter of 1934, when the federal government called upon the Air Corps to take over airmail service. The attempt failed after a series of highly publicized fatal crashes. The inability of the Air Corps to do something as apparently simple as delivering the mail without sustaining a number of fatalities alarmed many in President Franklin D. Roosevelt's administration.[46]

As a result of the airmail fiasco, former secretary of war Newton D. Baker was called upon to head a board to investigate the state of the Air Corps and to make recommendations. The advocates of airpower used the occasion to push for an independent air force, but the board was simply opposed to the idea of an independent air arm or a unified department of defense. The Baker Board determined that the problems of the Air Corps would be solved by more control, not less. Since the post of assistant secretary of war for air had been abolished early in the Roosevelt administration, the board advocated that duties such as individual training, procurement, and supply would be assumed by the chief of the Air Corps. For actual air operations, the GHQ Air Force would be established and would be responsible to the Army chief of staff in peacetime and commander of the field forces in a war. As a civilian on the Baker Board, James H. "Jimmy" Doolittle filed a minority report advocating the separation of the Air Corps from the Army. As an Air Corps Tactical School instructor, Captain George insisted that "so long as we have an air force subordinate to and controlled by officers whose entire experience has been had in ground warfare, we will find that the Air Force is considered only in connection with other branches of the ground Army."[47] The GHQ Air Force was, however, a first step toward the autonomy required to carry out the kind of mission the faculty of the ACTS envisioned—a mission far different from that currently prescribed by the War Department.[48]

The Air Service Field Officer's School was established at Langley Field, Virginia, in 1921. The school was renamed the Air Corps Tactical School in 1926 and moved in 1931 to Maxwell Field. The curriculum was originally designed to train field-grade officers in the Air Service and then was expanded to explore new ways to employ airpower. The training consisted of nine months of instruction that included the usual courses in logistics, communications, and ground tactics, but most of the 1,345 hours were devoted to practical flying, doctrine, and strategy as they applied to pursuit, bombardment, attack, and observation aviation. It was the aviation component of the curriculum that was most important. Since the Air Corps was required to accept current War Department military doctrine, the ACTS served as an almost surreptitious source for the unique military doctrine of the Air Corps.[49]

The instructors at ACTS did not restrict themselves to the expressed military doctrine of the War Department. If they had, the students would have limited themselves to studies in coastal defense and consequently would have been unprepared for the realities of military aviation in World War II. Rather they introduced their students to the underlying philosophy of war and in so doing hoped to explore new methods of waging it. In 1929 ACTS adopted the motto Proficimus More Irretenti (We Make Progress Unhindered by Custom). This motto was highly symbolic because by 1930 ACTS had shifted emphasis from the familiar pursuit aviation to bombardment aviation, which existed mainly in theory and depended on technology that had yet to be developed.[50]

In the early days, ACTS regarded pursuit aviation as central to air operations. This belief was summed up in the 1925–26 text entitled *Employment of Combined Air Force*: "Pursuit in its relation to the air service . . . may be compared to the infantry in its relation to the other branches of the Army. Without pursuit, the successful employment of the other air branches is impossible."[51] War Department doctrine had been based on the Clausewitzian principle as expressed in the Field Service regulations of 1923: "The ultimate objective in all military operations is the destruction of the enemy's armed forces by battle. Decisive defeat in battle breaks the enemy's will to war and forces him to sue for peace."[52] In 1926 ACTS amended this principle by stating that airpower could strike deep into enemy territory at the vital points of the enemy's infrastructure rather than merely targeting the enemy's military forces in a war of attrition. In 1930 the bombardment text stated, "Bombardment formations may suffer defeat at the hands of hostile pursuit, but with a properly constituted formation, efficiently flown, these defeats will be the exception rather than the rule."[53] The 1931 bombardment text expressed the belief that the bomber could operate day or night, singly or in mass, with or without pursuit support, and that defense against hostile pursuit could be maintained by supporting fire from machine guns of aircraft flying in close formation. The attitude was more succinctly expressed by 1st Lt Kenneth N. Walker in a lecture in the bombardment course: "Military airmen of all nations agree that a determined air attack, once launched, is most difficult, if not impossible to stop."[54] This shift in emphasis from pursuit to bombardment was the result of two factors: the air war theories of the time and the state of aviation technology.

There is no doubt that General Mitchell's ideas concerning airpower had a profound effect on doctrine formulated at ACTS. The court-martialed general's writings and testimony were well known among the faculty at ACTS, many of whom had had direct contact with him. In fact, Lieutenant Walker and Capt Robert Olds had served as aides to Mitchell. These two men were responsible for formulating a major portion of ACTS bombardment doctrine. Their work prompted historian Robert T. Finney to conclude that these two instructors "consciously or unconsciously" provided "the covering for the skeleton built by Mitchell."[55] As noted in chapter 1, Mitchell leaned more and more in his later years toward the ideas of Douhet, so much so it is difficult to distinguish Mitchell's ideas from those of Douhet.

Controversy still surrounds the role of Douhet's theories in the formulation of strategic bombing doctrine at ACTS. There is no doubt that Douhet's writings were available to the students at ACTS as early as 1923; and in light of this, it is inconceivable that the Air Corps officers who constituted the faculty and student body at ACTS would not search out every possible source in a field in which so little work had been done. At the very least, Douhet's theories were transmitted through the influence of Mitchell. There is no doubt that Douhet's ideas were familiar to those who taught and studied at ACTS.[56]

A distinction must be made, however, between being familiar with Douhet's concepts and accepting them totally. Douhet's advocacy of attacking an enemy's vital center and his belief in a self-defending bomber became a part of American airpower doctrine, but his hellish vision of initial attacks against the enemy civilian population was all but rejected out of hand. Even Mitchell thought a few gas bombs could paralyze the population of a city, but ACTS refused to accept this particular concept for a number of reasons. In later years, Hansell explained one reason for this rejection: "The idea of killing thousands of men, women, and children was basically repugnant to American mores. And from a more pragmatic point of view, people did not make good targets for the high-explosive bomb."[57] Ronald Schaffer explains another reason for the rejection of attacks directed toward civilians: "Selective bombing also fit very well the kind of equipment and bombing techniques the Air Corps was developing, and it seemed the most efficient way of using the nation's scarce military resources."[58] New technologies had made it easier for the Americans to avoid the politically unacceptable idea of bombing civilians; therefore, Douhet was influential at ACTS in terms of formulating basic concepts, not in terms of designing a specific strategic bombing doctrine. As so often happens in military aviation, the existing technology determined the parameters of the doctrine that would direct it.

In technological terms the bomber of the 1930s was indeed the queen of the skies. With the B-10 and later with the B-17 Flying Fortress, both of which could achieve speeds of two hundred miles per hour or better, there were no pursuit aircraft in existence that could overtake the bombers from the rear. For pursuit aircraft to be successful against bombers, they would have to meet them head on. Without a sufficient early warning system this was all but impossible, and radar was as yet unknown. Even if by chance the pursuit aircraft overtook the bombers, it was believed that the defensive armament of the bombers could easily deal with the attacking aircraft. It was also believed that the bombers could fly well above enemy antiaircraft fire, thus making the defense of the bomber virtually assured. When the Sperry and Norden bombsights were introduced in 1933, the apparent reality of high-level, precision bombing was complete. Pursuit aircraft simply could not prevail against such bombers as the B-17.[59]

When Hansell became a student at ACTS, only about one quarter of the students admitted were below the rank of captain, and those who were accepted had to have an efficiency rating of not less than "excellent." This was an important career boost for Lieutenant Hansell. Of the 59 graduates in Hansell's class, six would later play a part in his professional and personal life. These fellow students included Muir S. "Santy" Fairchild, Byron Gates, Barney Giles, Laurence S. Kuter, Hoyt S. Vandenberg, and Reginald Vance, Hansell's brother-in-law. For some officers who attended ACTS, the year of duty at the school was a time of reflection and rest. This was not the case for Hansell because the atmosphere at the school in 1934–35 was supercharged with debate over the future of airpower in general and the Air Corps in particular.[60]

The faculty at ACTS had a profound impact upon Hansell. Having just left the Three Men on a Flying Trapeze team it is surprising that he did not become a protégé of Chennault, but rather he was won over by the bombardment advocates. The year as a student at ACTS transformed Hansell from "Pursuit Possum" into a true advocate of bombardment aviation. Five officers were responsible for the conversion. Col John F. Curry, the commandant of the school, impressed Hansell as did Lt Col Harold George and Capt Robert Webster. Maj Donald Wilson and Lt Kenneth Walker also had a vicarious impact on Hansell. Even though both Wilson and Walker had left the faculty at the end of the previous year, their influence and writings were still important. It was these five men who guided Hansell in the development of his views on strategic bombing.[61]

Historian Conrad Crane explained the two prerequisites for creating new military doctrine: "First, higher authorities must realize the need for change and support new ideas. Second, a small and creative group of thinkers must work together to synthesize a body of thought expressing a new approach to war."[62] The General Staff certainly had not realized the need for a new air doctrine, but Colonel Curry both realized the need and had the means of providing a setting for the formulation of air doctrine without interference from Washington. In 1933–34 Curry had organized the academic program into three departments: Air Tactics, Ground Tactics, and Basic and Special Instruction. Air Tactics, naturally, received the most

Martin B-10 Bombers

attention with emphasis on attack, bombardment, pursuit, and observation aviation. Hansell later characterized Curry as a "stalwart leader". . . who should be listed among the best."[63]

Of all the instructors at ACTS, Harold George certainly had the greatest impact on Hansell, so great that Hansell later referred to him as a "prophet of air power." George's most important contribution to the strategic air doctrine being formulated at Maxwell was his ability to state the new objective of air war. He and Kenneth Walker had developed an air war theory consistent with the theories of Douhet, Trenchard, and Mitchell: airpower could decide the outcome of war. Before the President's Commission on Aviation in 1934, George explained the new interpretation of an old Clausewitzian theory: "The object of war is now and always has been the overcoming of the hostile will to resist. The defeat of the enemy's armed forces is not the ultimate object in war; the occupation of his territory as a military operation is not necessarily the object in war. Each of these is merely a means to an end, and the end is overcoming his will to resist. When that will is broken down, when that will disintegrates, then capitulation follows."[64] This belief made two bold assumptions. First, since the pure Douhetian theory of direct attacks against civilians had been rejected, the bombers would have to hit highly selective targets. Second, the bombers would have to reach the targets without being shot down.[65]

In a 1933 lecture Donald Wilson stated that the goal was to "select targets whose destruction would disrupt the entire fabric of an enemy's economy and thereby discommode the civilian population in its normal day-to-day existence and to break its faith in the military establishment."[66] Wilson knew from his own railroad experience that the destruction of a few vital links could disrupt the flow of material; therefore, if one identified and destroyed the truly vital links, the objective of disruption of the civilian population could be achieved. Later, George and Webster examined New York City and concluded that if 17 specific targets within the city's transportation and utility system were destroyed, the city would no longer be habitable. This would achieve the objective Douhet had proposed without the destruction and casualties, thereby avoiding any semblance of immorality.[67]

Hansell's mentors naturally assumed that this sort of decisive strategic bombing could take place without serious opposition from enemy pursuit or antiaircraft fire. Wilson felt that in most cases the enemy air force could be passed up unless it threatened one's own base of operations or if enemy air defenses were too strong. According to George, in the unlikely event that an enemy air force had to be dealt with, the solution was to seek out and destroy the enemy on the ground. In fact, he discounted the threat of pursuit aviation altogether and expressed his opinion that air-to-air combat was an anachronism: "The spectacle of huge air forces meeting in the air is a figment of the imagination of the uninitiated."[68] The mutual supporting fire from close formation along with speed and altitude would make the bomber practically invulnerable and make a pitched air battle a thing of the past.[69]

By the time of Hansell's graduation from ACTS, the basic premise of the school was complete, "Independent strategic air action against a hostile industrial nation could achieve the ultimate aim of destroying the will of an enemy to resist."[70] The bomber could reach its targets in daylight, destroy them, and return to base without serious opposition from enemy defense forces. Hansell and his classmates had been present at the creation of America's new air doctrine. They had sat at the feet of George and Webster and had been nurtured on the ideas of Walker and Wilson. When Hansell joined the faculty of ACTS in 1935, he was ready not only to advocate the new doctrine but also to expand upon it.[71]

Hansell served as an instructor at ACTS from 1935 to 1938, completing three years of the usual four-year tour. Col Arthur G. Fisher was commandant of ACTS from 1935 to 1937, followed by Brig Gen Henry C. Pratt. More important than the commandant, however, was the head of the Department of Air Tactics and Strategy. That office was held by Colonel George during the 1935–36 school year and then by Colonel Wilson for the 1936–37 and 1937–38 school years. By the mid-thirties the Air Force course was the vehicle through which the theories of airpower and air war were expounded, and it was considered to be the most important course in the curriculum. Hansell, as a lieutenant, was assigned to the important position of instructor in the Air Force section. The section chiefs during Hansell's three years were first Harold George, then Donald Wilson, and finally Muir Fairchild. Many future Air Force leaders, such as John Cannon, Ira Eaker, Newton Longfellow, Elwood R. Quesada, Nathan F. Twining, Kenneth Wolf, Orvil Anderson, Earle E. Partridge, and a host of lesser-known officers, were students of Hansell's. Hansell found himself in company with the most important advocates of strategic air war in the United States Army and, for that matter, in the world.[72]

Hansell's first real test of loyalty to bombardment aviation in general and the Air Corps in particular came in 1936 when Major Chennault began recruiting Air Corps fliers for his famous Flying Tigers. The Chinese government made it profitable for Americans to join their struggle against the Japanese. Luke Williamson and Billy McDonald, frustrated at not receiving regular commissions, had already joined Chennault. One day Chennault called Mrs. Hansell and asked to see Pos. When Chennault arrived, she prepared tea for the two but remained close at hand so she could hear the conversation. Chennault offered Hansell a position in his expedition. Hansell promptly turned him down, citing his career and, most of all, the fact that he did not wish to leave his family. Chennault, impatient with his subordinate's attitude, informed Hansell that he too had a wife and children and that he was leaving them and that Hansell could do the same. At that point Mrs. Hansell burst into the room and ordered Chennault to leave at once without saying another word and promptly showed him to the door. This removed all doubt about Hansell's new career choice and alienated Chennault for the rest of his life.[73]

With George and Chennault together at ACTS the debate between bombardment and pursuit reached its peak. The many social gatherings were often excuses to debate the issues of the day. Hansell was popular only among a small circle of friends; his opinionated views often brought him into conflict with others. Gatherings were often held at the Hansells' quarters, and the debates would continue late into the evening and often erupt into violent arguments. Hansell's son, Tony, recalled being told to go to sleep but finding it impossible because of the noise the adults were making downstairs. Once at a dance a well-meaning officer asked Mrs. Hansell to dance in order to suggest that she "tell Possum to get his head out of the clouds." True to form, Mrs. Hansell furiously terminated the dance. She knew that her husband was obsessed with the potential of bombardment and, whether she agreed or not, she stood by Possum and his quest.[74]

With the departure of George and Chennault in 1936, the atmosphere at ACTS became somewhat less combative, although Kuter, Hansell, and Fairchild could be just as vociferous. Just prior to George's departure, Hansell and several friends obtained a gallon of six-week-old Alabama moonshine and treated their mentor to an informal party. Episodes like this were not rare at Maxwell Field. The officers would abstain from alcohol all through the work week, but on the weekends they would often find time to party. The Hansells particularly enjoyed the company of the Kuters and the Vandenbergs. Even though Hoyt Vandenberg was a pursuit advocate, he "played the role of the arbitrator, referee, placator, and soother."[75] Once a swimming party was so wild that the commanding officer at Maxwell almost made Hansell and his companions foot the bill for draining and refilling the base pool. The friendships forged at ACTS would last a lifetime.[76]

Hansell enjoyed the parties at Maxwell, but he took his duties as instructor in the Air Force section very seriously. The course consisted of five parts: Principles and Tactical Doctrine for Combat Aviation, Antiaircraft Defense, Air Warfare, Air Forces in the Army, and Air Force Operations. His lectures were meticulously arranged with close attention given to every detail. In February 1938 Wilson sat in on a lecture and wrote a complimentary critique of it, reminding Hansell to stress the necessity of an independent air force. Hansell naturally echoed the air doctrine established by Wilson and his contemporaries but added his own touches. Since the Air Corps was supposed to be a defensive force, Hansell often created hypothetical situations in which the United States was being invaded from Canada's maritime provinces or from European colonies in the Caribbean and challenged his students to respond to the threats through detailed map exercises in which they would apply the principles of air warfare against imaginary enemies. The training was as practical as possible for American military forces in the late 1930s.[77]

Hansell was also very careful to advocate his ideas and still tacitly remain within the confines of existing War Department doctrine. For example in April 1938 Hansell gave a lecture entitled "The Influence of Air Force on Land Warfare." In the lecture he conceded that "the ultimate objective of all military operations is the destruction of the enemy's armed forces by battle," but concluded the lecture by saying, "If, by the application of air power, we can deny to the enemy ground forces the essential munitions for waging a conclusive land operation, if in other words, we can isolate the troops on the battlefield from their essential supplies, then we will have had a profound influence upon the conduct of land warfare, and will have made a maximum contribution toward the object of war, whether or not the air force is ever actually seen on the battlefield."[78] Even though this departure from War Department doctrine was not very subtle, Hansell did exhibit an awareness of the necessity of operating within the system.

Hansell took great care to communicate the new principles of strategic air war and their historical background. He often relied on Helmuth Karl Bernhard Moltke's definition of strategy—"the art of applying the means available to the attainment of the end desired." Hansell would then lead his students through what he called the three basic factors in the conduct of war: (1) the end desired; (2) the means available; and (3) the application of the means. The end desired was always to break the enemy's will to resist; the means available was the air force; and application of the means was the destruction of carefully selected targets.[79] Hansell saw war as a science, which, even though it was unpredictable, was governed by discernable principles. In the introduction to "The Employment of Offensive Force," he stated, "It is simply not possible to formulate doctrine that will meet every purpose and every situation. However, it is perfectly feasible to outline *principles* which will meet every purpose and every situation."[80]

Hansell was totally dedicated to using the principles he taught to achieve the goal of breaking the enemy's will to resist. In a lecture given in April 1938, he explained the very essence of his strategic thinking. He declared that there were

two general methods by which air forces might exert conclusive action through air warfare: (1) by disrupting the life of the civil populace, denying to the people the normal conveniences which have become essential to modern life, and hence causing such suffering as to make the civil populace prefer the acceptance of peace terms to endurance of further hardship; in other words, breaking the enemy's will to resist; (2) by paralyzing the industrial machinery which must be relied upon to sustain the *means* to fight—the armed forces. This latter method, by emasculating the means to fight, also eventually breaks the "will to resist." The breakdown of the national economic structure may break the will to resist by either or both of these methods.[81]

Hansell believed that if the enemy population was convinced that their own forces were incapable of defending them, they would cause an end to the hostilities by placing pressure upon their government. Yet Hansell steered clear of Douhet's advocacy of direct attacks on the civilian population. In his lecture, "The Aim in War," he declared, "We may find the Air Force charged with breaking the will to resist of the enemy nation. Let us make it emphatically clear that that does *not* mean the indiscriminate bombing of women and children."[82] ACTS did, however, make provision for attacks upon nonspecific targets within cities, which amounted to attacks upon women and children. Yet attacks of this nature were to be used only as a "last resort" and were intended to make the cities "untenable" rather than to target the people themselves. Hansell and his associates had no intention of waging a war of wholesale murder.[83]

The only way to avoid wholesale murder in strategic air war was to strike specific targets. Hansell and his colleagues were very confident that this could be accomplished. In one lecture Hansell boldly declared, "There is at present time, we believe, no structures which cannot be destroyed by bombs," but he went on to add, "Bombs will accomplish the desired result only if they are detonated in the proper places. No amount of skill or proficiency in other ways can compensate for failure to deliver the bombs with sufficient accuracy."[84] In order to strike the targets, those targets must first be identified. Hansell identified the desired targets: "Civil structures such as power plants, factories, water works, and other structures are quite vulnerable to small bombs." In Hansell's opinion, these targets were "almost impossible to disperse and cannot be concealed."[85]

Hansell may seem to have been oversimplifying the situation, but the faculty at ACTS had already begun to tackle the enormous problem of target selection. Since American military intelligence carried out on foreign nations was strongly discouraged, Fairchild and Webster undertook an analysis of American industry to test the concept of the vital point. Hansell assisted and made an important discovery. He found that a particular highly specialized spring used in the manufacture of controllable pitch propellers was manufactured by one particular firm, and that a shortage of that spring had brought a large portion of American aircraft production to a halt. Hansell indicated that that example had set the pattern for target selection, since precision targets that were critical for basic industry were sought. Targets of this type were later referred to by critics as "panacea targets" and the search for them later made the ball-bearing facilities at Schweinfurt, Germany, infamous.[86]

Targeting is pointless if the aircraft cannot reach the target because of enemy opposition, yet little attention was paid at ACTS to this problem. Hansell's lectures reveal a lack of concern over enemy opposition in the air: "The Pursuit Section here at the School . . . feels that units of perhaps 12 to 15 pursuit airplanes might engage bombardment units of almost any size. Of course, with a numerical inferiority the defending pursuit may not shoot down many bombers."[87] As we have seen, the level of pursuit technology of the time did not offer much promise of a viable defense against bombers. Because of the lack of early warning systems in the 1930s, Hansell estimated that a city would need at least 900 pursuit aircraft to provide adequate defense. He came to the conclusion that "it is not feasible to provide pursuit defenses on a broad scale that are capable of adequate defense against enemy bombers."[88] Yet he did caution that the students should be careful about accepting that type of general statement. Technology was constantly changing and no one could tell what the future might hold. But at that time Hansell pointed out that bombers would have the advantage of initiative in the absence of early warning. He did seem to recognize the potential value of pursuit escort for bombers, but concluded that "although accompanying pursuit is highly desirable, it cannot normally be counted upon in attacks against the interior because of the limited range of pursuit aviation."[89] At any rate, since pursuit aviation lacked the capacity to attack strategic ground targets, Hansell believed it should not be included in a striking force. His attitude toward pursuit aviation is best summed up in the following: "Perhaps someone will invent a death ray or some such device that will obliterate airplanes in flight—when that time comes there will be a defense against this new instrument—the air force."[90]

It is certain that most of Hansell's ideas were far from original; they reflect the work being done at ACTS and can be traced to his mentors such as George and Wilson. Yet as a junior officer Hansell did make some unique contributions. In some lectures he explored the use of chemical weapons to neutralize the air bases and bridges of invading forces although he assumed that these actions would only occur during an actual invasion of the United States and that the use of poison gas would come only out of desperation.[91] In another project Hansell put his engineering skills to use by preparing curves of probability from which he derived the probable number of bomb hits on a target, based on a given number of bombs dropped with an average rate of accuracy.[92] Hansell's greatest contribution was the demonstration of a talent that would serve him well later—gathering and understanding foreign military intelligence. In his lectures, he would routinely compare the theory being taught at ACTS with actual air combat in China and Spain. For example, he stated that the Spanish Civil War did not apply to aerial warfare (at least not to strategic bombing) because since both sides desired the occupation of the country, air forces alone could not possibly achieve the desired objective.[93] Hansell also had a firm grasp of the principles of economic warfare. In a speech given around 1938 to the Montgomery, Alabama, Chamber of Commerce, he offered insight into Germany's reasons for approaching another war: "Germany's prosperity is dependent upon the acquisition of raw materials and markets. Hence Germany's national policy is necessarily concerned with obtaining these essentials."[94]

In retrospect, many mistakes were made by the men who developed the air war theories at ACTS. They overestimated the effect of bombardment on the civilian population. (Hansell wrote, "We know from our analysis of our own vulnerability to air attack that our national structure might be almost completely disrupted in a very brief period of time.")[95] Target selection was to be far more difficult than was thought at the time, and they overrated the destructive power of explosive bombs. ACTS also missed the mark in its evaluation of enemy fighter opposition in the mistaken belief that bombers alone could successfully penetrate enemy air space with minimal losses. The airpower pioneers at ACTS were true to their motto because they were unhindered by custom, but they were hindered by a rapidly changing technology and a rapidly changing world situation.

It must be remembered, however, that the faculty at ACTS operated in the realm of pure theory. Their work was at best preliminary because they were not called upon to make actual strategic or operational plans. The equipment on which they based their doctrine was as yet untested, as in the case of the B-17 and its bombsights. They had confidently touted the virtues of the self-defending bomber, yet power turrets and .50-caliber defensive guns were not yet available. The real value of the work done at ACTS is that a small group of talented military thinkers were given the opportunity to explore the potential for a powerful new weapon—airpower.

In later years Hansell reflected on the importance of his work at ACTS: "If our air theorists had had knowledge of radar in 1935, the American doctrine of strategic bombing in deep daylight penetrations would surely not have evolved." He went on to add, "Our ignorance of radar was surely an asset in this phase."[96] One might question his conclusion, but it is clear that the work done at Maxwell Field produced the Air Corps's plan to deploy America's vast airpower resources during World War II.

Notes

1. *Atlanta Journal*, 6 June 1943; and *Atlanta Constitution*, 6 June 1943.

2. Col Haywood S. Hansell III, interviewed by author, 16 February 1992; DeWitt S. Copp, *Forged in Fire: Strategy and Decisions in the Air War over Europe, 1940–1945* (New York: Doubleday & Co., 1982), 403; and interview with Barney Giles, File K239.0512, Air Force Historical Research Agency (AFHRA), Maxwell AFB, Ala.

3. Hansell III; Mrs. Haywood S. Hansell Jr., interviewed by author, 21 March 1992; and Dennett Hansell, interviewed by author, 21 March 1992.

4. Ibid.

5. Ibid.

6. Ibid.

7. Haywood S. Hansell Jr., *The Strategic Air War against Germany and Japan: A Memoir* (Washington, D.C.: Government Printing Office, 1986), vii.

8. Hansell III; Mrs. Hansell; and Dennett Hansell.

9. Ibid.

10. Col Haywood S. Hansell Sr. to Haywood S. Hansell Jr., letter, 29 May 1918, from the Hansell family's private collection.

11. Hansell III; Mrs. Hansell; and Dennett Hansell.

12. Hansell III; Mrs. Hansell; Dennett Hansell; and "Exalted Sense of Ethics," an unidentified article from the Hansell family's private collection.

13. Sydney Shalett, "This Possum is Jap Poison," *The Saturday Evening Post*, 25 November 1944, 17.

14. Ibid.

15. Hansell III; Mrs. Hansell; and Dennett Hansell.

16. Ibid.

17. Ibid.

18. Ibid.; and Shalett, 94.

19. John F. Shiner, *Foulois and the U.S. Army Air Corps, 1931–1935* (Washington, D.C.: Office of Air Force History, 1983), 32.

20. Hansell III; Mrs. Hansell; and Dennett Hansell.

21. Accident Reports, File 200.3912-1, AFHRA, Maxwell AFB, Ala.

22. Shalett, 95.

23. Unidentified newspaper article from the Hansell family's private collection.

24. James Parton, "*Air Force Spoken Here*": *General Ira Eaker and the Command of the Air* (Bethesda, Md.: Adler & Adler, 1986), 179; and Hansell III.

25. Mrs. Hansell.

26. Ibid.

27. Ibid.

28. Ibid.

29. Ibid.

30. Capt Harold L. George to the commandant, Maxwell Field, Alabama, letter, 24 November 1933, Haywood S. Hansell Jr. Papers, microfilm edition, AFHRA, Maxwell AFB, Ala.; and C. W. "Bill" Getz, ed., *The Wild Blue Yonder: Songs of the Air Force*, 2 vols. (San Mateo, Calif.: Redwood Press, 1981), DE-14, 15, F-15, 16, O-4, 5, 6.

31. Martha Byrd, *Chennault: Giving Wings to the Tiger* (Tuscaloosa, Ala.: University of Alabama Press, 1987), 41–42.

32. DeWitt S. Copp, *A Few Great Captains: The Men and Events that Shaped the Development of U.S. Airpower* (Garden City, N.Y.: Doubleday & Co., 1980), 321.

33. Byrd, 41.

34. Ibid., 41–42.

35. Ibid., 42.

36. Hansell III.

37. Shalett, 95.

38. Byrd, 41–42.

39. Ibid., 43–59.

40. Ibid., 45.

41. Ibid., 45–46.

42. Wesley Frank Craven and James Lea Cate, eds., *The Army Air Forces in World War II*, vol. 1, *Plans and Early Operations, January 1939 to August 1942* (1949; new imprint, Washington, D.C.: Office of Air Force History, 1983), 26.

43. Ibid., 26–29.

44. Ibid., 29.

45. Ibid., 29–30.

46. Ibid., 30–31; and Shiner, 144.

47. Shiner, 203.

48. Craven and Cate, 29–32.

49. Thomas A. Fabyanic, "A Critique of United States Air War Planning, 1941–1945" (PhD diss., Saint Louis University, 1973), 2–3; Robert T. Finney, *History of the Air Corps Tactical School, 1920–1940*, USAF Historical Study 100 (Maxwell AFB, Ala.: USAF Historical Division, Air University, 1955), 6, 7, 28; and Hansell, *Strategic Air War*, 6, 7, 17.

50. Finney, vii, 28.

51. Fabyanic, 5.

52. Finney, 30.

53. Fabyanic, 25.

54. Finney, 32, 33.

55. Ibid., 27.

56. Ibid.; Fabyanic, 15; Thomas H. Greer, *The Development of Air Doctrine in the Army Air Arm, 1917–1941* (Washington, D.C.: Office of Air Force History, 1985), 50–51; Robert Frank Futrell, *Ideas, Concepts, Doctrine: A History of Basic Thinking in the United States Air Force, 1907–1964* (Maxwell AFB, Ala.: Aerospace Studies Institute, 1971), 63; and Conrad C. Crane, *Bombs, Cities, and Civilians: American Airpower Strategy in World War II* (Lawrence, Kans.: University Press of Kansas, 1993), 17–18.

57. Hansell, *Strategic Air War*, 13–14.

58. Ronald Schaffer, *Wings of Judgment: American Bombing in World War II* (New York: Oxford University Press, 1985), 29.

59. Finney, 33–35.

60. Ibid., 42, 72–73.

61. Ibid., 57–58.

62. Crane, 19.

63. Ibid.; Haywood S. Hansell Jr., "Harold George: Apostle of Air Power," in *Makers of the United States Air Force*, ed. John L. Frisbee (Washington, D.C.: Office of Air Force History, 1989), 76–77; and Hansell, *Strategic Air War*, 7.

64. Hansell, "Harold George," 77.

65. Haywood S. Hansell Jr., *The Air Plan that Defeated Hitler* (Atlanta: Higgins-McArthur/Longino and Porter, 1972), 4, 23, 32.

66. Finney, 31.

67. Michael S. Sherry, *The Rise of American Air Power: The Creation of Armageddon* (New Haven: Yale University Press, 1987), 53; Crane, 19–20; and Hansell, "Harold George," 78.

68. Greer, 56.

69. Hansell, *Air Plan*, 44–45; and Finney, 37.

70. Fabyanic, 45.

71. Finney, 36; Crane, 19; and Hansell, *Air Plan*, 12.

72. Finney, 21, 23–24, 58–61, 64–77.

73. Byrd, 62; and Mrs. Hansell.

74. Hansell III; and Mrs. Hansell.

75. Phillip S. Meilinger, *Hoyt S. Vandenberg: The Life of a General* (Bloomington, Ind.: Indiana University Press, 1989), 19.

76. Ibid.; and Mrs. Hansell.

77. Haywood S. Hansell Jr., "Air Force—Course Outline"; Lt Col Donald Wilson to 1st Lt Haywood Hansell, letter; and Haywood S. Hansell Jr., "Employment of Offensive Force." These documents are from the Hansell Papers, AFHRA, Maxwell AFB, Ala.

78. Haywood S. Hansell Jr., "The Influence of Air Force on Land Warfare," Air Corps Tactical School, Maxwell Field, Ala., April 1938.

79. Haywood S. Hansell Jr., "The Air Force and Its Characteristics," Hansell Papers, AFHRA, Maxwell AFB, Ala.

80. Haywood S. Hansell Jr., "The Employment of Offensive Air Force," Hansell Papers, AFHRA, Maxwell AFB, Ala.

81. Hansell, "The Influence of Air Power on Land Warfare."

82. Schaffer, 30.

83. Hansell, *Strategic Air War*, 10.

84. Hansell, "The Air Force and Its Characteristics."

85. Ibid.

86. Finney, 32–35; Sherry, 54.

87. Haywood S. Hansell Jr., "The Employment of Defensive Force," Hansell Papers, AFHRA, Maxwell AFB, Ala.

88. Ibid.

89. Haywood S. Hansell Jr., "Tactical Offense and Tactical Defense," Hansell Papers, AFHRA, Maxwell AFB, Ala.

90. Ibid.

91. Haywood S. Hansell Jr., "Air Operations—Counter-Air Force," Hansell Papers, AFHRA, Maxwell AFB, Ala.

92. Hansell, *Air Plan*, 18.

93. Hansell, "Tactical Offense and Tactical Defense."

94. Haywood S. Hansell Jr., "The Air in War," Hansell Papers, AFHRA, Maxwell AFB, Ala.

95. Hansell, "Air Operations—Counter-Air Force."

96. Greer, 60.

Chapter 3

Planning

Hansell's ideas concerning aerial warfare were well established by the time he left ACTS in 1938. Yet, as an Army officer, he knew he had to follow the prescribed Army path to success. An important step on that path was admission to the Army Command and General Staff College (CGSC), Fort Leavenworth, Kansas. It was an honor to be accepted because graduation from this institution was the harbinger of subsequent promotions and positions of responsibility. Fewer than one in 10 West Point graduates became generals; the path to a star led through Leavenworth. Hansell was particularly honored because he entered the CGSC as a first lieutenant. Most students were majors or lieutenant colonels.[1]

CGSC's mission was to instruct Army officers in every aspect of their profession with the ultimate objective being the ability to command division- and corps-size units. The students participated in map exercises, planned and led attacks, conducted reconnaissance, defended strong points, and perfected techniques of logistics, especially supply and transportation. The focus was, of course, on ground-based combat arms. Many Air Corps officers found the instruction boring and outdated.[2]

In the 1930s the instructors at CGSC failed to discuss airpower adequately. Only five of the 158 conference periods were dedicated to aviation, and these five periods taught airpower concepts from 1923. The best Hansell could expect from the experience was the promise of future promotion. Eaker and other graduates from the school jokingly referred to the nearby prison as the "big house" and the Command and General Staff School as the "little house" for reasons that were, for them, painfully obvious.[3]

If the intellectual atmosphere was confining, the living quarters were even more so. The Hansell family moved from the spacious quarters at Maxwell Field to a little apartment that had formerly been a bachelor officer's quarters. The place was so small that a stairway leading to another apartment upstairs

57

separated the Hansell's two bedrooms from the kitchen and dining room. Mrs. Hansell referred to the apartment as a "public hallway" which forced her to get fully dressed to go from her bedroom to her own kitchen. Being a first lieutenant in a field officer's world plainly had its disadvantages.[4]

The Hansells even found it difficult to keep up the social pace at Leavenworth. Since there was very little to do at the Army post itself, the officers had to make the expensive trip to Kansas City if they were to enjoy any nightlife. The Hansells could afford to make the trip only a few times while they were at Leavenworth. But, since Leavenworth had been an old frontier post, Possum got a chance to practice his horsemanship and play polo to his heart's content. Mrs. Hansell became even more involved in horseback riding and continued to take instruction in the subject, mostly to please her husband.[5]

The year at Leavenworth lived up to Hansell's expectations in one respect. On 2 May 1939, he was promoted to captain. He did not find the experience at Leavenworth as stimulating as his studies at ACTS, but he had paid his dues and could go on to more interesting and important assignments. By the time he graduated in June 1939, he was ready to load Dotta and Tony into his new 1939 Oldsmobile and set out for his new assignment in Washington.[6]

It is said that soldiers prepare for war and pray for peace, but in the years between 1937 and 1941, the very kind of war for which Hansell and his contemporaries were preparing became shocking reality. The July 1937 incident at Marco Polo Bridge plunged Japan even deeper into China. The Munich crisis of 1938 had given Adolf Hitler another victory in his drive to create his greater Germany and had also shown President Franklin Delano Roosevelt (FDR) the need for a larger air force. FDR originally proposed a 10,000-plane Air Corps but by April 1939 had been forced by political considerations to scale the plan down to a 6,000-plane force.[7] By 1 September 1939 Europe was at war, and by the spring of 1940 France was fighting for her life. These events prompted President Roosevelt to call for an air force of 50,000 aircraft. By December 1941 the British were struggling to prevent the invasion of England and fighting to maintain their lifeline in the Mediterranean. The Russians had retreated to the very gates of Moscow after suffering unimaginable losses. American foreign policy had gone from staunch isolationism to participating in a de facto naval war against Germany and actively working to isolate Japan. Hansell arrived in Washington to witness the astonishing growth of the Army air arm. As Wesley F. Craven and James L. Cate describe the situation, "The whole story of Air Corps activity in the period 1939–41 may be conceived as a race against time in a desperate effort to overtake Axis air forces which had long been on a war basis."[8]

The Hansells moved into a townhouse at 4457 Greenwich Parkway, just west of the Georgetown University campus. This picturesque home was a far cry from the cramped facilities at Leavenworth. Hansell's new assignment was in the munitions building located between the Washington Monument and the Lincoln Memorial at the present location of Constitution Gardens. George and Eaker were working for Arnold also in the munitions building. At first Hansell's function was public relations, but soon he was given a far more important assignment as Eaker's assistant. Eaker was executive to the chief of the Air Corps, a position that placed Hansell very close to the center of power in the command structure. Eaker had earned the trust of General Arnold and, as Hansell later put it, "Ira . . . was living literally hand in glove with Arnold."[9] Next in line was Col Carl A. "Tooey" Spaatz, Arnold's operations officer. Eaker said of the Arnold-Spaatz relationship that whereas Gen Robert E. Lee had a number of lieutenants, Arnold had only one—Spaatz. Arnold had been given the nickname "Happy" because he apparently had a permanent smile on his face. This "smile" was misleading because Arnold was a hard-driving leader who expected nothing less than perfection from his staff. As Eaker later stated, "He'd have fired his own mother if she didn't produce."[10]

Washington (and indeed the nation) was dominated by one figure in the years immediately preceding and during World War II—President Roosevelt. Hansell gradually became an admirer of the president but only after the war began. Hansell did not like FDR's New Deal because he thought it was socialism and that it abandoned his father's (and his own) Protestant work ethic. In 1940 he supported Wendell L. Willkie, probably because the Democrat-turned-Republican had promised an independent air force. But once FDR committed himself to the rapid expansion of the Army Air Forces, Hansell became, as usual, a team player.[11]

The social climate in Washington was more stimulating than that at Leavenworth, but Hansell still found time for his favorite nonflying pursuit, polo. Once at Fort Meyer, Virginia, Possum was engaged in a heated polo match when his horse accidentally collided with the horse ridden by Col George S. Patton Jr., commander of the 3d Cavalry Regiment. Patton furiously dismounted, stopped the match, and began to yell at Possum declaring that he might be a good pilot but that he "wasn't worth a damn as a polo player." Witnessing this scene from the stands, Mrs. Hansell leaned over the rail and yelled, "You can't talk to my husband like that!" Thus a 37-year-old captain and his wife brushed shoulders with a future legend.[12]

Even though the Air Corps was expanding rapidly, General Arnold had his hands tied in terms of the essential function of intelligence gathering. As late as 1939, he was not privy to the G-2 reports of the War Department General Staff unless he read the reports in the G-2 office. He was not allowed to remove the reports from the office. Arnold took his concerns to the Army chief of staff, Gen Malin Craig, who allowed Arnold to establish his own assistant military attachés for air at United States embassies in major world capitals. Arnold established the Air Force Intelligence Division in November 1939 and placed Captain Hansell and Maj Thomas D. "Tommy" White in charge of setting it up.[13]

Hansell and White divided the Intelligence Division into two broad areas of responsibility. White would be in charge of the assistant military attachés, while Hansell undertook the area of strategic air intelligence and analysis. He took up the very task in strategic air planning that Douhet considered to be the essence of air strategy—targeting. He set up three subsections: (1) the analysis of foreign air forces, including size, composition, equipment, disposition, tactical doctrine, and proficiency; (2) the analysis of airports and air bases throughout the world, including maps and weather data; and (3) the preparation of economic, industrial, and social analyses of major foreign powers, an undertaking that involved the difficult task of target selection and preparing target folders.[14] The magnitude of the task was well understood by Hansell, who stated, "We had to proceed on our own, pioneering in one of the most difficult, critical, and challenging areas in the field of intelligence."[15]

The War Department G-2 offered Hansell and White no help whatsoever. Not surprisingly, G-2 vigorously opposed the collection and analysis of this type of information, arguing that "it did not relate to proper military intelligence." In addition to this problem, the assistant military attachés for air ran into trouble collecting information. For example, during the invasion of Poland the only information came from the press, conversations with colleagues, and a knowledge of German air doctrine and tactics, none of which could reveal what was actually happening at the front. Yet Hansell dutifully analyzed the reports, most of which were little better than reading the *New York Times*. Never one to back down from a challenge, Hansell committed himself to finding new ways of gathering information on his own.[16]

In July 1940 Hansell was appointed chief of the Operations Planning Branch, Foreign Intelligence Section. On 15 March 1941, he was promoted to the temporary rank of major. With new authority and rank, Hansell set out to solve his intelligence-gathering problems. Rising concern about Hitler prompted a number of civilian experts to accept Army commissions. Hansell was able to acquire the services of Dr. James T. Lowe, a specialist in diplomatic history. He also lured Maj Malcom Moss, an expert in oil production who had traveled widely and seen many potential targets first hand.[17]

Hansell divided the world into theaters and collected intelligence on the interior of the selected countries themselves in order to prepare air operations against specific targets. He and his newly acquired experts set out to study the industrial-economic structure of Nazi Germany by focusing on electric power, steel production, petroleum products, the aircraft industry, and transportation systems. The problems presented by this project were exacerbated by a limited budget and the fact that Germany was already at war and thus under a cloak of secrecy.[18]

Major Moss suggested concentrating on the electric plants and systems as primary targets in an air war against Germany. He recalled that since many United States banks had underwritten the construction of electric facilities in pre-Nazi Germany, the banks would have drawings and specifications of such targets. Hansell was delighted because Moss had "tapped a gold mine." They used the bank sources along with scientific journals and trade magazines to put together a comprehensive study of the German electric-power system, including aiming points and bomb sizes. Progress on petroleum and synthetic oil plants was made partly through the same sources and partly through individuals who had worked in Germany, Romania, and the Middle East. After much effort, this shoestring intelligence operation had produced target folders on all the major target systems. Without an extensive intelligence network, adequate funding, or adequate support, Hansell had accomplished a most difficult task indeed.[19]

Hansell's efforts were not necessarily appreciated at the time. When his staff prepared a project to survey the Burma Road to explore the possibilities of supplying China in order to conduct air operations from there, the War Department G-2 section got hold of the proposal and forwarded it to the chief of staff. The deputy chief of staff, Maj Gen William Bryden, wrote his critique in his own hand when he returned the plan: "If the Intelligence Division of the Air Corps has nothing more practical to do than this, we will give them a job."[20] When the incident came to the attention of General Arnold, he responded by writing, "I am inclined to agree with General Bryden." Hansell had had his first brush with Hap Arnold. There would be many more such clashes between the doctrine-oriented Hansell and the pragmatic Arnold.[21]

Hansell's work on target systems was remarkable, especially considering the lack of support he received. The efforts were somewhat less successful when it came to an analysis of German transportation systems because of the extent of the rail and canal systems. Perhaps the greatest benefit of this intelligence work was to reinforce Hansell's convictions about the ideas formulated at ACTS. He later wrote of his experience as intelligence chief: "I was motivated by a number of convictions to turn out maximum effort to the defeat of Hitler. A year's study as head of the Strategic Air Intelligence Section of A-2 led me to a firm belief that Germany was susceptible to defeat from the air."[22]

Hansell's intelligence also included British sources. On 28 November 1940, he had a conversation in Spaatz's office in Washington with Air Commodore John C. Slessor, who answered a number of questions about strategic bombing as it had been practiced thus far in the war. Slessor agreed with Hansell's ideas totally, even to the point of endorsing precision bombing over area bombing. Since the Operations Planning Branch of the Intelligence Division was just being organized in London, it was suggested that a visit by Hansell to that facility would "greatly facilitate the organization and operation of this function." Hansell's next important mission would be as an observer in England.[23]

When Hansell departed for London, Dotta was seven months pregnant and had seven-year-old Tony and 10-month-old Lucia to care for. He hated to leave, yet the trip was important for the development of American strategic airpower and for his career. Just before his departure he was authorized by the War Department to investigate the efficiency and capability of foreign commercial airlines and military air forces. He was rated both as an aircraft observer and a technical observer for the occasion.[24]

Hansell found that he was in his element in London, "I got a tremendous cooperative reception; couldn't have been finer."[25] He found that the British could go through a day filled with terror and difficult decisions and still find time for tea in the afternoon. This was very much in line with Hansell's southern upbringing, and he was never more at home. He even began using the strictly British term "chap" in his conversation and writing, and it is obvious that the British had won a true friend and advocate. Much of Hansell's time was spent with Gp Capt A. C. H. "Bobby" Sharp, who welcomed him into the inner chamber of RAF intelligence. After working 16-hour days, the RAF officers would take time to talk to the young American major about British air operations and, more importantly, British strategic targeting.[26]

The real work of Hansell's visit consisted of examining German-facility target folders that had been prepared by the British. Surprisingly, he found that he was better informed than the British on German electric power, petroleum, and synthetic products, although the British knew more about

German aircraft and engine production, the actual strength of the Luftwaffe, and the German transportation system. He also examined British base construction because the American-British Conversations (ABC) had already discussed an Anglo-American bomber offensive. By the end of July he had collected a large amount of intelligence materials consisting mostly of very valuable target folders. The problem was how to transport nearly 500 pounds of classified foreign intelligence on loan from a nation at war to a "neutral" nation. The material was finally shipped to the States in a medium bomber.[27]

More important than the target folders was Hansell's firm conviction that the ideas he and his colleagues had formulated at ACTS had the potential to win the war. In spite of what Slessor had said in Spaatz's office, the basic difference between the British and Americans was the argument about area bombing at night and daylight precision bombing. It was true, Hansell wrote, that "both German and British bombers proved vulnerable to fighters, but they were medium bombers, poorly armed and flying at a relatively low altitude."[28] American long-range, heavy bombers would be much better armed and fly at much higher altitudes. Their tight formations and concentrated firepower would provide an adequate defense. Hansell also had newfound faith in the British ability to hold out, even in the face of the prospect of imminent Soviet collapse. As he later wrote, "A tour in England as an observer of the war convinced me Britain would fight and go on fighting so long as there was one ray of hope. We would supply that ray."[29]

While Hansell was collecting this vast amount of material, two significant events occurred. First, the German invasion of Russia was unbelievably successful for the Germans. Hundreds of thousands of Russians were being taken prisoner, and the German panzer divisions were driving deep into Soviet territory. It appeared to be only a matter of time before the Soviet Union went the way of France. Second, President Roosevelt had requested that the War and Navy Departments prepare overall production requirements necessary to defeat America's potential enemies. The first hint Hansell had that something important was transpiring was a cablegram ordering him home from England immediately.[30]

The world situation in the summer of 1941 was truly desperate. The Soviet Union appeared to be on the verge of collapse, and without Germany's distraction by the Russian front, the British and Commonwealth forces could have no reasonable hope of victory. Only the intervention of the United States could improve the situation. The Japanese also threatened to open yet another front in the Pacific. President Roosevelt had taken important steps to involve the United States short of war beginning in 1937 and more recently with the Neutrality Act of 1939, which incorporated the "cash-and-carry policy." Gradually America became more and more involved. The destroyers-for-bases deal was followed by the nation's first peacetime draft and, in March 1941, by the Lend-Lease Act. All the while, the Roosevelt administration was tightening the screws on Japan through ever-tougher sanctions.

The United States had no intention of being caught without a strategic plan. In early 1941 the Americans and British had a series of "conversations" that established the basic strategy should there be an Anglo-American alliance. The final report, known as ABC-1, was submitted on 27 March 1941 by a US staff committee and representatives of the British chiefs of staff. The basic premise of the report was that the industrial and economic might of the United States would be used to support the British and all other nations that opposed the Axis (Germany, Italy, and Japan). Germany was identified as the main enemy, and it was agreed that the resources of the Allies would first be directed against Germany. By the end of April 1941, the War Plans Division of the General Staff had completed Rainbow No. 5, which was the culmination of planning that had begun in the autumn of 1939. Rainbow No. 5 accepted the general concepts of ABC-1 in that, in the event of war, the United States and her British Allies would open an offensive in the Atlantic while maintaining a strategic defense against the Japanese in the Pacific.[31]

On 9 July 1941, President Roosevelt sent a letter to the secretaries of War and the Navy requesting an estimate of overall production requirements needed to defeat the Axis. He wanted only an estimate of desired munitions production and the mechanical equipment that would be required for victory. He went on to write, "I am not suggesting a detailed report but one that, while general in scope, would cover the most critical items in our defense."[32] What he got, however, was one of the most important military documents produced by the United States in World War II.[33]

The plan would have to include requirements for the air forces, but it was at first unclear how the so-called Air Annex to what became the Victory Program would be written. Lt Col Clayton L. Bissell, an air officer assigned to the War Plans Division of the General Staff, sought only informal assistance from the new Air Staff of the Army Air Forces. Lt Col Harold George had strong objections to this because his own Air War Plans Division of the Air Staff had been in existence for nearly three weeks, and he felt that his staff should prepare the Air Annex. Brig Gen Leonard T. Gerow, head of the General Staff's War Plans Division, met with General Arnold to discuss the plan, at which time Arnold suggested that Colonel George's Air War Plans Division be given the task so the General Staff's War Plans Division would be free to deal exclusively with ground forces. Gerow agreed, only requiring that the air planners remain within the guidelines set down by ABC-1 and Rainbow No. 5.[34]

Colonel George was summoned to Arnold's office and informed that he and his tiny staff had the task of preparing the Air Annex, but that he would have to work quickly because Arnold was prepared to depart for destinations unknown, even by him. Arnold was scheduled to return on 12 August 1941, and the document had to be completed by then, just nine days hence. Arnold would end up at Argentia, Newfoundland, for the famous Argentia Conference. So while Roosevelt, Churchill, and their staffs hammered out a grand strategy for winning World War II, George and three other officers would give them the tools to accomplish the task.[35]

Events had been moving so rapidly that the air plans could not keep up with them. In May of 1940 a 24-tactical-group air force had been envisioned, but in July that plan was upgraded to 54 groups. In June 1941 all Army aviation was concentrated into the United States Army Air Forces, giving Arnold more control over the air arm. Yet, even with this unprecedented growth and limited autonomy, there was no guarantee that the Army Air Forces would not be restricted by the current

War Department doctrine, which stated that air forces existed to carry out Army missions. Just like field artillery or the engineers, the air force might be relegated to simply supporting the infantry. The fact that George and his team were writing the Air Annex meant that for the first time the air force mission would be determined by airmen.[36]

On Monday, 4 August 1941, George assembled his team—Laurence Kuter, Ken Walker, Possum Hansell, and himself—with no time to spare. Each of these four men had served together at Maxwell Field and had taught at ACTS. To a man, they believed that strategic bombing could win the war, and now they had the chance to draft a plan that could put into practice the principles they had taught. George assumed direction of the project himself. Kuter, who was on loan from the G-3 (operations) Division of the General Staff Corps, concentrated on calculating the forces necessary to meet the mission. Walker was the expert on probabilities of bombing accuracy. Having just returned from England as America's foremost expert on targeting, Hansell began the difficult, delicate, and key job of target selection.[37] The success of the plan was dependent upon the team, and, as Hansell later reflected, "Actually the plan was the fruit of seven years of working together, rather than seven days. Without our previous service together on the faculty of the Air Corps Tactical School it would have been quite impossible to produce a plan of this magnitude in so brief a period."[38]

Hansell had just returned from England when he immediately became immersed in the writing of AWPD-1. Mrs. Hansell, now eight months pregnant, could not understand what Possum was doing that was so important. "I couldn't bring myself to believe that it wasn't just a job you got paid for," she later remembered. She saw him only once during the period and had absolutely no idea what her husband was working on. She resented his absence deeply and could not believe his total dedication to the job.[39]

The old munitions building where the team worked was uncomfortable in the best of times, but that nine-day period was unbearably hot, with temperatures of 90°F each afternoon. The ubiquitous Westinghouse oscillating fans did little to mitigate the heat. It was perhaps even worse in the penthouse office in which the team did their work. Hansell said, "Literally, when you put your hand down on your desk, your papers would stick to it. It was terribly difficult and unpleasant."[40] They were at their desks from early morning until midnight all through the process. Tempers flared under the heat and the pressure of the deadline. At one point Walker angrily took Hansell to George's desk and exploded at the younger officer. Hansell was red-faced and ready to "tear down the penthouse." George gave the two a moment to cool off and then grinned at Walker and said, "Well, Ken, you're right. But you know, the trouble we've always had with ol' Possum is that he's right, too, once in a while."[41] Walker and Hansell cooled down and forgot the incident.

The war situation in August 1941 played a significant role in determining AWPD-1. It was thought that the Soviet Union was on the brink of collapse and could not last until the spring of 1942. This would once again make Britain the focus of German attention. But even with the Russian campaign in full force, the Germans were seriously threatening Britain's lifeline in the Mediterranean and the Atlantic and had sunk or damaged 459,000 tons of British shipping in July 1941. If Great Britain fell, hopes for victory against Germany would fall as well.[42] Hansell felt that "delay had already reached the danger point; it might already be too late."[43]

With no time to waste, George and his team adopted the bold premise that a massive bombing campaign against Germany would debilitate the German war machine and topple the German state. The strategic bombing campaign would also assist a land invasion of Western Europe, if that should become necessary. As historian William Snyder observed, the writers of AWPD-1 believed that "most industrial societies are hostage to the continuing operation of a few critical industrial systems, such as electric power plants and distribution networks. Destruction of these 'vital centers' weakens both the enemy's will and capacity to conduct modern war."[44] If the Army accepted it, this principle would give the air force more independence and the promise of actually winning the war.[45]

Both ABC-1 and Rainbow No. 5 had anticipated an air attack from England as the earliest American offensive action but did not offer a detailed statement as to how that mission was to be accomplished. In addition to the offensive against Germany, George and his team also had other tasks to perform. First of all, they had to defend the Western Hemisphere, mainly from a possible Japanese attack on the west coast. Then the air force was to maintain a strategic defense in the Pacific, allowing the Navy to bear the brunt of any operations against the Japanese. This presented a most complicated problem in terms of size, composition, equipment, disposition, and organization of the air forces.[46] Not only must the forces be created, they must be used properly. And Hansell observed, "Moreover, it was axiomatic that the employment must make its maximum contribution in support of our overall national policy."[47]

President Roosevelt had requested an estimate of the amount of equipment that must be produced to win the war. The Air War Plans Division came up with some impressive estimates. AWPD-1 called for 68,416 aircraft of all types, including 11,853 combat aircraft and 37,051 trainers. The anticipated attrition rate was 2,133 aircraft per month. The force would require 2,118,635 men of whom 179,398 would be officers and 1,939,237 enlisted personnel. The plan called for 135,526 pilots, navigators, bombardiers, observers, and machine gunners. On the ground in support roles would be 862,439 technicians; 60,153 nonflying officers; and 1,106,798 nontechnical personnel.[48]

Numbers of aircraft were basically what the president required. George's Air War Plans Division went further, however, to produce an incredibly detailed plan as to how these planes and personnel would be deployed against the Axis. They could not afford to allow the Army and Navy to set the air priorities because, as Craven and Cate state, "It is apparent, however, that the air planners were less interested in the problems of the defensive in the Americas and the Pacific than in the war in Europe."[49] In fact, the most important air mission listed in AWPD-1 was "to wage a sustained air offensive against German military power."[50]

AWPD-1 was centered around the strategic bombing of Germany, and the attention given to the numbers indicates that the planners devoted almost their entire attention to that task. In World War I, air planners had ignored such Clausewitzian frictions as weather, mechanical problems, attrition rates, and replacement requirements. The Air War Plans Division developed an elaborate system to determine as accurately as possible just what size force they would need in the strategic campaign. Based on British climatological records, the planners determined that the strategic bomber force could count on only five operational days per month. They estimated the number of aborts due to mechanical failure and determined the aircraft replacement rate. The critical estimate was how many bombers would be required to knock Germany out of the war. The planners estimated that it would require 220 bombs to destroy a target 100 feet square. For planning purposes they assumed that a bomber would carry only a single bomb. Each group would include 70 aircraft of which only 36 would be available for a given mission. Under normal conditions it would take six groups to destroy a target, but when the estimated bomb error under combat conditions (a factor of five) was calculated, 30 would be required to destroy a target.[51]

For example, if 50 generating plants were to be destroyed, 30 groups would be required for the task, which would equal 1,500 individual targets per group. Assuming that the weather would allow eight operational days per month (three more than could be expected, according to British experience), it would require 32 groups or 2,240 operational aircraft to destroy the targets within six months. Eventually the Air War Plans Division determined that there would be 154 individual German targets, which would ultimately require 6,860 heavy bombers.[52]

The Air War Plans Division did not simply draw these numbers from a hat. A detailed bombing plan had been established by the planners. The first and most important assumption of the plan was, as Hansell put it, "that since the German state was supporting one of the greatest military operations of all time, it was under great internal stress."[53] If the bombing could strike the most critical target systems in the German economy, the Germans would be forced to terminate military operations because of a paucity of equipment and petroleum products and the loss of any means of transporting what resources were left. The planners estimated that the Army could not possibly mount offensive operations in northwestern

Europe in less than two and a half years after M day (mobilization day), but that the Air Corps could begin operations within one year of M day. The first tasks of the Air Corps operating out of England and the Middle East would be to attain air superiority by attacking air bases, aircraft factories, and light metal industries. The next task performed during the buildup was to undermine the war-making foundations of Germany. Finally, in an intensive six-month bombing campaign, the strategic bombing forces would tenaciously attack selected target systems in Germany and German-occupied Europe with large concentrations of bombers using precision-bombing techniques.[54]

D day (the invasion of northwest Europe by the Allies) could not be conducted before the spring of 1944. Thus if the strategic campaign yielded the results the planners envisioned, the invasion itself would be unnecessary. Yet they feared that if the heavy bomber forces were diverted from their strategic targets to support the invasion, the chance to defeat Germany with airpower alone would be lost. They allocated, therefore, what they felt would be adequate tactical forces to be used in conjunction with the ground forces. Those forces would include 13 groups of A-20 light bombers, two photo-reconnaissance groups, 108 observation squadrons, nine transport groups, and five pursuit groups based in the United Kingdom. The Air War Plans Division hoped that this tactical air force would free the bombers to carry out the true purpose of AWPD-1.[55]

Since the ultimate objective of AWPD-1 was to force the capitulation of Germany through strategic bombing, the selection of targets was of the utmost importance. Hansell was the foremost targeting expert in the Army Air Forces. Drawing from his experiences as a student and instructor at ACTS, as an air intelligence expert, and as an observer of British air operations and intelligence, he accepted the task of selecting targets for the AWPD-1 plan with the confidence of a professional. He set out to find the answers to the myriad questions that accompany the task of targeting: What were the important links in the German economy? Which targets were most vulnerable? Which targets would be most difficult to harden?

Which targets within a given target system should be hit first? How often should the targets be hit?[56]

He had only a few days to complete the task; nonetheless, Hansell was well prepared. As he later recalled, "After putting as many pieces of the puzzle together as were available to us, we pinpointed some 154 targets which, we felt, would disrupt or neutralize the German war-making capability, provided, of course, they could be destroyed or kept out of operation."[57] These targets were divided into four broad target systems, which were listed in order of priority—the electric power, the inland transportation, the petroleum industry, and the civil population of Berlin.[58]

Hansell estimated that the destruction of 50 electric-generating stations in Germany would result in denying Germany 40 percent of her electric-power generating capacity. This would "in all probability cause the collapse of the German military and civil establishment."[59] He further estimated that destruction of the 50 targets would require fifteen hundred group missions over the prescribed six-month period. Major Moss's assessment of the German electrical system had been invaluable to Hansell, and he made full use of it. As historian James C. Gaston wrote, "At 1:30 [P.M.] on Thursday, 7 August, the gentle, red-haired Southerner knew more than Rudolph Vogel."[60] Of course, Hansell realized there would be problems with targeting electrical systems such as generating plants and switching stations. The generating plants were bound to be heavily defended; the stations were small and difficult to hit from high altitude. Dams were vulnerable but difficult to get to.[61] Even though, as we shall see, this target system was later rejected, it had much merit. As historian Alan Levine noted, "The only [German] weak spot, perhaps, was a strained electrical power system. Otherwise, there were few weak points in the German war economy, and they were not obvious."[62]

Hansell's analysis of German inland transportation systems divided this target system into two categories: inland waterway transportation and rail transportation. He determined that inland waterways moved 25 percent of the total freight carried in Germany. He estimated that the destruction of nine locks, three ship elevators, and inland harbor facilities at Mannheim and Duisburg would paralyze the existing inland waterway establishment. In terms of rail transportation, Hansell estimated that the destruction of 15 marshalling yards and 15 other "sensitive points within the rail net" would cause the "disintegration and failure of the transportation system in Germany." This was significant since Hansell estimated that 72 percent of German traffic was by rail. Thus with 17 targets in the German inland waterway system and 30 targets in the German rail system, their destruction could be ensured with 1,410 group missions.[63]

Hansell was very sanguine about the prospects of destroying the German petroleum industry. He pinpointed 27 synthetic oil plants which, according to Hansell, accounted for "nearly 50 percent of Germany's crude petroleum." Since the Luftwaffe, German army, and Kriegsmarine were so dependent on petroleum, oil, and lubricants, the destruction of these plants would all but halt their supply of gasoline. Most importantly, he estimated that 80 percent of the aviation gasoline came from these plants. The plants were located in central and western Germany, and thus would be more easily targeted. Therefore, with only 810 group missions, the petroleum industry of Germany would be practically useless.[64]

The most controversial of Hansell's target systems was the proposed attack on the civil population of Berlin. Only in the event that the whole structure of the German state "seemed on the verge of collapse" would the attack be ordered.[65] In fact, it was not given much attention in AWPD-1:

> Immediately after some very apparent results of air attacks on the material objectives listed above or immediately after some major setback of the German ground forces, it may become highly profitable to deliver a large scale, all-out attack on the civil population of Berlin. In this event, any or all the bombardment forces may be diverted for this mission. No special bombardment force is set up for this purpose.[66]

Here Hansell maintains that the attack *may* become highly profitable. Later he wrote, "We stressed the point that until that time [Germany on the verge of collapse] there was reason to doubt the efficacy of simply bombing civilians."[67] Yet, since Germany had surrendered in 1918 in part because of civil unrest following setbacks on the battlefield, there was reason to believe that such an attack was justified, but only under certain conditions. Hansell went so far as to point out that no bombardment force was set up for the purpose. But, as Conrad Crane points out: "This one-time exception to general policy was sanctioned only as a way to end the war quickly, but late in the war this concept of an aerial *Todestoss* (deathblow) would prove a potent lure for American leaders, helping to sanction the use of the atomic bomb."[68] Hansell had allowed the one tiny crack in his strategic bombing doctrine that would ultimately change the entire concept of strategic bombing in the eyes of many highly placed American Air Force generals.

Before any of these target systems could be attacked in strength, AWPD-1 listed an "intermediate" target: the Luftwaffe. The plan, however, was not for air-to-air combat because at ACTS these men had dismissed the very idea of great battles between aircraft; and, as Hansell had put it at ACTS, no "death ray" had yet been invented. The only way for a strategic air force to destroy fighter opposition was to destroy the German aircraft industry and depend on the defensive fire of the American bombers.

Hansell identified 18 large aircraft assembly plants, six large aluminum plants, and six magnesium plants, which were the heart of the German aircraft industry. After 113 group missions in the six months of the air offensive, the German fighter threat would, according to the plan, be greatly diminished. Hansell acknowledged the success of British fighters over the German bombers in the Battle of Britain, but he concluded that the size of the German aircraft along with their deficiency in defensive armament contributed to their failure. The American bombers would be technologically superior to any aircraft the Germans had used against Britain, and the American aircraft would have sufficient defensive firepower.[69]

This is not to say that the Air War Plans Division overlooked the possibility of escort fighters. On the contrary, the subject was surprisingly thoroughly explored. The document conceded, "It has not yet been demonstrated that the technical improvements to the bombardment airplane are or can be sufficient to overcome the pursuit airplane, permitting day operations in the face of strong pursuit opposition." It went on to acknowledge, "The importance of day attacks is recognized in scoring hits against vital targets. It is unwise to neglect

development of escort fighters designed to enable bombardment formations to fight through to the objective."[70]

In its simplest form, AWPD-1 called for 12 groups of B-29s
(very heavy bombers), 20 groups of B-17s (heavy bombers),
and 10 groups of B-26s (medium bombers) to be based in the
United Kingdom. An additional 12 groups of B-29s would be
based in the Middle East. The plan even made provisions for
the giant B-36, which could bomb Europe from bases in the
United States. As it turned out, B-29s would not be ready for
the air war in Europe, and B-36s would be the intercontinen-
tal bombers of the postwar period, but Hansell and his colleagues had prepared a detailed plan that they believed would
win the war.[71]

Thus the watershed document of America's air strategy in
World War II was completed by the deadline of 1:30 P.M. on
Sunday, 12 August 1941. Hansell's contribution was crucial,

B-29 Very Heavy Bomber

B-26 Medium Bomber

not only for preparing the document but also in giving it lasting value as a war plan. As Gaston observed, "Hansell's analysis was clean, thorough, and intelligent—exactly what was needed."[72]

After World War II, AWPD-1 came under criticism for a number of flaws. Craven and Cate's classic study of the Army Air Forces in World War II found the plan to be deficient in that it did not allocate sufficient forces for strategic defense in the Pacific, while providing for too much hemispheric defense in the Americas. Of course, there was the argument that Germany was not defeated by airpower alone and that the invasion support was weak in fighters. While it is difficult to argue with these conclusions, they overlook the most fundamental flaw in AWPD-1.[73]

Hansell's assumption that the German war economy was under "great internal stress" was the fundamental error of the plan. As economic historian Alan S. Milward observed,

Seen from outside its frontiers National Socialist Germany was a country which had already geared its economy to the more absolute limit of war potential. It was widely assumed that the German state in 1939 had long been fully prepared for a major war and that Germany's economic resources were wholly engaged in the purpose of war. All Allied strategic planners started from this assumption, but nothing could have been farther from the truth.[74]

The error, of course, was not Hansell's alone. Germany, using blitzkrieg methods to fight short, decisive wars, had placed no greater wartime commitment on her economy than that which would have been expected during peacetime in 1938. This information shocked many when it was discovered after the war. Hansell's estimation of numbers of targets, numbers of group missions, and identification of subtargets within such target systems as the petroleum industry was inadequate. More than 6,860 bombers would be needed, more bombs would be required, and more time allotted to complete the missions because of unacceptable weather.[75]

The most obvious error in AWPD-1 was its omission of fighter escorts as an integral part of the plan. Hansell himself expressed regrets that fighters were not included. "Neither AWPD-1 or AWPD-42 called for escort fighters, and patently this was the greatest deficiency in both plans. . . . We did not think it possible to build an airplane that had [a] couple thousand miles of range, that would also have the maneuverability to enter into combat with an airplane that has simply come up from the ground into the target area."[76] The inability of the bomber to defend itself would lead to a 21 percent loss at Schweinfurt, and the Luftwaffe would be destroyed in the end by escort fighters, not by destroying German aircraft factories.[77] Yet, the planners had used the best information available at the time and, as Hansell later related, "We were told that [escort fighters would be impossible] by most of the aeronautical people with whom we had dealt . . . and the air strategy people accepted the concept that we are going to have to fight our way through to defend ourselves simply because it was either that or give up."[78]

Other criticisms of AWPD-1 have emerged. Historian Barry D. Watts, considering the method in which the numbers were estimated, added his criticism of the overall strategic scope of the document: "I would, therefore, argue that their thinking was mechanistic in character—more akin to that of artillery officers laying out a plan of fire against inanimate targets than to classical, Clausewitzian strategists."[79] Hansell later admitted that the authors of AWPD-1 had concentrated on winning the war with the fewest American casualties and had paid little attention to "what happened afterward."[80] But it is certain that in preparing the air campaign against Germany they had adhered to principles of strategic air war they had earlier espoused. After all, Clausewitz's objective was to compel an enemy to yield by using the appropriate level and type of violence against him. The Air War Plans Division had planned a revolutionary method of achieving that objective, but the ideas had clearly come from the ACTS in the 1930s. George, Hansell, and the others had enjoyed the rare opportunity of seeing their air war theories actually take wing.

It is true that tactical air support, airlift, reconnaissance and observation, and air defenses had been slighted, but even the most severe critics of the strategic air war admit that the plan was appropriate for the situation. In their critique of the relationship between American bombers and their escort, historians Stephen L. McFarland and Wesley P. Newton maintain that "AWPD-1 projected figures that staggered the imagination, but proved to be remarkably accurate."[81] Given the time constraints, lack of resources, and limited staff, it is quite remarkable that four men could produce the American air plan for World War II in only nine days and forecast US combat groups within 2 percent, and the total number of officers and men within 5.5 percent. AWPD-1 had predicted a total of 44 bombardment groups and 21 fighter groups in Europe. The actual numbers were 60 and 44, respectively. More importantly, the United States would deploy its air forces against Germany in accordance with AWPD-1 with only surprisingly minor adjustments.[82]

The completed plan was not especially attractive because there simply was no time for glossy maps, charts, or eye-catching presentation. The 23 copies of the document were mimeographed, numbered, and kept under tight security. Barely meeting the deadline, AWPD-1 was deposited with the War Department General Staff at midnight, 12 August 1941.[83] Finally submitting the plan must have given the four men a tremendous sense of relief. Hansell later described the experience:

> It is far beyond my ability to adequately describe the frustrations, disappointments, fragile hopes, determination, and soaring zeal that were mixed in the cauldron to make AWPD-1 and the plans modifying it. The frantic efforts to meet deadlines, the disagreements, the uphill fight against entrenched and hostile opinion, the dedicated crusade for the new role of air power, the slumbering dread that we might be wrong—that we might persuade our leaders to take a path that would lead to disaster—put a heavy burden on all of us.[84]

Even after AWPD-1 was submitted, there was certainly no guarantee that it would be accepted since it would mean that the War Department would have to abandon or seriously modify its doctrine concerning Army aviation. Since the proposal came from a subordinate element of the Army, Hansell imagined that the War Department General Staff would consider it "brash beyond belief."[85] But the time constraint was placed upon the War Department General Staff as well, and since it was very busy putting together the Artillery Annex, Cavalry Annex, Medical Annex, and on and on, it passed the Air Annex without comment. In fact, Hansell suspected that the War Department General Staff was actually unaware of just what George's team had written into the plan.[86] Hansell later commented, "They [the War Department General Staff] were so busy trying to complete the rest of it themselves[,] I think if we had gotten it in earlier, it probably would have been thrown out."[87]

George realized the importance of selling the plan to his superiors, so he had his team prepare a highly polished presentation. The presentation was memorized after hours of editing and practice. No notes were used, only charts; each member of the group literally memorized all the facts and figures necessary to make his point. George introduced the presentation; Hansell gave the intelligence analysis and summary of targets; Kuter explained the force necessary to achieve the objectives; and Walker described the base requirements. George then concluded the presentation by taking questions. They practiced and polished the presentation until it was ready for its first live audience.[88]

The first formal presentation was to Brig Gen Harry L. Twaddle, G-3 (operations) of the War Department General Staff. General Twaddle and several members of his staff met with the Air War Plans Division in George's extemporized war room in the munitions building. The presentation took two hours and went very well. At least, Twaddle accepted it graciously enough. Perhaps the most important aspect of the meeting is that it helped the Air War Plans Division work out any bugs and polish its delivery.[89]

Two days after presenting the plan to General Twaddle, George's team gave their presentation to General Gerow and undersecretary of war for air Robert A. Lovett. Lovett was sympathetic to the plan, but the team had some apprehension about Gerow. But, as Hansell put it, "General Gerow showed himself to be a broad-minded, intelligent, and high-minded officer concerned primarily with the overall success of American forces."[90] In other words, Gerow agreed with Hansell. On 22 August 1941, they presented the plan to Maj Gen George Brett, chief of the Air Corps; General Gerow, General Fairchild, and Col Don Wilson were present.[91]

On 30 August 1941, AWPD-1 was presented to Gen George C. Marshall, General Arnold, Mr. Averell Harriman, and members of the General Staff. This was a critical point because Marshall could have "with a gesture" dismissed the entire plan. After the presentation there were questions about production, and even though Marshall showed great interest, he still appeared to be unconvinced. When all the arguments had been exhausted, Marshall said simply, "Gentlemen, I think the plan has merit. I would like for the secretary and assistant secretaries to hear it." To Hansell and his colleagues these words were "like music to our ears."[92]

On 4 September 1941, the Air War Plans Division presented the plan before Mr. William Knudsen, head of the Office of Production Management, along with five of his division chiefs and Mr. John Biggers, the president's Lend-Lease representative. This meeting resulted in the most rigorous questioning they had experienced. The problem was manufacturing capabilities. Mr. Knudsen took issue with some of the intelligence estimates based on the resources available in Germany. The most controversy surrounded Germany's production capacity, but the Air Materiel Command had provided facts and figures to rebut most of the criticism.[93]

Finally, on 11 September 1941, the team briefed Secretary of War Henry L. Stimson. This was an informal briefing held in Mr. Stimson's office with only General Marshall present. Having had a private meeting with George before the actual meeting, the secretary was already sold on the plan. His response all but guaranteed presidential approval: "General Marshall and I like the plan. I want you gentlemen to be prepared to present it to the president. I will speak to him about the date. Thank you for coming to my office."[94] This day (11 September) turned out to be a particularly important day in the life of Maj Haywood Hansell. The plan for which he had prepared for years became a reality, and his son Dennett was born.[95]

On 25 September 1941, Secretary of War Stimson forwarded the Victory Program, which included the Air Annex or AWPD-1, to the president. At that same time, isolationist Sen. Burton K. Wheeler of Montana obtained a copy of the Victory Program. According to Wheeler, he was approached by an unnamed Army captain who was concerned at the accelerated pace of preparations for war and who brought him an actual copy of the still-secret Victory Program. The senator was angered by the activist stance the president and the military had taken and felt that it was his duty to reveal the plan to the people. He showed his copy to correspondent Chesly Manly of the *Chicago Daily Tribune*. On 4 December 1941, the headlines of the *Tribune* proclaimed the existence of a war plan.[96] Hansell was shocked to see that "much of the secret information [he] had gathered in England was spread before the world in the pages of a newspaper."[97]

Stimson attacked the party responsible for the leak as having a lack of "loyalty and patriotism" and, at first denied that the report had any authorization from the government. Arnold was "ruthless" in his efforts to track down the leak. All members of the Air War Plans Division, including Hansell, were investigated, but Major Kuter seemed the most likely suspect. The FBI examined Kuter's papers closely and interrogated him at length, but in the end he was exonerated. The "Army captain" was never identified and the source of Wheeler's information remains a mystery.[98]

This breach of security could have been disastrous. Upon obtaining the information about the Victory Program in the *Chicago Daily Tribune* and other papers, the Germans prepared "Fuhrer Directive Number 39" on 11 December 1941, which proposed terminating the Russian campaign and concentrating forces in the Mediterranean to deny the Americans bases in the region. Furthermore, there would be a development of massive air defenses around Germany and increased naval attacks on American shipping. Clearly the scoop in the *Daily Tribune* had warned the Germans of American intentions in waging the war in Europe. But on 19 December, Hitler fired Field Marshal Walter von Brauchitsch, commander of the German army, and took command himself with renewed determination to defeat Soviet Russia, thus negating the effect of the security leak.[99] On 4 December newspaper publisher Col Robert R. McCormick had called the *Tribune* story "the greatest scoop in the history of journalism."[100]

The manner in which Hansell learned of Pearl Harbor later became the subject of an Associated Press article. As the Hansells drove along a Virginia highway near Washington on the afternoon of 7 December 1941, they listened to a presentation of Gilbert and Sullivan's comic opera, "The Mikado." The announcer broke into the broadcast to announce, "The Japanese have attacked Pearl Harbor." After the announcement, the production of "The Mikado" continued, adding to the air of "unreality."[101] The attack on Pearl Harbor would, of course, have a profound impact on Hansell's career. Not only would he be given new and much greater responsibilities, he would also see AWPD-1 retain its validity even after the attack on Pearl Harbor had radically altered the Army and Navy portions of the Victory Program. It had always been the plan for the American Pacific Fleet to at least maintain a strategic defense against Japan, but now the battleships were in the mud of Pearl Harbor and the American public was clamoring for offensive action against the Japanese. In addition to this, the recent German successes in the Soviet Union had cast some doubt on the "Germany first" principle.[102]

On 22 December 1941, the Arcadia Conference was convened in Washington among members of the combined chiefs of staff in order to define Allied strategy more clearly. George and Hansell were assigned to meet with representatives from the RAF. Along with the British, George and Hansell prepared the groundwork on which AWPD-1 would be executed. Hansell was an ideal choice for this assignment because one of the British representatives was Gp Capt Bobby Sharp, whom Hansell had known since his tour in England in July. Together the Americans and British laid out a tremendous air program that would accommodate 3,000 bombers, a number no one believed possible at that time. As Hansell put it, "the British played ball 100 per cent" and soon began the work of preparing aerodromes for the Americans in Britain.[103]

The Arcadia Conference had accepted, on 31 December 1941, a paper that outlined the Allied strategy. The agreement reaffirmed ABC-1 and Rainbow No. 5: American war production would provide the materials for war; lines of communications would be protected; Germany would be isolated primarily by blockade and bombardment; the main offensive against Germany would continue to be developed; and a strategic defense would be maintained against Japan at the same time. This was the agreed-upon strategy, but public sentiment in the United States demanded an offensive against the Japanese. The Navy was in full agreement with public opinion. There was always a chance that the Europe first priority would slip away, with profound implications for all services.[104]

Promotions had come quickly for Hansell. On 5 January 1942, he was promoted to the rank of temporary lieutenant colonel and on 1 March 1942, he became a temporary colonel. Following the Arcadia Conference, Hansell became chief of the European branch of the Air War Plans Division. During this time George, Hansell, and Walker realized that an independent air force was out of the question on practical grounds because they did not have enough time to prepare their own ordnance, supply, communications, or medical units. They submitted a plan to the War Department by which the Army would be divided into three branches—Army Ground Forces, Army Air Forces, and Army Service Forces. Much to their surprise, the plan was accepted and became the established Army organization all through World War II.[105]

In April 1942 Colonel Hansell was named to a post in the War Department General Staff. He was assigned to the new

Joint Strategic Committee, which consisted of eight members, four from the War Department and four from the Navy Department. The chairmanship of the committee alternated between Navy Capt Oliver Reed and Army Col Ray Maddocks. All members were expected to divest themselves of service allegiances and prejudices. Hansell, unable to divest himself of his firm belief in strategic airpower, noted that he was the only graduate of ACTS. Hansell shared a desk with a naval aviator, an arrangement that allowed them to share ideas.[106] Hansell described the meetings: "We had the damnedest battles you ever heard of, till two or three o'clock in the morning. But it was a common meeting ground and people did say what they meant, and out of it came compromises . . . and sometimes quite well."[107]

Just as the Joint Strategy Committee was called to order one morning early in its existence, "a burly Marine captain entered, bearing a locked and sealed briefcase. He wore side arms and an armed guard accompanied him. With much ceremony he removed a message from his briefcase and received a signed receipt. The message was from the Joint Chiefs of Staff (JCS) by way of the Joint Plans Committee. It was a masterpiece of directness and simplicity asking in effect: 'What should be the strategic concept of the conduct of the war?'"[108] The committee's first task was to come to some understanding of just how badly the war was going for the Allies, so they received a presentation from the Joint Intelligence Committee. The prospects were gloomy at best. The collapse of Russia was predicted for the spring of 1942, and the Allies fully expected the Germans and Japanese to join hands in Karachi, India, within the year. Since Europe appeared to be a lost cause, most members of the Joint Strategy Committee favored a strategic offensive in the Pacific and a strategic defense in the Western Hemisphere. Hansell, most unwilling to see his strategic campaign against Germany abandoned, worked with Lt Col Albert Wedemeyer through many hours of heated debate to convince the Joint Strategy Committee that the Germany-first strategy of ABC-1, Rainbow No. 5, and the Arcadia Conference was the only strategy to adopt. The decision process had been accelerated after the JCS impatiently sent a message demanding an answer to their question. Finally, although originally three-fourths of the committee was for abandoning Europe, Hansell and Wedemeyer convinced their colleagues that Germany was by far the more dangerous enemy.[109]

This was not the end of their disagreement, however. The Joint Strategy Committee accepted the Germany-first principle, but then suggested sending a strategic bombing force to guard the route between Hawaii and Australia. Not only was this an inappropriate way to deploy bombers, it would have taken away from the proposed mission of the yet-to-be-formed Eighth Air Force. A majority of the committee voted to form such an air unit, but Hansell dissented, thus causing the first "split-paper," and the joint chiefs were not pleased. General Arnold called Hansell into his office for an official "personal admonition," which went into Hansell's military record. Later Hansell and Wedemeyer were able to convince the committee of the folly of wasting bombardment aircraft on ocean patrols. The admonition remained in his record, but he was awarded the Legion of Merit for his services in air intelligence and air war planning.[110]

The value of the Joint Strategy Committee is problematic, but it did give Hansell even more experience in high-level planning. In August 1942 at the personal request of Gen Dwight D. Eisenhower, Hansell was transferred to the European theater of operations; his mission would be to transform his plans into action against the Germans. When Hansell arrived in Europe he was in a unique position to ensure that AWPD-1 was indeed the plan of action in the air war against Germany. After all, AWPD-1 was the embodiment of the military concepts fashioned at the Air Corps Tactical School in the 1930s, and Hansell's quest was to make his vision of air war a reality.[111]

Notes

1. Geoffrey Perret, *There's a War to be Won: The United States Army in World War II* (New York: Random House, 1991), 190–211.

2. Phillip S. Meilinger, *Hoyt S. Vandenberg: The Life of a General* (Bloomington, Ind.: Indiana University Press, 1989), 18.

3. Ibid.

4. Mrs. Haywood S. Hansell Jr., interviewed by author, 21 March 1992.

5. Ibid.

6. Haywood Hansell, personnel file, Record Group 18, File 201 (Washington, D.C.: National Archives); and James C. Gaston, *Planning the American Air War: Four Men and Nine Days in 1941* (Washington, D.C.: National Defense University Press, 1982), 20.

7. Jeffery S. Underwood, *The Wings of Democracy: The Influence of Air Power on the Roosevelt Administration, 1933–1941* (College Station, Tex.: Texas A&M University Press, 1991), 125–37.

8. Wesley Frank Craven and James Lea Cate, eds., *The Army Air Forces in World War II*, vol. 1, *Plans and Early Operations, January 1939 to August 1942* (1949; new imprint, Washington, D.C.: Office of Air Force History, 1983), 106.

9. Maj Gen Haywood S. Hansell Jr., interviewed by Murray Green, 2 January 1970, US Air Force Academy Library, Colorado Springs, Colo.

10. James Parton, *"Air Force Spoken Here": General Ira Eaker and the Command of the Air* (Bethesda, Md.: Adler & Adler, 1986), 115.

11. Haywood S. Hansell III, interviewed by author, 16 February 1992; and Hansell, Green interview.

12. Mrs. Hansell.

13. Haywood S. Hansell Jr., *The Air Plan that Defeated Hitler* (Atlanta: Higgins-McArthur/Longino and Porter, 1972), 49.

14. Ibid., 50.

15. Haywood S. Hansell Jr., *Strategic Air War against Germany and Japan: A Memoir* (Washington, D.C.: Government Printing Office, 1986), 22.

16. Hansell, *Air Plan*, 50; and "Daily Report of Military Operations, 15 September 1939," from the Military Attaché in Berlin, filed in the Haywood S. Hansell Jr. Papers, microfilm edition, AFHRA, Maxwell AFB, Ala.

17. Hansell, *Air Plan*, 50; and Hansell, *Strategic Air War against Germany and Japan*, 23.

18. Brig Gen Haywood Hansell Jr., interviewed by Bruce C. Hopper, 5 October 1943, Spaatz Papers, Library of Congress, Washington, D.C.; and Hansell, *Air Plan*, 51.

19. Hansell, *Air Plan*, 51–52; and Thomas A. Fabyanic, "A Critique of United States Air War Planning, 1941–1945" (PhD diss., Saint Louis University, 1973), 51.

20. Hansell, Hopper interview.

21. Haywood S. Hansell Jr., *Strategic Air War against Japan* (Maxwell AFB, Ala.: Air War College, Airpower Research Institute, 1980), 20–21.

22. Ibid., 53.

23. "Conversation with Air Commodore Schlesser [sic]," 4 December 1940, File 167.6-51, AFHRA, Maxwell AFB, Ala.

24. Orders for Maj H. S. Hansell from the War Department, Office of the Chief of the Air Corps, 7 July 1941, Hansell Papers, AFHRA, Maxwell AFB, Ala.

25. Hansell, Hopper interview.

26. Hansell III; Mrs. Hansell; and Hansell, *Strategic Air War against Germany and Japan*, 25.

27. Hansell, *Air Plan*, 53; and Hansell, *Strategic Air War against Germany and Japan*, 24–25.

28. Hansell, *Air Plan*, 53.

29. Hansell, *Strategic Air War against Germany and Japan*, 53.

30. Hansell, *Air Plan*, 54; and Hansell, Hopper interview.

31. Craven and Cate, 136–41.

32. President Roosevelt to the secretary of the Navy, letter, 9 July 1941, AWPD-1, Tab A, File 145.82-1, AFHRA, Maxwell AFB, Ala.

33. Craven and Cate, 132.

34. Hansell, *Air Plan*, 65–67.

35. Ibid., 65; Hansell, *Strategic Air War against Germany and Japan*, 30; Gaston, 3–4; and Geoffrey Perret, *Winged Victory: The Army Air Forces in World War II* (New York: Random House, 1993), 49.

36. Hansell, *Air Plan*, 2–3, 63–67.

37. Craven and Cate, 146; Hansell, *Air Plan*, 69–70; and Hansell, Hopper interview.

38. Haywood S. Hansell Jr., "General Laurence S. Kuter 1905–1979," *Aerospace Historian*, June 1980, 92.

39. Mrs. Hansell.

40. Gaston, 22.

41. Ibid., 58.

42. Hansell, *Air Plan*, 92.

43. Ibid., 71.

44. William P. Snyder, "Developing Air Power Doctrine: An Assessment of the Air Corps Tactical School Experience," paper presented at the Annual Conference of the Society for Military History, Fredericksburg, Va., 10 April 1992, 4.

45. Ibid., 2; Hansell, *Air Plan*, 55, 76; and Robert Frank Futrell, *Ideas, Concepts, Doctrine: A History of Basic Thinking in the United States Air Force, 1907–1964* (Maxwell AFB, Ala.: Aerospace Studies Institute, 1971), 106.

46. Craven and Cate, 147.

47. Hansell, *Air Plan*, 54–55.

48. Craven and Cate, 132, 149; and Hansell, *Air Plan*, 88.

49. Craven and Cate, 148.

50. AWPD-1, Tab 1.

51. Hansell, *Air Plan*, 77, 86–87; and Fabyanic, 59–60.

52. Fabyanic, 60; and AWPD-1, Tab 2.

53. Hansell, *Air Plan*, 74.

54. Ibid., 71–78; and Craven and Cate, 148.

55. Hansell, *Air Plan*, 87; and Craven and Cate, 149.

56. Hansell, *Air Plan*, 79.

57. Ibid., 85.

58. AWPD-1, Tab 2.

59. Ibid.

60. Gaston, 32; Rudolph Vogel was the director of the Reisholz electrical power station near Dusseldorf.

61. Hansell, *Strategic Air War against Germany and Japan*, 35; and Hansell, *Air Plan*, 81.

62. Alan J. Levine, *The Strategic Bombing of Germany, 1940–1945* (Westport, Conn.: Praeger Publishers, 1992), 20.

63. Hansell, *Air Plan*, 82; and AWPD-1, Tab 2.

64. AWPD-1, Tab 2; and Hansell, *Air Plan*, 82.

65. Hansell, *Air Plan*, 93.

66. AWPD-1, Tab 2.

67. Hansell, *Air Plan*, 93.

68. Conrad C. Crane, *Bombs, Cities, and Civilians: American Airpower Strategy in World War II* (Lawrence, Kan.: University Press of Kansas, 1993), 26.

69. AWPD-1, Tab 2.

70. Ibid.

71. Hansell, *Strategic Air War against Germany and Japan*, map opposite pages 36 and 37.

72. Gaston, 34.

73. Craven and Cate, 149.

74. Alan S. Milward, *War, Economy and Society, 1939–1945* (Los Angeles: University of California Press, 1979), 23–24.

75. Ibid., 26; and Fabyanic, 61–62.

76. Hansell, Green interview.

77. Snyder, 18–20.

78. Hansell, Green interview.

79. Barry D. Watts, *The Foundations of U.S. Air Doctrine: The Problem of Friction in War* (Maxwell AFB, Ala.: Air University Press, 1984), 22.

80. Futrell, 134.

81. Stephen L. McFarland and Wesley P. Newton, *To Command the Sky: The Battle for Air Superiority over Germany, 1942–1944* (Washington, D.C.: Smithsonian Institution Press, 1991), 74.

82. Hansell, *Strategic Air War against Germany and Japan*, 103, 113.

83. Hansell, *Air Plan*, 89; and Gaston, 97.

84. Hansell, *Strategic Air War against Germany and Japan*, 112.

85. Hansell, *Air Plan*, 89.

86. Ibid.; and Hansell, Green interview.

87. Hansell, Green interview.

88. Hansell, *Air Plan*, 81; and Hansell, Hopper interview.

89. Hansell, *Air Plan*, 90; and Gaston, 80–82.

90. Hansell, *Air Plan*, 93.

91. Ibid., 95.

92. Hansell, *Air Plan*, 95.

93. Ibid.

94. Ibid., 96.

95. Mrs. Hansell.

96. Hansell, *Air Plan*, 96; Burton K. Wheeler, *Yankee From the West* (Garden City, New York: Doubleday & Co., 1962), 33–34; and *Chicago Daily Tribune*, 4 December 1941.

97. Hansell, *Air Plan*, 96.

98. Hansell, Green interview; and Gaston, 97.

99. Gaston, 101–3.

100. Wheeler, 34.

101. "Flying Fortress Chief of USAAF In England Goes Raiding Himself," n.d., Hansell family's private collection.

102. *Washington Post*, 11 December 1941; and Hansell, *Air Plan*, 96.

103. Hansell, *Air Plan*, 98; Hansell, Hopper interview; and Craven and Cate, 234–41.

104. Hansell, *Strategic Air War against Germany and Japan*, 54–55.

105. Hansell, Hopper interview; and DeWitt S. Copp, *Forged in Fire: Strategy and Decisions in the Air War over Europe, 1940–1945* (New York: Doubleday & Co., 1982), 135.

106. Hansell, *Strategic Air War against Germany and Japan*, 45–46.

107. Hansell, Hopper interview.

108. Hansell, *Strategic Air War against Germany and Japan*, 48.

109. Ibid., 45–53.

110. Ibid., 53–56.

111. Ibid., 57.

Chapter 4

The Frictions of War

General Arnold wanted his inner circle of younger generals to have combat experience. He remembered all too painfully his own unsuccessful efforts to get a command at the front during World War I. He sent Kuter and Hansell to Europe, but he did so with the understanding that they would return to Washington within the year. Colonel Craig recommended Hansell for the job as air planner for Eisenhower, the new commander of the European theater of operations. Hansell and Eisenhower were not strangers; the two had worked closely together in Washington while Hansell was setting up the Air Intelligence Office. In July 1942 General Eisenhower had requested that Hansell be transferred to his headquarters in London, and by August the details had been worked out.[1]

Eisenhower requested Hansell's promotion to brigadier general because he was aware that the British members of the United States-United Kingdom Air Planning Committee were of air-vice marshal and air-commodore rank, and he wanted the American member to have at least equal status. When Hansell arrived in London in August, Brig Gen Frank O. "Monk" Hunter, commander of the VIII Fighter Command, had the honor of being the first to pin a star on Hansell's epaulet. Hansell assumed the dual roles of air planner for Eisenhower and deputy theater air officer under General Spaatz. Spaatz wanted Hansell to make sure that Eisenhower's views concerning air planning reflected his own. To make sure that he could use Hansell to mold Eisenhower's development of air strategy, Spaatz had Hansell live with him in his comfortable house at Bushy Park in London as did Col Lauris Norstad and Col Hoyt Vandenberg.[2]

The question Hansell had to answer was whether Eisenhower would ignore the strategic use of heavy bombers and lean toward using them tactically in support of the ground forces. Actually, on 21 July 1942, some weeks before Hansell arrived, Eisenhower had defined the mission of the Eighth Air Force as supporting the invasion of the Continent, and there is no evidence to suggest that Hansell had any success in changing Eisenhower's mind concerning the use of airpower. Hansell settled in to a hectic schedule at the European theater of operations, United States Army (ETOUSA) headquarters, 20 Grosvenor Square, London. There TSgt James Cooper was assigned to handle all of Hansell's personal and confidential correspondence and would remain with the general until June 1943. Cooper remembered General Hansell as a pleasant, immaculately dressed officer, who was very busy with a number of pressing projects, ranging from planning for the buildup of airpower in the Mediterranean to more diplomatic duties involving the RAF and even the British royal family.[3]

The late summer of 1942 was indeed a busy one for Hansell and the other staff officers at ETOUSA. The buildup of US forces in England and the preliminary plans for an early invasion of the Continent (the Bolero, Sledgehammer, and Roundup operations) were in the planning stages, as were Operation Sickle, the buildup of the Eighth Air Force, and Operation Torch, the invasion of North Africa. This flurry of activity brought men of differing personality and opinion together, and inevitably there were clashes between them. Hansell was present on 7 August 1942 when Generals Patton and Doolittle arrived at ETOUSA headquarters to discuss Torch. Doolittle got off on the wrong foot by lecturing Eisenhower on the necessity of securing, preparing, and supplying air bases in North Africa. Doolittle recalled, "From the first moment I sensed that Ike had taken an immediate dislike to me. Once again, I had the uncomfortable feeling of being an illegitimate offspring at a family reunion."[4] The personality clash between Eisenhower and Doolittle had little impact on Hansell, but the diversion of strategic air resources from England to Africa had a tremendous impact on him.[5]

Hansell soon learned that the strategic bomber force was being diverted from its intended strategic purpose by a number of "overriding" concerns. First, by August 1942 the Germans had a fleet of 240 operational U-boats, and the safety of the convoys sailing to England and those that would be sailing to North Africa was certainly in doubt. The U-boat factories and bases had to be bombed, thus diverting the heavy bombers from the original target lists. To make matters worse, 15 combat groups originally scheduled to go to England were sent to the Pacific. In addition to these problems, the Eighth Air Force had to prepare the Twelfth Air Force for Operation Torch in North Africa. Hansell found himself so caught up in the myriad of operations that he was not making policy as much as he was carrying out the very dispersion of strategic bomber forces to which he was so opposed.[6]

Eaker's VIII Bomber Command flew its first heavy-bomber mission on 17 August 1942, with Eaker flying along in "Yankee Doodle," the lead aircraft in the second flight. The B-17s bombed the rail yards at Rouen, France, without loss. Hansell flew his first combat mission on 20 August 1942 in the wake of the 19 August commando raid on Dieppe, France. Twelve B-17s were detailed to bomb the Longeau Marshalling Yards at Amiens, France. Hansell had received permission to go on the mission only at the last minute and had arrived at the field only a half hour before takeoff. As he hurriedly prepared for the mission, he was not issued the proper equipment.[7]

Seated in the radio compartment, Hansell flew in the B-17 commanded by Maj Paul Tibbets. Brig Gen Newton Longfellow had accompanied Tibbets on an earlier mission, and when a crew member was wounded the general had, as Tibbets saw it, interfered with the operation of the aircraft. For this reason Tibbets had decided to have any future passengers ride in the radio compartment. As they flew over France, Hansell discovered that his oxygen mask was not functioning properly and took his gloves off to repair it, thus causing a painful frostbite to his hands. The mission itself was a milk run, but when they arrived back at base Hansell was in great pain.[8] Tibbets later remembered the mission very differently, reporting that, "We had the usual trouble with flak and fighters and everything and when we got back, Hansell was down on the floor, sitting on the radio compartment, and he was paralyzed. He could not move. We had to pick him up. He had his hands wrapped around his knees and that's the way we carried him off the airplane. We couldn't unfreeze him until the medics got ahold of him and did something and got him loose. He was paralyzed with fear."[9] There was certainly an element of fear in any mission over enemy-held territory, but Hansell was suffering from frostbite, not terror. The medics were administering first aid to a physically injured man. In a letter to Arnold on 27 August 1942, Spaatz acknowledges Hansell's injury and his contribution to the daylight bombing: "Hansell has been doing a splendid job. He accompanied the Amiens raid and froze his hand. His and Eaker's opinions in what can be accomplished with daylight bombing have the added value of personal experience."[10]

When Hansell returned to Grosvenor Square, a letter from General Eisenhower awaited him congratulating him upon his promotion to brigadier general, and he resumed work on plans for the Twelfth Air Force and operations for the Eighth Air Force. At midnight of 26 August, Hansell awoke Spaatz with news of a cable from General Marshall. The Army chief of staff had ordered Hansell to obtain bombing data and return to Washington within 48 hours.[11] The president had called for an "immediate detailed war plan" (AWPD-42), and Marshall stressed, "Urgency requires his moving in a matter of hours." The final line of the cable had to be very sobering for Hansell: "The results of the work of this group are of such far-reaching importance that it will probably determine whether or not we control the air."[12]

On 25 August 1942, President Roosevelt had requested that General Arnold submit "his judgment of the number of combat aircraft by types which should be produced for the Army and our Allies in this country in 1943 in order to have complete air ascendancy over the enemy."[13] The report was to be made through General Marshall, thus prompting the 26 August cable. Hansell indeed took the cable seriously and left at the earliest opportunity along with Col Harris Hull, head of the intelligence section at VIII Bomber Command, and RAF Gp Capt Bobby Sharp, Hansell's old associate.[14]

Unlike AWPD-1, which was drawn up to plan a potential war, AWPD-42 was to be prepared in order to meet ongoing crises. The Japanese had carved out a large empire in the Asiatic-Pacific theater and the battle for Guadalcanal had just begun, with the outcome very much in doubt. Tobruk, Libya, had fallen and Egypt had not yet been saved at El Alamein. The Russians were falling back as the German armies neared Stalingrad and the oil fields of the Caucasus. In addition to these problems, the German U-boats had sunk 589 vessels in the first months of 1942, a loss that amounted to 3,210,000 gross tons; Great Britain was threatened with collapse. It was in this crisis atmosphere that Hansell and his new team set about to revise AWPD-1.[15]

Hansell was to head the planning team for AWPD-42, but most of the AWPD-1 team was available for consultation—Maj Gen Hal George, Brig Gen Laurence Kuter, Brig Gen Kenneth Walker, and Lt Col Malcom Moss. The time pressure was similar to the one that had driven AWPD-1; Hansell and his team had only 11 days to complete AWPD-42.[16]

The basic strategy behind AWPD-1 continued in AWPD-42— to undermine and destroy "the capability and will of Germany to wage war by destroying its war-supporting industries and systems." Strategic offense would be used against Germany, while strategic defense would be used against Japan and, as Craven and Cate observed, there was little essential change between AWPD-1 and AWPD-42 at a strategic level. Yet military necessity dictated some important changes in the structure of the plan. It was feared that Russia would collapse at any time, and since airpower was the only area in which the Allies had a numerical superiority, it would be up to the air forces to hold Germany at bay while the surface forces grew. This meant that strategic airpower would have to be used to bomb U-boat facilities and provide air support for surface forces in the Mediterranean and the Pacific. The Eighth Air Force would have to alter its target list and make provisions to work more closely with RAF bomber command.[17]

The intended purpose of AWPD-42, like that of its predecessor, was to project aircraft production needs. Hansell and his team more than doubled the required production over AWPD-1's projected total of 68,416 aircraft of all types to 146,902 aircraft of all types to be built in 1943. The actual total was eventually lowered to 127,000 airplanes; 80,500 of which would be combat types. These figures included aircraft for the Army Air Forces, the Navy, and our Allies. The types of aircraft included tactical, training, liaison, transport, gliders, and bombing aircraft. Seventy-six heavy bomb groups were projected with a total 1943 production of 3,648 B-17s and B-24s. The 10,000-mile B-36 was dropped from the plan because

Hansell and his planners realized that Great Britain would be secure and could provide 130 air bases.[18]

AWPD-42 also called for 230,243 officers and 1,554,104 enlisted men for the Army Air Forces; 1,140,363 tons of bombs; 4,888,941 gallons of gasoline; and 17,421,507 ship tons in order to transport all its necessities to the battle fronts in 1943. Hansell and his team then projected the number of Army Air Forces' aircraft that would be needed in each theater of operations. The United Kingdom got the lion's share with 7,268 aircraft; North Africa was allotted 824; the Middle East was given 448; the Far East received 676; and the China-Burma-India theater was projected to have 950.[19]

Like AWPD-1, AWPD-42 went beyond production requirements to produce a plan for the use of strategic bombers. A fairly detailed analysis of a bombing campaign against Japan was drawn up. It projected that 51,480 bomber sorties against 123 Japanese target systems would bring the Japanese empire to its knees. The B-29 would not be ready until late 1944, but neither would bases that were within range of Japan. The revisions in AWPD-1's list of target systems would have a more immediate impact since the strategic air war against Germany was still the first priority.[20]

As in the first plan, AWPD-42 placed German aircraft factories, Luftwaffe airfields, and industries that supported aircraft production at the top of the list. This "intermediate" target list was important because even AWPD-42 did not include fighter escort. It was still believed that the bomber was self-defending, but perhaps more important, it was not thought possible to design an escort fighter that would have the range to cover B-17s and B-24s over Germany. The Eighth Air Force had only completed six missions prior to writing AWPD-42, and there had been no opportunity to evaluate the defensive power of the Luftwaffe.[21]

U-boat facilities replaced electric power as the number two target system. U-boat attacks on Atlantic convoys had created a crisis in the Allied camp and deep concern over future operations, particularly Torch. Thus the expedients of war had altered Hansell's target list, but politics also played a part. Hansell later expressed his reason for placing submarines so high on the target list: "It [the placing of submarines as the

96

B-24 Bomber

number two target system] also recognized the concern, interest, and power of the naval leaders whose authority would influence adoption of the plan by the Joint Chiefs if and when it was submitted to them."[22] Hansell considered the targeting of submarines a deviation from strategic bombing doctrine, but he was forced by circumstances to accept this compromise.

Transportation targets remained number three on the target list, but electric power had fallen to fourth place. Hansell had revised the details of the plan to bomb German power plants. He had reduced the total number of electric targets from 50 to 37 because of more complete intelligence. The planners had also added switching stations, whereas before they had only included generating stations. They also added turbine houses as subtargets because their replacement would require 18 months to two years. Hansell maintained that electric targets were of utmost importance since no industry could function without electricity, and he undoubtedly hoped to return electricity to a place of prominence on the target list as soon as the U-boat menace subsided. Target system five was petroleum, and sixth place went to rubber.[23] Morale was not discussed as a target system as it had been in AWPD-1, but it was hoped that attacks on electric power would have an adverse effect on the daily lives of the civilians and thus have an enormous effect on morale.[24]

There was no time for formal presentations. Hansell simply sent the secret document to the Government Printing Office where it would be reproduced and bound in Morocco leather. Thirty copies were to be produced, with the first 15 carrying the names of the recipients in gold letters. Number one went to President Roosevelt, number two to Secretary of War Stimson, and so on. Presidential adviser Harry Hopkins's copy was number six. Hopkins obtained his copy around one o'clock on the morning it was to be delivered to Generals Marshall and Arnold. After reading it in the wee hours of the morning, Hopkins met with President Roosevelt at breakfast and reported favorably on the document. The president then called Stimson to inform him that he approved of the plan, but the secretary had not seen the plan yet himself, so he called General Marshall. Marshall too was in the dark and quite angry because of it. Hansell received a call from two of Marshall's staff officers who had to report to the angry general in one hour and did not have time to read the plan, so Hansell outlined the plan over the phone.[25]

Hansell knew that he would soon be the object of General Marshall's wrath so he sought and received an immediate audience with General Arnold and requested to return to England immediately. Arnold replied, "Seems to me you're in a hell of a hurry. But O.K. Go ahead." Hansell called Hal George at the Air Transport Command and within an hour he was airborne for England. Hansell recalled, "The comparative safety of the combat zone was a welcome haven. General Marshall seldom lost his temper, but when he did, three thousand miles was none too great a margin of safety."[26]

AWPD-42 was completed on time, and it differed from AWPD-1 only in terms of numbers and adjustments to target priorities. Even though the planners had to make provisions for an invasion of the Continent, they still believed that Germany could be defeated by strategic airpower alone. The results of the early raids had caused too much optimism because the planners saw no need for fighter escort and tended to be too optimistic about bombing accuracy. Yet its most significant problem had little to do with strategy. Hansell and his team had enough confidence to deal with the Germans—dealing with the US Navy was another matter.[27]

Even though AWPD-42 took naval aviation into account in projecting production, the chief of naval operations, Adm Ernest J. King, objected to the plan because the Navy did not participate in writing it. General Kuter knew as early as September that there was a problem with AWPD-42. In a letter to Spaatz he expressed his concern, "It is perfectly clear that we cannot build the AWPD-42 program . . . and at the same time build unlimited numbers of Monitors and Merrimacs or infinite numbers of shields, spears, and chariots."[28] On 30 September he wrote Hansell informing him that "AWPD-42 has hit a serious snag. The plan blew up on 24 September when the navy rejected it in its entirety."[29] AWPD-42 was never accepted by the joint chiefs, but Harry Hopkins bought it and persuaded President Roosevelt and Secretary Stimson to accept all requirements other than those of the US Navy. The plan, though unaccepted, became the pattern for expansion in the American aircraft industry.[30] Even more important, the idea of strategic bombing survived. As General Arnold wrote to Spaatz, "The principle objectives of the air forces in this new plan as well as in the old one are to be attained by *precision bombing*" (emphasis in original).[31]

Hansell's return to Washington had not afforded him a lengthy visit with his family. Mrs. Hansell recalled seeing him only once during the two weeks he worked on AWPD-42, and she could not understand what could be more important than time with the family. As we have seen, he left as quickly and as unannounced as he had arrived and left Dotta with three children in the midst of the usual childhood crises and wartime rationing. She hated being in Washington without Possum and referred to the experience as "unadulterated hell." Christmas 1942 was bleak for the Hansell family. Ethyl Kuter, wife of General Kuter, offered Dotta the Kuters' more comfortable quarters at Fort Myer for the holidays, where Dotta and the children enjoyed a Christmas dinner of cheese sandwiches. This was a difficult time for Mrs. Hansell, but she worked hard to keep her despair from the children. In early 1943 Dotta developed pneumonia and all three of the children got sick at the same time. Possum's sister, Susan Vance, called from Tampa, Flordia, each day for 10 days, but Mrs. Hansell pretended all was well. Finally Mrs. Arnold took it upon herself to contact Mrs. Vance and inform her of her sister-in-law's plight. Susan arrived the next day and took charge. She checked Dotta into Walter Reed Army Hospital; sublet the house; found new tires for the car (a miracle in wartime); and made arrangements for the care of Tony and Lucia. Susan then took Dennett, who was still sick, back to Tampa on the train. When she regained her health, Mrs. Hansell drove the other two children to Florida and eventually settled in the quiet community of Indian Rocks, where Possum would later join them.[32]

Hansell had been absent from London during much of the preliminary planning for Operation Torch. Soon after he returned, the Torch air plan was issued and revealed a major weakness: there was no single air commander. Whereas Eisenhower had Adm Andrew B. Cunningham as the naval commander, the air units would be split up between two commands. Air Marshal Sir William Welsh would command the Eastern Air Command and Doolittle would command the Twelfth Air Force. With most of the strategic planning completed, it fell upon Hansell and others to cannibalize the Eighth Air Force to strengthen Junior, the code name for the Twelfth Air Force.[33]

The Ninth Air Force provided the Twelfth with headquarters for the XII Fighter, XII Bomber, and XII Service commands. Once they arrived in England, the corresponding commands were placed under the care of the Eighth Air Force. In addition, the Eighth handed over two fighter groups and four heavy bomber groups, leaving only five groups of B-17s and two groups of B-24s. Yet the remaining groups gave up essential equipment such as bomb-loading equipment and transport vehicles to the Twelfth. One-third of the Twelfth's 27,356 men came from the Eighth. Hansell was appalled at the sight of the strategic air forces being subjected to "scatterization" and commented, "Our fears were realized. Political necessity was more compelling than military strategy. The invasion of

North Africa produced a diversion of strategic air forces away from the air offensive against Germany."[34] He found the whole affair to be "demoralizing."[35]

Not only was VIII Bomber Command devoting half its time to XII Bomber Command, but now Hansell had to draw up plans for it to begin bombing U-boat bases in the Bay of Biscay, France, in order to protect the Torch invasion armada. On 29 October 1942, Eisenhower decided to rectify the one major weakness in the Torch air plan by naming Spaatz as theater air commander. Spaatz intended to move Ira Eaker up from VIII Bomber Command to command the Eighth Air Force. Hansell was given the job of preparing and sending the cablegram setting these events in motion. The next day Hansell met with Doolittle and Spaatz to go over the final plans, only to learn that at that late date Spaatz was unclear as to "where, when, and what" the Twelfth Air Force was to do. On 1 November Hansell, along with Brig Gen Asa N. Duncan, began a strategic study of the Mediterranean area by directing the A-2 (intelligence) and A-5 (plans) sections to explore the major strategic questions arising from Torch.[36]

On 8 November 1942, the British and Americans invaded French Northwest Africa. Eleven days later, on 19 November, Spaatz and his staff prepared to fly to the scene of battle. Three copies of the secret documents Spaatz would need were made and placed in three weighted briefcases, one each being attached to the arms of Hansell, Duncan, and Kuter. Each of the three would fly in a different airplane. Hansell flew in Spaatz's B-17 without incident, but the plane carrying General Duncan crashed in the Bay of Biscay, and even though Kuter's plane circled the wreckage, there was no sign of survivors.[37]

Immediately after the invasion began, Eisenhower required that the Eighth Air Force be ready for operations in North Africa, should that become necessary. Even though this did not materialize, 75 percent of the Eighth Air Force's supplies were diverted to North Africa. While in Africa Hansell did his final staff work for Eisenhower; and by 23 November, Spaatz, Kuter, and Hansell were back at Bushy Park where Hansell learned that he would be given command of 3d Bombardment Wing (medium) and Kuter would take over the coveted 1st

Bombardment Wing (heavy). Eaker would take the helm at Eighth Air Force and General Longfellow would take VIII Bomber Command. Spaatz would join Eisenhower in the Mediterranean.[38]

Hansell arrived at the headquarters of the 3d Bombardment Wing at Elveden Hall, northeast of Cambridge, England, at seven o'clock on the evening of 5 December 1942. The 3d Wing consisted of only one group of B-26 medium bombers. These aircraft already had a bad reputation that had earned them the nicknames of "Widow Maker," "Baltimore Whore," and "Flying Prostitute." The references to the world's oldest profession came about because the B-26 Marauder's wing span was so short that it "had no visible means of support." The Marauder could carry 3,000 pounds of bombs 500 miles at 265 miles per hour, but it was indeed a tricky aircraft to fly and had caused many training fatalities. More recently the B-26 had had a cruel introduction to flying over German-occupied France when aircraft from the 319th Group, on their way to Africa on 12 November 1942, suffered poor navigation in bad weather. Two planes were lost over Cherbourg, France. This action seemed to jinx the Marauder, and the legend of the mishap had grown out of proportion among the B-26 crews.[39]

The 3d Wing, operating airfields at Bury Saint Edmunds and Rattlesden, England, consisted of the 322d Bombardment Group and the 42d Service Group. Hansell's main task was to get his wing ready for combat as soon as possible. By the second day of command, he was in conference with his group commanders and had inspected most of their facilities. His greatest problem was eliminating the crews' fear of the B-26. Although he had never flown one himself, on 7 December he began his education in flying the Marauder. He invested every possible hour in becoming comfortable with his new charge, flying from air base to air base. On 11 December he flew to the RAF station at West Raynham and spent the night discussing low-altitude tactics with the British. Both the Americans and British had used similar aircraft at low altitudes and had achieved good results. The RAF was instrumental in giving Hansell the benefit of its experience in medium bombers. They advised that the aircraft fly at no more than 1,500 feet and to approach the target as close to the ground as possible (at "0" feet in Air Force terminology).[40]

After only a week in command, Hansell wrote to General Longfellow explaining that he had had no opportunity to conduct operations and that he was worried about aborts and a lack of spare parts and batteries. On 13 December he got a chance to perform a service he always enjoyed—diplomacy. He paid a social call on Lady Elveden and the Duke and Duchess of Grafton. Yet his duties were usually more mundane. He was concerned about a surprise air attack on his command post and went to some length to see that it had antiaircraft protection. He also participated in training exercises in DB-7s (earlier versions of A-20s) and found birds to be a major problem around his bases. Practice missions were conducted when the weather permitted, but they were often disappointing. On one such mission the group missed its target by over half a mile—the target was Elveden Hall! With much trial and error the practice missions were going better and better. Just as the 3d Bombardment Wing was shaping up for an operational mission, Hansell was called to command the 1st Bombardment Wing (heavy), the premier command in the Eighth Air Force.[41]

At this time the Eighth Air Force consisted of the VIII Service Command (which dealt with maintenance and supply), the VIII Fighter Command, and VIII Bomber Command. The VIII Bomber Command was divided into wings, with each wing consisting of numbered groups, and each numbered group consisting of four numbered squadrons. In January 1943 General Eaker could count on two heavy bomber wings: the 1st (which was equipped with B-17s) and the 2d (which was equipped with B-24s). Since there were only two B-24 groups operational, the burden fell on Hansell's 4th Bomb Wing.

Hansell arrived at the headquarters of the 1st Wing on 2 January 1943. Brampton Grange, located near Huntingdon, had been a hunting lodge and, therefore, had no heat. Hansell later described his quarters as "the most uncomfortable living accommodation in England." Yet Brampton Grange was located at the hub of Hansell's airfields. The 303d Bombardment Group was at Molesworth; the 91st at Bassingbourn; the 305th at Chelveston; the 306th at Thurleigh; and the 92d at Alconbury.[42]

Douglas A-20 Bomber

Eaker knew that it took men with the proper temperament to command a bomber force, and in the winter of 1942–43 he was afflicted with a shortage of such personnel. In a letter to General Arnold's chief of staff, Eaker explained his reasons for calling Brig Gen Frederick L. Anderson back to England to replace Hansell at the 4th Bomb Wing, "There is a great dearth here of suitable Group Commander, Wing Commander and senior Air Force and Bomber Command personnel. We are doing the best we can with what we have."[43] General Kuter had been sent to North Africa to assume command of the Allied Tactical Air Force, which left Hansell and Longfellow to bear the burden of operational command. There was, however, a potential problem concerning giving Longfellow VIII Bomber Command. Both Hansell and Kuter outranked him, but any anxiety concerning Hansell was soon put to rest. As Hansell recalled, "Eaker asked me if I had any objection to subordinating myself to an officer who was junior to me. I was so anxious to be in Bomber Command I would work for anybody."[44] General Longfellow was not well liked; Hansell felt that Longfellow "had the general attitude of a British Sergeant Major—constant criticism and domineering demand."[45] It was clear that Longfellow was a poor choice for VIII Bomber Command. Eaker covered for Longfellow, serving in effect as both air force and bomber command commander, treating Longfellow more like an operations officer than a commanding general.[46]

As of 2 January, Hansell had only four operational heavy bomber groups. Col Curtis E. LeMay's 305th, Colonel De Roussy's 303d, Colonel Wray's 91st, and Colonel Armstrong's 306th were all experienced and ready for missions. The oldest bombardment group in the Eighth Air Force, the 92d, was no longer operational. Lieutenant Colonel Sutton's group was in the process of moving from Bovingdon to Alconbury, but its major problem was high operational losses. Hansell had to work hard to keep this group together. As Hansell recalled, "VIII Bomber Command wanted to deactivate the Group. I objected. I did not want history to report that a US heavy bombardment group had been destroyed in combat. The 92d was finally rebuilt and the group carried on a worthy record."[47] In theory the 1st Bomb Wing would have 160 B-17s available for operations, with usually around 72 aircraft being launched for any given combat mission. In addition to the two B-24 groups of the 2d Bombardment Wing, Hansell's wing was the entirety of the Eighth Air Force. This was a far cry from the aircraft requirements laid down by the Air War Plans Division.

Operation Sickle (the buildup of the Eighth Air Force in England) was adversely affected by needs in other theaters of operations. Two heavy bombardment groups were sent from England to the Twelfth Air Force in North Africa. Two additional heavy bombardment groups slated for the Eighth were sent to the Asiatic-Pacific theater. Lt Gen Frank M. Andrews, the new European theater of operations commander, and General Eaker resisted any shift of forces but were unable to retain the promised strength. Another problem was a lack of available shipping, which prevented the transport of the ground personnel and equipment necessary to establish new groups.[48]

In spite of all the setbacks, Hansell remained optimistic about his prospects with the 1st Wing. "The theories and doctrines of the Air Corps Tactical School had been pursued with an inspiring faith in spite of disappointments and the shocking effect of air battles of unprecedented dimensions."[49] He had before him an opportunity to do what few dreamers ever have even a chance of realizing—to make his air doctrine work as he and his colleagues had planned at Maxwell Field. Yet, the reality of the strategic and supply problems were not lost on him. As he later reflected, "But now, when the real opportunity to apply strategic air power was at last a reality, other influences rose to frustrate its realization."[50]

Hansell flew his first mission as commander of the 1st Wing on 3 January 1943, the day after he took command. The objective was the U-boat facilities of the Penhouet works at Saint-Nazaire, France. Seventy-two B-17s from the 1st Wing took off, accompanied by 13 B-24s from the 44th Bombardment Group of the 2d Bombardment Wing. Hansell's wing suffered eight aborts, giving him only 68 bombers over the target. The 44th group lost six of its 13 B-24s to aborts, giving the 2d Wing only seven bombers over the target.[51]

The bomb run from the initial point to the target was complicated by 115-miles-per-hour head winds. Flying straight and level in the face of heavy opposition was a nine-minute ordeal. After the Spitfires departed, the Luftwaffe pressed the attack from the front—head-on attacks with a closing speed often in excess of five hundred miles per hour. In addition to this, the antiaircraft fire or flak (short for *Flieger Abwehr Kannonen*) was particularly deadly because the Germans introduced the highly effective "predicted barrage." Before 3 January they had utilized the "continuous following" or "trial and error" method. The new development was much more deadly and American losses due to flak increased thereafter.[52]

Seven of Hansell's 68 B-17s were shot down. The seriousness of the losses was undoubtedly pressed home to Hansell because each of his two wing men was shot down in flames during the action. The bombers claimed to have destroyed 12 German fighters and probably destroyed 18 more, but even this inflated "score" could not belie the fact that Hansell had lost more than 10 percent of his force. The survivors heroically battled their way home, many in stricken aircraft. Some flew off course in the confusion and were forced to land in Wales.[53]

Initial bombing results seemed to be good. Three hundred and forty-two 1,000-pound high-explosive bombs had been released over the target, 26 of which landed within 1,000 feet of the target, destroying a small torpedo warehouse and damaging the dock area. A ground report claimed that the Penhouet works were put completely out of action, but, in reality, the submarine base was unfazed by the attack and "work proceeded without let or hindrance."[54]

Hansell was clearly shaken by the ordeal; he recognized that there was a lack of discipline in formation flying, which had caused not only poor bombing results but also weakened the mutually supporting defensive fire of the B-17 formations. Determined to improve the efficiency of his unit, Hansell set out to correct the problems that had made the Saint-Nazaire raid a near disaster. He clearly was not satisfied with the raid, and shortly after the event he expressed his intentions, "It was quite apparent that we are going to have to solve our own problems in our own way, because there was no support, there was no recourse but to abandon it [daylight bombing]."[55] Hansell had no intention of giving up on the theories of daylight precision bombing he had espoused at ACTS, but now the old ACTS motto, *Proficimus More Irretenti* (We Make Progress Unhindered by Custom), was probably more a source of anxiety than pride.

The 1st Bombardment Wing was not the precision strategic instrument it was designed to be. In the brief time General Kuter had been in command, he had begun to address problems that he had inherited. Colonel LeMay, with Kuter's encouragement, had designed the basic idea behind the "combat box" and each of the groups had been working on its navigation and bombing accuracy. Yet Hansell's evaluation of his wing's performance set the tone for his first weeks in command, "I was shocked at the performance of the Wing,"[56] he later recalled. The bombing was erratic, and, in spite of many brave deeds he knew, as DeWitt Copp observed, "that heroism was not enough to bring destruction to the submarine pens."[57]

On 4 January 1943, Hansell called a meeting of his group commanders. This meeting set the standard for meetings that were conducted after each bomber mission. Hansell called the group commanders' meetings "trial[s] by fire" and added, "I dreaded them, as I am sure all the others did also, because the essential ingredient of our effort to learn by experience—and learn quickly—was absolute honesty. The mistakes had to be acknowledged. It was a soul-searing ordeal."[58] The meetings were open to criticism and recommendation, and any subject was open to discussion, except that of abandoning daylight bombing of selected targets. The meeting included group commanders, group leaders, group navigators, group gunnery officers, the lead bombardier, the operations officer, and group staffs. Eventually, the meetings would be limited to Hansell and his group commanders. They would discuss what mistakes they had made and how they could learn from the experience.[59] Hansell later confessed, "Only too often it was glaringly apparent that I had not used the best judgment and the costly results born of those errors in the actual mission itself could be traced all too easily to my mistakes."[60] This readiness to accept personal responsibility was characteristic of his honesty and clear-eyed objectivity.

Beginning at the first meeting, Hansell established standard operating procedures (SOP) that would be used by each group in the wing. These "SOPs" included take off and assembly, route to target, target exposure, return to England, and landing at bases. No detail was too small to be addressed. If there was a problem on one mission, the SOP would be changed for the next mission. Once Hansell had made a decision, the group commanders were given "absolutely no discretion for deviation until the next meeting." Hansell termed this doctrine *flexible rigidity*. The motto Hansell selected for the 1st Bombardment Wing expressed his expectations for the bomber crews: "Put the Bombs on the Target."[61]

Hansell realized that the most critical tactical problem he faced was the penetration of German air defenses. With no long-range escorts available, the bombers would have to rely upon their defensive firepower enhanced by their formations. It had already been determined that an element of 60 B-17s was too unwieldy, and a simple element of three offered little defensive firepower. When Hansell came on board, he found that Kuter was already experimenting with the combat box. Three aircraft comprised an element, two elements comprised a squadron, and three squadrons comprised a group, thus creating a combat box of 18 aircraft, which was the smallest unit for defensive purposes and the largest that could be handled on the bomb run. Hansell then created two tactical combat wings of three combat boxes each. These were tactical units, which were led by the senior group commanders and did not affect the administration of the 1st Bomb Wing. Colonel LeMay commanded the 101st Combat Wing, and Colonel Armstrong commanded the 102d.[62]

Before the war, bombing practice was by individual sighting runs by individual aircraft—in theory this would produce the greatest accuracy. Peacetime theory also called for the bombers to weave from side to side and at varying altitudes to avoid enemy aircraft and antiaircraft fire. These practices would not work in actual combat. With the combat boxes and wings being utilized, Hansell standardized the practice of "bombing on the leader." This would provide the greatest bombing accuracy while producing the most effective defensive fire. Each combat box would separate from its combat wing at the initial point, complete the bomb run, and reassemble at the rally point. The lead bombardier of each combat box would control the bomb run, and all aircraft in the combat box would release their bombs when he did.[63]

In the absence of fighter escort, the heavy bombers had to be self-defending. Close formations were essential for that defensive fire, but Hansell soon learned that the gunnery in the 1st Wing was lacking. He found the gunners to be "woefully ill-trained" and sought to remedy the situation by establishing a gunnery school. The British Air Ministry provided a site where war-weary B-17s could tow targets, and LeMay provided the gunnery instructor. Hansell recalled the situation: "The gunnery instructor was slightly tougher than Curt [LeMay], and I spent much of my time keeping him from being court-martialed for his treatment of his students."[64] When they attempted to test gunnery against head-on attacks, the gunners shot the A-20 target plane down instead of the intended target it was towing. Because of weather restrictions, most 1st Bomb Wing gunners got their gunnery practice in combat.[65]

The toughest problem the aircrews encountered was indeed the head-on attacks. The solution was to make field modifications of B-17s by placing flexible, handheld 50-caliber machine guns in the nose of the aircraft. The chin turret of the B-17G did not arrive in England until September

1943. Another solution was the YB-40, a "destroyer escort" version of the B-17. By placing an additional turret to the aft of the aircraft and providing more machine gun ammunition it was believed that this new aircraft could "shepherd" the bombers to and from the targets. This solution proved to be less than satisfactory.[66] The other problems that confronted 1st Wing gunnery officers included air-to-air bombing (an attempt by the Germans to down American bombers with aerial bombs), long-range cannon fire, and long-range rocket fire. There would be no satisfactory defense against these German tactics until the escort fighters appeared.[67]

Hansell was quite effective in establishing combat doctrines for formation flying, bombing, and defensive gunnery. These practices would serve the Eighth Air Force, for the most part, for the rest of the war. Yet Hansell realized that he was also the commander of the 1st Wing, and that meant that he would have to exercise strong, decisive leadership where it counted— in combat. He determined that he, his commanders, and his staff would fly no more than one mission in five. This amounted to about one mission per month. General Kuter had flown no missions because of his knowledge of ULTRA, but Hansell had no such impediment. (ULTRA was the designation for the signals intelligence derived from the radio communications that the Germans encrypted on their high-grade decipher machine called *ENIGMA*.) His next mission would be his closest brush with death and establish him as a general who led from the bomber formation, not the desk.[68]

The B-17 in which Hansell chose to fly the next mission was the *Dry Martini II*, usually piloted by Capt Allen V. Martini. On the morning of 13 January 1943, however, Martini was ill and unable to fly. Maj Tom H. Taylor, commander of the 364th Bombardment Squadron, volunteered to fly as pilot. The objective for the day was the Fives locomotive works at Lille, France. *Dry Martini II* was in the first position, second element, third squadron. The formation flew to 27,000 feet and received moderate to heavy flak over Saint-Omer. The fighter attacks soon followed, as the 305th Bomb Group history recorded, "The yellow-nosed FW 190s, who became known as the 'Abbeville Kids,' were present in unpleasant numbers, concentrating their attacks on the nose of our aircraft and coming in pairs."[69] Just after "bombs away" a lone FW 190 came in at eleven o'clock level and fired directly into the cockpit. A 20-mm shell struck Major Taylor in the head, killing him instantly. A shell fragment hit the copilot, 2d Lt Joseph Boyle, wounding him in the leg, while flying glass from the explosion lacerated his face.[70]

At that point the *Dry Martini II* dove out of formation and fell 2,000 feet. Boyle thought that the engines were gone, but after he pulled Major Taylor's body from the controls, he managed to level the aircraft off. Just as Boyle learned that two of his crewmen were also wounded, another FW 190 made a head-on attack into the nose of the B-17, blasting the oxygen masks from the faces of the navigator and bombardier. Both men recovered their masks and continued firing for their lives. The interphone was mostly knocked out, allowing communication only between the copilot, tail gunner, and navigator. Even though the aircraft was out of formation and had its hydraulic system shot away, Boyle, much to his credit, managed to bring the stricken *Dry Martini II* back to Chelveston. Hansell, probably positioned in the radio compartment during the action, left the business of managing the aircraft back to base to the crew. Having come very close to death, Hansell would always know what it meant to send young men in B-17s over German-occupied Europe.[71]

Seventy-two B-17s from the 1st Bomb Wing had attacked Lille with the loss of only one aircraft. The bombing results were good, with the official report stating, "very severe damage was inflicted."[72] The raid was also a step forward for the new tactics. Hansell sent LeMay's 305th Group a copy of his memorandum concerning the raid, in which he praised the crews for improved air discipline and better formation flying. The results of the raid were very encouraging, but there were many more raids to follow and many more lessons to learn.[73]

On 18 January 1943, Eaker received orders from Arnold to report to Casablanca, Morocco, at once. The Casablanca Conference had been under way since 14 January, and Prime Minister Winston L. Churchill had convinced President Roosevelt to commit the Eighth Air Force to night bombing. Eaker arrived on the 19th and lost no time in making his case before Churchill. His arguments included the fact that the

Eighth Air Force loss rate was lower than that of the RAF Bomber Command; the Eighth was not trained for night operations; day bombers could accomplish missions the night bombers could not; day accuracy was five times greater than night; and day bombing would destroy German fighters. Churchill countered with a number of questions: Why had there been so many aborts? Why so few missions? Why were the Army Air Forces and the RAF not given the same directive and the same tactics? and, most importantly, Why had American bombers not bombed Germany? Eaker explained that inexperience, the Torch diversions, poor weather, and the concentration on U-boat targets had all contributed; but he promised that targets in Germany would soon be attacked and that, with a combination of Army Air Forces and RAF strategic bombing attacks, the Allies would bomb the Germans "around the clock."[74]

The idea of bombing Germany "around the clock" appealed to Churchill, and thus Eaker preserved the Eighth Air Force for daylight operations. On 21 January, CCS 166/1/D, the Casablanca Directive, was issued. It declared that the ultimate air objective was "the progressive destruction and dislocation of the German military, industrial and economic system, and the undermining of the morale of the German people to a point where their capacity for armed resistance is fatally weakened."[75] The document was, however, interpreted three ways. The RAF saw it as a further endorsement of urban attacks. The Army Air Forces saw it as a reaffirmation of daylight strategic bombing. The top-level commanders viewed the purpose of strategic airpower as preparation for invasion. In spite of the partisan interpretations, the Casablanca Directive was, as historian Thomas Fabyanic observed, "firm approval of the air strategy by the CCS and the highest Anglo-American leadership."[76] The top five targets on the target list were (1) German submarine construction yards, (2) the German aircraft industry, (3) German transport, (4) oil plants, and (5) other targets in the German war industry.[77]

At that point in the strategic air war, it was primarily up to Hansell to carry out the directive. On 23 January the 1st Wing launched a disappointing mission to the Lorient and Brest U-boat facilities in France. Seventy-three 1st Wing aircraft were dispatched, of which only 54 bombed the target. Fourteen of the 73 B-17s aborted the mission and no damage was reported to the submarine pens. Five B-17s were lost—nearly 7 percent of the force. The major mission of January 1943 was the raid on Wilhelmshaven, Germany. Churchill wanted an American daylight attack on Germany, and it was up to Hansell and his 1st Wing to deliver. Sixty-four of Hansell's B-17s set out for the target and only six aborted. German defenses were so confused that a British observer termed them "pathetic." Even though German fighters were out in force, only one B-17 was lost, and the gunners downed as many as seven enemy attackers. The U-boat yards were not seriously affected by the attack, but the Eighth Air Force had made its long-anticipated appearance over Germany.[78]

February's weather did not permit full operations. After two false starts because of unfavorable weather, Hansell's bombers set out for Emden, Germany, on 4 February. This raid proved to be more costly than the first; 39 B-17s bombed Emden, stirring up a "hornet's nest" of Me 110s and Ju 88s in addition to the usual Me 109s and FW 190s.

This was the first time the Germans had sent twin-engined fighters into the battle against American bombers and the first time air-to-air bombing was used. Five B-17s were lost. Other problems surfaced as well. The electrically heated suits failed, causing 43 cases of frostbite, nine of them severe. The unheated machine guns even froze up in the battle.[79]

On 4 February 1943, Gen Frank Andrews assumed command of European theater of operations, United States Army. Soon after his arrival in England he toured the 305th Group at Chelveston. Hansell was there to greet him. This was the first time the two men had met, and they got acquainted as they "munched on a muffin and discussed bombing tactics."[80] Andrews had been commander of the GHQ Air Force in the 1930s, and now, as ETOUSA commander, he promised to promote the interests of the Eighth Air Force. There were numerous other meetings between Hansell and Andrews at Brampton Grange, and Hansell was thoroughly impressed by his new theater commander.[81]

On 14 February the 1st Wing launched a mission to Hamm, Germany, but the aircraft had to turn back because of cloud cover. On 16 February Hansell's B-17s attacked Lorient, otherwise known as "Flak City." Eighty-nine heavy bombers bombed the target, but the results were disappointing. Enemy opposition was as fierce as ever, with enemy fighters and flak accounting for the crippling of six B-17s. On 26 February Hansell launched an attack intended for Bremen, Germany, but cloud cover forced the bombers to release their loads on Wilhelmshaven, Germany. The flak was not effective, but the fighters attacked in strength, one Me 109 attempting an air-to-air bomb attack. Of the seven B-17s lost, six were possibly to enemy fighters. The final mission of February was to Brest on the 27th. Hansell flew this mission in the *Tony H*, a bomber he had named for his son. He had himself photographed in front of the aircraft bearing his son's name; Tony was thrilled to receive a copy of the photo. This mission was termed a "milk run" because there were no losses. The only unusual aspect of the mission came when the Germans sent a radio message causing the 305th Group to turn back. February had been frustrating for Hansell. Fourteen field orders had been cut for the groups and nine of those had been canceled, at times varying from seven hours to 30 minutes before takeoff. Bombs had actually been dropped on four of the five missions flown.[82]

By March 1943 the 1st Wing was showing the signs of the attrition it had suffered in the first months of the year. Prior to 1 February the entire Eighth Air Force had received only 20 replacement crews to compensate the loss of 67. By spring some groups were down to 50 percent strength. Missions could be launched only if there were enough fresh, trained crews, but by March an estimated 73 crews were "war weary."[83] Hansell described his dilemma:

> During the early period when the bomber units of the Eighth were finding themselves and tempering their quality in the heat of combat, success or failure hung upon the human factor, which had to sustain the greatest strain of all, the morale of the combat crews—The morning after each mission saw the breakfast table growing smaller. By March the crews of the initial groups were less than half strength. Each mission was costing between five and six percent in combat casualties, and missions were running at the rate of five missions per month.[84]

Even though Hansell did not have the minimum of 300 bombers considered necessary to carry out strategic operations, progress was made in March. The operations research section of the Eighth Air Force endorsed the "bombing on the leader" method already employed by the 1st Wing. Also in March the Eighth began to employ automatic flight-control equipment and bombardiers reported much improved accuracy.[85]

The 1st Wing flew nine missions in March. On 4 March they struck Hamm, the first Eighth Air Force objective in the Ruhr Valley. One group returned without dropping its bombs, but three struck the target with unusual accuracy against light opposition. Four B-17s were lost in that action. On 6 March Hansell's bombers struck Lorient and reported direct hits on railway targets. On 8 March Hansell flew in a B-17 piloted by 1st Lt John Carroll on a mission to bomb the railway yards at Rennes, France. With the loss of only one B-17, the 1st Wing cut the marshalling yards at both ends and caused a complete standstill for three or four days. Normal traffic could not be resumed in the yards for an additional two weeks.[86] A newspaper reporter, Charles F. Danver, was present when Hansell returned from the mission and reported that a corporal offered the general a sandwich: "General Hansell helped himself to one of the brown triangles and inspected its contents. 'Why do they cut this stuff so thin?' he grumbled. And he promptly bit off a big mouthful. A young staff lieutenant asked him about the mission. 'It was a fine trip,' he said as casually as if the raid had been an automobile ride in the country."[87]

The next two missions were described as milk runs. Hansell's bombers struck Rouen on 12 March and Amiens on 13 March. On 18 March the 1st Wing attacked the U-boat yards at Vegesack, Germany. Seventy percent of the bombs fell within 1,000 feet of the target. Hansell had had cameras installed on each aircraft to record bomb damage. This way the bomb groups could compete, and, as Hansell pointed out, "The competition had a salutary effect."[88] There had been 15 U-boats in varying degrees of construction, seven of which were damaged severely, one capsized, and six others slightly damaged. At the time, it was estimated that the Bremer Vulkan Yards would produce only four additional U-boats in a six-month period. This estimate of the long-term effect proved to be too sanguine, but the strike photos had been accurate. Andrews and Eaker had traveled to Brampton Grange to await word on the raid, which certainly made the results very gratifying for Hansell. On 22 March the 1st Wing struck the U-boat yards at Wilhelmshaven with a loss of two aircraft. The marshalling yards at Rouen were attacked on 28 March with a loss of one. On 31 March the shipyards at Rotterdam, Netherlands, were struck, with three B-17s lost due to a midair collision. Considering the resources available to Hansell, March had been a good month.[89]

The Casablanca Directive had firmly established the concepts upon which the Allies would build their strategic air offensive, but a comprehensive plan had yet to be worked out. On 23 March 1943, Arnold appointed Hansell chairman and director of a committee that would write the Combined Bomber Offensive (CBO) Plan. Gen Frederick Anderson, Air Commodore Sidney O. Bufton (director of bomber operations at the British Air Ministry), Gp Capt Arthur Morley, Maj Richard Hughes, Maj John Hardy, Lt Col A. C. "Sailor" Agan, and Col Charles Cabell all served on the committee. Beginning on 3 April, the team met at Bushy Park for 10 days, at the end of which they had prepared the air war plan that would direct the Pointblank operations over Europe.[90]

Hansell was the ideal leader for such a team. He had experience in air intelligence, had contributed significantly to AWPD-1, and had directed AWPD-42. Yet, in spite of these antecedent plans, General Arnold had added a new variable into Hansell's equation—the Committee of Operations Analysts (COA). In December 1942 Arnold had directed Col Byron E. Gates of the Office of Management Services to form a group of operations analysts to determine the "rate of progressive deteriorization" and when that deteriorization would have progressed to a point to allow the invasion of northwestern Europe. Civilian experts and newly commissioned Army Air Forces' officers were assembled for the task. Members of the committee included Lt Col Malcom Moss (Hansell's former associate), Lt Col Guido R. Perera, Mr. Elihu Root Jr., and a host of other experts. Arnold was unclear in his directive as to specifically what he wanted, but on 8 March 1943 the committee submitted a report that set forth the industrial objectives, the destruction of which, in their opinion, would fatally weaken Germany.[91]

The COA used a clearly articulated methodology based on the scientific method. There were three steps in the process of target selection. Step one studied the German economy to find its relationship with the war effort. Step two sought to eliminate as many target facilities as possible, taking care to ensure that they were being eliminated for good reason. Finally, step three listed each industry in order of priority of bombing and listed each target within a given industry. The COA goal was to discover the "keystone" or "bottleneck" that supported the German war effort. Unlike the AWPD-1 and AWPD-42 plans, the COA did not have to concern itself with force or production requirements. It dealt exclusively with targeting.[92]

The findings of the COA became the basis for the CBO Plan. Hansell was shocked when he saw the new target priorities, and Eaker originally considered the COA to be at least a nuisance and possibly even dangerous. Target number one was the German aircraft industry. An entirely new target system, ball bearings, was given second place. Petroleum products came in third, followed by grinding wheels and crude abrasives at fourth. Nonferrous metals such as copper, aluminum, and zinc were at fifth. Sixth place went to synthetic rubber and seventh went to submarine yards and bases. Hansell's electric power system had been relegated from second place in AWPD-1 and fourth place in AWPD-42 to 13th place in the COA report.[93]

Even Craven and Cate characterize the omission of electric power as "curious," but the COA reasoned that "in almost no instance is any single industry dependent upon one generating plant but rather upon a network which pools the greater part of the electrical energy within an area."[94] According to their estimates, 60 targets would have to be destroyed to keep the Rhine-Ruhr and central Germany areas inoperable. In retrospect it was certainly a mistake to underrate the value of electric targets, but as Craven and Cate point out, this came not "from a lack of prescience but of adequate information regarding the situation as it currently prevailed."[95] Hansell, as chairman and director of the CBO planning committee, could have elevated the status of electric power as a target system.

117

He later explained his reason for not pursuing the issue: "The Planning team was reluctant, however, to challenge the intelligence structure which bore such wide and vital support. If the credibility of that intelligence base were seriously impaired, the entire structure of the Air Offensive might be brought down. As a result, the team made no effort to include the German electric power system in the CBO plan."[96] At this point, even Eaker had come to believe that electric power targets were small and costly objectives.[97]

Hansell and his team estimated that the destruction and continued neutralization of 76 precision targets within six target systems would "gravely impair and might paralyze the western AXIS war effort." Because of the continued boat threat, submarine construction yards and bases ranked as the number-one target system. The German aircraft industry ranked second. Ball bearings, oil, and synthetic rubber ranked third, fourth, and fifth, respectively. Military transport vehicles ranked sixth. The CBO committee finally recognized the very real threat from German fighters, realizing that they could make both daylight and night bombing unprofitable. Therefore, German fighter strength was no longer an intermediate target, but second in priority. The report also specifically called for a "very deep penetration at Schweinfurt." The idea of such an attack had originated with the COA and was an important part of the CBO Plan.[98]

With the operational experience of the Eighth Air Force behind them, the CBO planners did not have to rely upon highly theoretical calculations as the AWPD planners had. They determined that their objectives would be achieved through a four-phase plan. In phase one (April–July 1943) the missions would be limited to the range of fighter support, which meant that the submarine yards would be the targets. In phase two (July–October 1943) 1,192 heavy bombers would commit 75 percent of their effort to fighter assembly and aircraft factories within a radius of 500 miles, while committing 25 percent of their efforts on submarine facilities. In phase three (October 1943–January 1944) forces would deploy 1,746 heavy bombers, enough to perform all assigned tasks. In phase four (beginning in early 1944) forces would commit 2,702 bombers on the combined offensive. The plan was quite realistic and contributed to a generally successful bombing campaign.[99]

Hansell wrote the final draft of the CBO Plan himself. General Andrews gave the plan his "unqualified" endorsement as did the chief of the Air Staff and the Royal Air Force Bomber Command. General Eaker took the plan to Washington and presented it to the Joint Chiefs of Staff on 29 April 1943. The Navy objected, but on 4 May 1943, the JCS approved the CBO Plan. On 14 May the JCS presented the plan to the Combined Chiefs of Staff (CCS) at the Trident Conference in Washington. It was the understanding of the CCS that the plan would culminate with a cross-Channel invasion on 1 May 1944. Thus Hansell had written the plan that effectively ended his dream of defeating Germany with strategic airpower alone. Electric power would not be a priority target; the invasion was now the object of the air offensive; and the report recognized the bomber's vulnerability to fighters. Hansell was, above all, a good soldier. When given an order he did his best to carry it out. In essence, he had written a plan that met the necessities of war but that did not reflect his true vision of the proper use of an independent strategic bomber force.[100]

Hansell returned to Brampton Grange to face another enemy—the weather. Only four missions were flown in the month of April because of unfavorable weather conditions. On 5 April bombers attacked the Renault motor vehicle and armament works at Billancourt, Paris, inflicting damage that cost the Wehrmacht 3,000 trucks and effectively shut the factory down for some time. Four B-17s were lost in the action. The next day industrial and aviation facilities at Antwerp, Belgium, were bombed with a loss of four Flying Fortresses. On 16 April the port areas of Lorient and Brest were struck with a loss of four bombers. On 17 April the 1st Bomb Wing struck the Focke-Wulf factory at Bremen. According to the returning crews, "Enemy fighters attacked in great force and with great determination after the bombers had passed the I. P. [initial point], continuing their attacks until 1355 when the bombers were 30 or 40 miles out to sea on the way home."[101] Six fortresses from the 91st Group and 10 from the 306th were shot down, a loss of 15 percent of the attacking aircraft. Bomb damage was extensive, however, with half the factory being destroyed.[102]

Hansell truly enjoyed the public relations side of his job. In April he hosted the king and queen of England during their visit to the 91st Bomb Group at Bassingbourn. On another occasion, the *Atlanta Constitution* ran a story showing Possum's generosity. "He escorted [the duchess of Gloucester] around, said goodby. When she got in her car she discovered a little pile of chocolate bars and canned peanuts—rarities even among royalty in England today. Hansell had gotten them from the post canteen and sneaked them into the car."[103] The article even shed some light into Possum's personal habits: "He often works from 8:30 a.m. until midnight or 1 a.m., taking time out for an occasional game of tennis or session with his phonograph records."[104] In May he had the pleasure of selecting the crew of the *Memphis Belle* to return to the United States. Hansell even made a brief appearance in William Wyler's famous film of the same name.[105]

The pace of the air war began stepping up in May. Five new B-17 groups—the 94th, 95th, 96th, 351st, and the 379th—arrived. General Anderson activated the 4th Bombardment Wing, but was forced to share Hansell's bases and maintenance facilities. Anderson even shared quarters with Hansell, but Possum welcomed his new comrade with enthusiasm because he knew that the new wing would mean bombing the enemy in mass.[106]

On 4 May 1943 Hansell flew his last combat mission. The target was Antwerp, and he flew in a B-17 christened *Chennault's Pappy*. The raid saw no losses, and as the aircraft returned across the Channel, Hansell sang "The Man of the Flying Trapeze" to the crew over the interphone. The name of the B-17 probably brought his stunt flying days to mind. At any rate he got poor reviews. "They didn't seem to think a hell a lot of my singing," Hansell reported after the mission.[107]

On 13 May the 1st Wing was joined by Anderson's 4th in a raid on northern France. Hansell's bombers struck the Poetz aircraft factory at Meaulte, France, with four losses. On 14 May the B-17s struck the shipyards at Kiel, Germany, and suffered eight losses, but the bombing was exceptional. And on 15 May cloud cover obscured the target at Emden, forcing the aircraft to bomb targets of opportunity, while suffering six losses. On 17 May, 80 of Hansell's bombers attacked Lorient. Four bombers failed to return.[108]

The losses were mounting rapidly. This fact had to be taking a heavy toll on Hansell. On 17 May 1943, Hansell visited his old B-26 unit, the 322d Bomb Group. At RAF request, a dozen Marauders launched for an attack on Dutch power stations. The attack would be made at tree-top level. One plane did not take off and one returned because of engine trouble, leaving 10 aircraft to continue the attack; all 10 were lost in the attack. "Possum Hansell would never forget the feeling of waiting with the others at the field in the fading light, knowing they were never coming back."[109]

On 19 May a raid on U-boat facilities at Kiel saw six losses. Three days later seven Fortresses went down over Wilhelmshaven. One hundred and forty-seven B-17s attacked Saint-Nazaire with a loss of eight. On 11 June 168 bombers struck the Wilhelmshaven U-boat facilities with a loss of eight. Hansell signed his last operational orders for the 1st Bomb Wing for the 13 June mission to Bremen. One hundred twenty-two bombers attacked the U-boat yards, suffering 26 losses—a loss rate of over 21 percent.[110]

General Eaker finally decided to relieve Longfellow as commander of VIII Bomber Command, replace him with Anderson, and give LeMay command of the 4th Bomb Wing. In a cable to Arnold, Eaker expressed his reasons for not giving the command to Hansell: "Hansell has been carefully considered for eventual Bomber Commander. He is nervous and highly strung, and it is doubtful whether he would physically stand the trials and responsibilities of the Bomber Command task."[111] Years later, when Hansell learned the reason he was passed over for command at VIII Bomber Command, he responded with this unpublished note: "This I find puzzling. The role of Bomber Commander from a comfortable headquarters near London is hardly as demanding as leader of a combat command in the field. If he had said that I was on the verge of exhaustion, having had combat command of a unit which had lost 170 percent of the bombers dispatched over a grueling, pioneering, period of six months, and had taken missions at the same rate as the Group Commanders, I would hasten to agree with him."[112]

Eaker had acknowledged that Hansell, more than Longfellow, had been responsible for heavy bomber operations in the Eighth Air Force. It could be that the stress of command had taken its toll on Hansell and he was indeed exhausted and Eaker perceived him to be nervous. There is yet another possible reason. Eaker later recalled that Arnold had stipulated that Kuter and Hansell would be returned to Washington after they had received operational experience.[113] At any rate, Hansell was not pleased with the news that he was going home. Eaker's aide and biographer, James Parton, recalled the scene: "Hansell took the bad news with grace after a two-hour session with Eaker at WIDEWING [Bushy Park], from which he emerged with face pale and lips pursed."[114]

Hansell left the command of the 1st Bombardment Wing with a true sense of accomplishment. His unit had taken terrible casualties. In the six months of Hansell's command, 56 men were killed in action, two died of wounds, 301 were wounded, and 1,752 men were missing. Total casualties amounted to 2,111 from a bomb wing of four groups that would ordinarily have only 1,600 combat personnel. The loss rate for the 1st Wing for the first five months of 1943 averaged 6.4 percent per mission of those aircraft actually attacking the target.[115]

What had all these brave young men accomplished? Sixty-three percent of Eighth Air Force bombs had fallen on submarine targets that the air force had not planned to bomb. The bombing itself was accurate, but the U-boat pens were much too thick for existing bombs—Kuter and Hansell had both considered larger ordnance the key to bombing U-boat facilities. On 4 May 1943 Adm Karl Doenitz observed, "You know that the towns of St. Nazaire and Lorient have been rubbed out as main submarine bases. No dog or cat is left in these towns. Nothing but the submarine shelters remain."[116] By the end of 1943, the Army Air Forces' surveys of strategic bombing yielded data that confirmed the fact that strategic attacks against submarine facilities were ineffective. By contrast, little more than 15 percent of Eighth Air Force bombs had fallen on German aircraft targets. Of seven attacks on the German aircraft industry, four were successful, the most notable example being the 17 April 1943 mission to the Focke-Wulf factory at Bremen. Attacks on Germany itself had been relatively successful, but very costly. The missions had not been escorted, but the Eighth had not been discouraged.[117]

Hansell's achievement lies in the fact that he led the Eighth Air Force in its formative days. He commanded all four of the B-17 groups in the 2d Bombardment Wing. He established the standard operating procedures, defensive formations, and bombing standards that carried the mighty Eighth through its history. He had, after all, commanded the forces that executed the first American daylight bombing raid on Germany, written two important war plans, and established the facilities that enabled the Eighth to expand. During his tour of duty in England, he received the Air Medal for completing five combat missions, the Distinguished Flying Cross for his leadership on the 8 March 1943 mission to Rennes, and the Silver Star Medal for his role on the 3 January 1943 raid on Saint-Nazaire. Yet, in spite of his successes, he was disappointed by the dispersal of bomber forces to Africa, the lack of reinforcements or replacements, the altering of the strategic target list, and the acceptance of the necessity of an invasion of the Continent. By any measurement, however, he had done his job well. In a critique of the effectiveness of the Eighth Air Force during this critical period, Craven and Cate point out that "at the end of May, the Eighth Air Force could look back over the record of the past five months with a certain degree of pride."[118] Hansell had, to a very large degree, made that pride possible and had, to the best of his ability, preserved the principles of daylight precision bombing, which he had helped formulate at the Air Corps Tactical School.

Notes

1. Haywood S. Hansell Jr., *Strategic Air War against Japan* (Maxwell AFB, Ala.: Air War College, Airpower Research Institute, 1980), v; DeWitt S. Copp, *Forged in Fire: Strategy and Decisions in the Air War over Europe, 1940–1945* (New York: Doubleday & Co., 1982), 277; and Dwight D. Eisenhower to Gen Thomas Handy, letter, 7 July 1942, *The Papers of Dwight David Eisenhower*, vols. 1–5, *The War Years*, ed. Alfred D. Chandler Jr. (Baltimore: Johns Hopkins Press, 1970), vol. 1, 364.

2. Haywood S. Hansell Jr., *The Air Plan that Defeated Hitler* (Atlanta: Higgins-McArthur/Longino and Porter, 1972), 100; Dwight D. Eisenhower to Gen George C. Marshall, letter, 11 August 1942, *Eisenhower Papers*, 364;

Copp, 277; and James Parton, *"Air Force Spoken Here": General Ira Eaker and the Command of the Air* (Bethesda, Md.: Adler & Adler, 1986), 179.

3. Wesley Frank Craven and James Lea Cate, eds., *The Army Air Forces in World War II*, vol. 2, *Europe: Torch to Pointblank, August 1942 to December 1943* (1949; new imprint, Washington, D.C.: Office of Air Force History, 1983), 213; James Cooper to the author, letter, 15 December 1991; Copp, 278; and James Cooper, telephone interview by author, 5 April 1992.

4. Gen James H. "Jimmy" Doolittle with Carroll V. Glines, *I Could Never Be So Lucky Again* (New York: Bantam Books, 1991), 277.

5. Craven and Cate, 45.

6. Ibid., 55, 61, 63, 243.

7. Roger Freeman, *The Mighty Eighth* (Garden City: Doubleday and Co., 1970), 12; and Copp.

8. Copp, 291.

9. Paul Tibbets, pilot of the *Enola Gay*, the B-29 that dropped the first atomic bomb, interviewed by Murray Green, 7 January 1970, Murray Green Collection, US Air Force Academy Library, Colorado Springs, Colo.

10. Carl A. Spaatz to Henry H. Arnold, letter, 27 August 1942, Henry H. Arnold Papers, Box 273, Library of Congress, Washington, D.C.

11. Dwight D. Eisenhower to Haywood S. Hansell Jr., letter, 27 August 1942, Haywood S. Hansell Jr. Papers, microfilm edition, AFHRA, Maxwell AFB, Ala.; Copp, 296; Harry Butcher, *My Three Years with Eisenhower: The Personal Diary of Captain Harry C. Butcher, USNR, Naval Aide to General Eisenhower, 1942 to 1945* (New York: Simon and Schuster, 1946), 78.

12. George C. Marshall to Carl A. Spaatz, cable, 26 August 1942, Arnold Papers.

13. Hansell, *Air Plan*, 100.

14. Ibid., 100–101.

15. Ibid.

16. Ibid., 102.

17. Copp, 298; Hansell, *Air Plan*, 102–3; and Craven and Cate, 277.

18. Hansell, *Air Plan*, 109; United States Strategic Bombing Survey Secretariat, "Memorandum on Bombardment Planning Documents (AWPD-1, AWPD-42) COA Report, Pointblank," 30 March 1945, Carl A. Spaatz Papers, Box 66, Library of Congress, Washington, D.C.

19. Hansell, *Air Plan*, 109–111; and "Memorandum on Bombardment Planning Documents."

20. Hansell, *Air Plan*, 108.

21. Copp, 298; Hansell, *Air Plan*, 107; and Thomas A. Fabyanic, "A Critique of United States Air War Planning, 1941–1945" (PhD diss., St. Louis University, 1973), 20.

22. Hansell, *Air Plan*, 106.

23. Ibid., 163; and Fabyanic, 106.

24. Fabyanic, 106.

25. Hansell, *Air Plan,* 111–12.

26. Ibid., 112.

27. Copp, 299; and Fabyanic, 101.

28. Laurence S. Kuter to Carl A. Spaatz, letter, 16 September 1942, Arnold Papers.

29. Laurence S. Kuter to Haywood S. Hansell Jr., letter, 30 September 1942, Arnold Papers.

30. Copp, 299; and Hansell, *Air Plan,* 105.

31. Henry H. Arnold to Carl A. Spaatz, letter, 3 September 1942, Arnold Papers.

32. Mrs. Haywood S. Hansell Jr., interviewed by author, 21 March 1992.

33. Craven and Cate, 53–55.

34. Hansell, *Air Plan,* 147.

35. Craven and Cate, 51–52, 231–33.

36. Craven and Cate, 54, 64, 237–38; Butcher, 157; and HQ ETOUSA to Assistant Chief of Staff (A-2 and A-5) from Haywood S. Hansell Jr., 1 November 1942, Spaatz Papers, Box 10.

37. Parton, 200–201; and Copp, 321.

38. Craven and Cate, 64, 65, 106; Parton, 200–201; and Carl A. Spaatz to Dwight D. Eisenhower, letter, 19 November 1942, Hansell Papers.

39. "Commander's Notes," Hansell Papers; and Freeman, 55.

40. Freeman, 55; "Commander's Notes"; and "Low Altitude Tactics," Royal Air Force paper, 16 December 1942, Hansell Papers.

41. Haywood S. Hansell Jr. to Newton Longfellow, letter, 12 December 1942, Hansell Papers; and "Commander's Notes."

42. Haywood Hansell, "Notes of a Heavy Bomber (B-17) Wing and Division Commander: 1st 6 Months of 1943—1st Bomb Wing, 8th Bomber Command," unpublished, undated manuscript in the Hansell family's private collection; and Freeman, 7, 46.

43. Parton, 212.

44. Ibid., 214.

45. Ibid.

46. Ibid., 203.

47. Hansell, "Notes," 1.

48. Craven and Cate, 311.

49. Hansell, *Air Plan,* 185.

50. Ibid.

51. "Mission Reports, 1st Bombardment Wing," Eighth Air Force Records, AFHRA, Maxwell AFB, Ala.; Craven and Cate, 250; and Copp, 331.

52. Craven and Cate, 251, 269; Copp, 322; and "History of the 305th Group," Box B-8, Curtis E. LeMay Papers, Library of Congress, Washington, D.C.

53. Craven and Cate, 251; Copp, 322; Hansell, "Notes," 2; and "History of the 305th Group."

54. Craven and Cate, 250–51.

55. Brig Gen Haywood Hansell Jr., interviewed by Bruce C. Hopper, 5 October 1943, Spaatz Papers.

56. Hansell, "Notes," 1.

57. Copp, 332.

58. Hansell, *Air Plan,* 139.

59. Hansell, "Notes," 5; and Hansell, *Air Plan,* 141.

60. Hansell, *Air Plan,* 140.

61. Copp, 332; Hansell, *Air Plan,* 140; and Hansell, "Notes," 5–7.

62. Hansell, *Air Plan,* 113–18; Hansell, "Notes," 3; and Craven and Cate, 266–67.

63. Hansell, "Notes," 6–7; Hansell, *Air Plan,* 118; and Craven and Cate, 272.

64. Hansell, *Air Plan,* 122.

65. Ibid., 123.

66. Once the B-17s had released their payloads, their weight diminished and thus their speed increased causing them to leave the heavier YB-40s behind.

67. Hansell, *Air Plan,* 125; and Craven and Cate, 265–66, 270.

68. Copp, 332; and Maj Gen Haywood S. Hansell Jr., interviewed by Murray Green, 19 April 1967, US Air Force Academy Library, Colorado Springs, Colo.

69. "History of the 305th Bomb Group."

70. Martin W. Bowman, *Castles in the Air: The Story of the B-17 Flying Fortress Crews of the U.S. Eighth Air Force* (Cambridge, England: P. Stephens, 1984), 37–38; Freeman, 23; "History of the 305th Bomb Group"; Wilbur H. Morrison, *The Incredible 305th: The "Can Do" Bombers of World War II* (New York: E. P. Dutton, 1962), 24–26; and "War Diary: 364th Bomb Squadron," AFHRA, Maxwell AFB, Ala.

71. Morrison, 26–29; "War Diary: 364th Bomb Squadron"; and Copp, 332–33.

72. "Mission Report," 13 January 1943.

73. Morrison, 33.

74. Wilbur H. Morrison, *Fortress without a Roof: The Allied Bombing of the Third Reich* (New York: St. Martin's Press, 1982), 111–16; and Craven and Cate, 300–303.

75. Craven and Cate, 305.

76. Fabyanic, 144.

77. Hansell, *Air Plan,* 170–71; and Craven and Cate, 305.

78. "Mission Reports," 23 and 27 January 1943; "Summary of Events, 1 January–31 January 1943," 1st Bombardment Wing, AFHRA, Maxwell AFB, Ala.; and Craven and Cate, 223, 264–65.

79. "Mission Report," 4 February 1943; "Summary of Events, 1 February–28 February 1943"; Craven and Cate, 324; and Freeman, 25.

80. Copp, 364.

81. Ibid.

82. Freeman, 26; Craven and Cate, 324–25; "Summary of Events, February 1943"; "Mission Reports," 14 and 27 February 1943; and Bowman, 42.

83. Craven and Cate, 309–10.

84. Hansell, *Air Plan*, 137.

85. Craven and Cate, 309–10, 342–43.

86. Craven and Cate, 318, 325–326; Freeman, 27; and "Mission Reports," 4, 6, and 8 March 1943.

87. "Danver Gets a Look at Puttsburghers Returning from Raid," unidentified, undated newspaper article from the Hansell family's private collection.

88. Hansell, "Notes," 8.

89. Craven and Cate, 314, 326, 327, 844; "Mission Reports," 18, 22, 28, and 31 March 1943; "Summary of Events, 1 March–31 March 1943"; and Copp, 364.

90. Craven and Cate, 348, 356; Hansell, *Air Plan*, 157; Parton, 252–53; and Copp, 383.

91. Craven and Cate, 348–54; and Hansell, *Air Plan*, 149.

92. Craven and Cate, 350–54; Fabyanic, 145–47; and "Memorandum on Bombardment Planning Documents," Tab C, 1.

93. Hansell, *Air Plan*, 158–64.

94. "Memorandum on Bombardment Planning Documents," Tab C, 2.

95. Craven and Cate, 362.

96. Hansell, *Air Plan*, 162.

97. Copp, 384.

98. "Plan for Combined Bomber Offensive from the United Kingdom," 14 May 1943, File 119.04-6, AFHRA, Maxwell AFB, Ala.; Craven and Cate, 367–69; and Fabyanic, 202.

99. "Plan for Combined Bomber Offensive from the United Kingdom"; Craven and Cate, 369–71; and Fabyanic, 202.

100. Hansell, "Notes," 16; Copp, 385; Craven and Cate, 365–66, 372–73; and Parton, 263.

101. "Mission Report," 17 April 1943.

102. "Summary of Events"; and "Mission Reports," 4, 5, 16, and 17 April 1943; and Craven and Cate, 316–19.

103. "Possums Don't Make Much Noise but US Bomber Boss in England Gets Around," *Atlanta Constitution*, 6 June 1943.

104. Ibid.

105. Ira C. Eaker to Henry H. Arnold, letter, 12 June 1943, Ira C. Eaker Papers, Box 18, Library of Congress, Washington, D.C.

106. Hansell, "Notes," 12; and Craven and Cate, 338.

107. "Atlanta General Turns Crooner on Big Raid—Gets 'Razzberries,'" unidentified, undated article from the Hansell family's private collection.

108. "Mission Reports," 4, 13, 14, 15, and 17 May 1943; and Craven and Cate, 314, 844–45.

109. Copp, 399.

110. "Mission Reports," 19, 21, and 29 May 1943, and 11 and 13 June 1943; and Craven and Cate, 845.

111. Copp, 403; and Parton, 272.

112. Hansell, "Notes," 16.

113. Hansell, *Strategic Air War against Japan,* v.

114. Parton, 287.

115. "1st Bombardment Wing Battle Casualties," File 525.391, AFHRA, Maxwell AFB, Ala.; and Craven and Cate, 317.

116. Craven and Cate, 316.

117. Ibid., 258, 317.

118. Ibid., 346.

Chapter 5

The Global Bomber Force

Even before Hansell officially left the 1st Bombardment Wing, a transatlantic struggle broke out between Arnold and Eaker over who was to retain Hansell's services. Air Chief Marshal Sir Trafford Leigh-Mallory had been named commander of the Allied Expeditionary Air Force (AEAF) in preparation for the invasion of France, and Eaker believed that Hansell would be an ideal deputy. Arnold was engaged in his own struggle in Washington and needed competent staff officers. Haywood Hansell was the man he wanted. Thus in mid-June 1943 a high-level "battle of the cables" was waged with the services of Hansell as the objective.[1]

On 19 June Arnold cabled Eaker that "Army Air Forces are being directly controlled by the Joint Chiefs of Staff and Combined Chiefs of Staff more and more each day." He indicated that he needed a high-level planner who would provide a balance that would counter the predominance of the Navy and Army ground forces on the combined and joint planning staffs. "On this high level, Brigadier H. S. Hansell is the type needed as the air officer to represent me."[2] The next day Eaker responded by agreeing with Arnold that Hansell was the man for the job in Washington, but "likewise there is no officer in the Eighth Air Force available for the job we have lately put Hansell on who would be satisfactory for the work he has to do and who would be, as he is, fully acceptable to the British and particularly to Air Marshal Leigh-Mallory."[3] On 22 June Eaker cabled Washington that he recommended that Hansell be retained in the European theater of operations for "the very important task to which he has just been assigned."[4]

Eaker's recommendation was accepted, but Hansell's duties as deputy commander of the AEAF, as events developed, would be nominal at best. Leigh-Mallory soon managed to offend many of the top Allied commanders and, as a consequence of this and the nature of the Allied command structure, the AEAF never achieved the prominence its title promised. In early July Eaker sent Hansell to Washington to promote a plan for a double bomber strike deep into the Continent against the aircraft factories at Regensburg, Germany, and Wiener-Neustadt, Austria. This plan soon became the infamous Regensburg-Schweinfurt mission. Hansell made the case for the plan before Arnold, and Marshall tentatively approved it on 19 July. Once Hansell went to Washington, however, there was little chance that he would ever assume a permanent assignment in the European theater of operations.[5]

After reporting to Arnold, Hansell received a well-deserved rest. Dotta and the children were at Indian Rocks, Florida, living across the street from her brother and sister-in-law, Reginald and Susan Vance. Possum contacted his wife, writing her that he would arrive at four thirty the next day. Excited at the news of his arrival, Mrs. Hansell made a trip to town to make preparations; she wanted their reunion to be special. Mrs. Hansell assumed that he would arrive in the afternoon, but when he arrived at the airport at four thirty in the morning there was no one to greet him. He took a taxi across the bay to Indian Rocks only to realize that he did not know the address. By that time it was six o'clock, and in desperation he had the taxi driver stop a milk truck and ask the driver. Luckily, the Hansell family was on the driver's route, and he led them directly to the house. Dotta was taken completely by surprise and was dressed in an old housecoat and curlers when the "conquering hero" returned.[6]

Time with the family at Indian Rocks was just what Hansell needed. He was exhausted by his experiences in Europe and showed obvious signs of stress. If an airplane flew by he would quiver and shake, but a steady diet of bananas and time in the sun soon relaxed him. Before long he and Dotta were in Atlanta, Georgia, and in the public eye. In an interview for the *Atlanta Constitution* Hansell described air combat: "Your apprehension is greater before you get into combat or flak though. After you get into the fight it's something like a football game, everything is all right." Indeed, everything was all right for Possum. He was with his family, he was in the good graces of General Arnold, and the press flattered him with lines like, "Hitler wishes 'Possum' Hansell would hurry up and go to Florida or even hotter climes." He was more than ready to get back to the business of strategic bombing.[7]

Mrs. Hansell, on the other hand, was fighting a battle of her own to raise three young children. At the end of the summer she moved to Tampa, Florida, in order to enroll the children in school. She was unhappy there, and within the year, she and the children moved to San Antonio, Texas, to be near her in-laws. Bearing the burden of the home front was made a bit harder by an act of insensitivity on the part of Possum. Mrs. Hansell had purchased a pair of earrings at Garfinkle's in Washington. She later referred to the purchase as "my one extravagance." Just before Possum left for England he asked her where she got the earrings because he wanted to take some to his English driver. In anger she threw the jewelry at him and to her surprise, he took them. At the time she was suspicious that he was in love with his driver, but she later realized that this was a harmless good deed offered by a hopeless romantic.[8]

Hansell returned to Washington to assist Arnold and his staff prepare for the Quebec Conference. It is probable that he had significant influence on the CCS 323 document entitled "The Air Plan for the Defeat of Japan." (The plan was based on the assumption that Germany would be defeated by the fall of 1944.) China and a number of Pacific islands were considered as bases. Operations were to begin in October 1944 and culminate in the frustration of Japanese strategic objectives by April 1945. The plan was hastily drafted in order to assure that the role of the B-29 was not neglected at the Quebec Conference.[9]

News of the loss of 60 bombers in the Regensburg-Schweinfurt raid arrived just two days before the Quebec Conference. This unfortunate turn of events placed Hansell in a familiar role: advocate of daylight precision bombing. Since Hansell was a wing commander fresh from the battle, Arnold saw him as an invaluable asset to have in the potentially hostile environment at Quebec. As expected, the British criticized Arnold for his persistence in daylight bombing. Hansell's greatest fear, however, was in losing the confidence of President Roosevelt. In a 24 August 1943 letter to Eaker, Hansell described how he "had the opportunity to contribute to the bomber offensive" from Quebec:

General Arnold took me up to the Citadel to see the President last week. I had about fifteen minutes uninterrupted opportunity to explain to him what we had done, how we were doing it, and what we expected for the future.

General Arnold asked me in the presence of the President whether I thought we could win the war by bombing alone. I replied that I felt it was necessary to have ground forces available to administer the devastated areas and they might encounter some opposition in establishing themselves in Europe even after interior Germany had begun to crumble. He seemed to accept this idea and made no comment.

I made an unsuccessful effort to have a message of congratulations sent by the President, himself, to the 8th Air Force on the Regensburg-Schweinfurt operation. I did describe its importance to the President. However, I do not think the message will be sent since it seems to establish a new precedent.[10]

Since the decision to invade northwestern Europe was made at the Quebec Conference, Hansell's confidence in the ability of strategic bombing to win the war alone seems to have fallen on deaf ears. President Roosevelt's refusal to send the message of congratulations might indicate that American strategic bombing operations were to some degree out of favor.[11]

Hansell, aware that Eaker was concerned about the fate of American strategic bombing, continued in his 24 August letter to encourage the Eighth Air Force commander: "I need not say how tremendously proud I was of [the] Regensburg-Schweinfurt operation. In spite of the very heavy losses, I believe it was completely justified and represents one of the turning points of the war. I believe that there is every confidence here that the 8th Air Force is going to do the job. Although you are very short now of personnel replacements, I do believe that General Arnold is doing everything in his power to correct that situation."[12] He then turned to his own future. Leigh-Mallory's appointment had been confirmed by the Combined Chiefs of Staff, and Hansell addressed his new role as deputy commander of the tactical air forces. Yet, his heart was still with strategic bombing and the mighty Eighth. He was opposed to giving the tactical role in Overlord (overall plan for invasion of Western Europe in 1944) to the Ninth Air Force—he felt that that role could be fulfilled by the Eighth Air Force. He concluded his letter to Eaker by stating: "Although my stay has protracted,

I believe it has paid dividends to the 8th Air Force. Certainly the opportunity to talk to the President about the bomber offensive was a gift from heaven."[13]

On 31 August he accompanied Arnold on an inspection tour of England. By 2 September the party was at Eaker's headquarters trying to make the best of a bad situation. Hansell was on hand on 6 September when the Eighth struck at Stuttgart, Germany, with the disastrous loss of 45 bombers. He returned to Washington with Arnold but was back in London in October. By this time it was probably obvious to Hansell that his future was no longer in the European theater of operations. In an interview given to the Eighth Air Force historian at Norfolk House on 5 October 1943, Hansell responded to a question about his present assignment: "Air Marshal Leigh-Mallory has been selected as the allied air commander and I am deputy commander. However, these things change so rapidly—when you get into this sphere, so many political angles to it, and so forth, that it may be all washed out."[14] General Arnold was absorbed with the B-29 project back in Washington and was having difficulty explaining to President Roosevelt why he was slow in deploying the aircraft in China. What he needed was an expert planner with combat experience and diplomatic skills. In October Hansell returned to Washington and was assigned as chief of the Combined and Joint Staff Division of Army Air Force Plans. Hansell's attentions now turned toward Japan.[15]

Hansell did not disappoint Arnold. When he took his seat on the Joint Plans Committee, he immediately had an objection to a statement he found in the proposed Joint War Plan against Japan. The statement read, "It has been clearly demonstrated in the war in Europe that strategic air forces are incapable of decisive action and hence the war against Japan must rely upon victory through surface forces, supported appropriately by air forces. Final victory must come through invasion of the Japanese home islands."[16] It was clear that the air force had had no advocate on the committee. Hansell at once took up the challenge and, as he later remembered, with much difficulty succeeded in amending the statement of basic strategy. The new description of the grand strategy against Japan read, "The possibility that invasion of the principal

Japanese islands may not be necessary and the defeat of Japan may be accomplished by sea and air blockade and intensive air bombardment from progressively advanced bases. The plan must, however, be capable of expansion to meet the contingency of invasion."[17]

Hansell had the plan to defeat Japan, and Arnold had the instrument—the B-29 Superfortress. Its $3 billion development project promised a bombing aircraft that was pressurized, could fly to 30,000 feet, and could carry a four-ton bomb load to a target 1,750 miles distant. The project had begun in November 1939, and after four years the aircraft was nearly operational. It was so complicated that more than the usual number of design flaws had to be ironed out, but it was important to get the aircraft into the war as soon as possible if Arnold's gamble was going to pay off. There were many doubts about Operation Matterhorn, which called for operating B-29s out of China. The basing of B-29s in China would cause tremendous logistical problems and place the heavy bomber bases in danger of being captured by Japanese ground forces. In September 1943 (before Hansell joined the team) the combined staff planners had concluded that Matterhorn was unfeasible from a logistical point of view alone.[18]

General Arnold had requested that the Committee of Operations Analysts draw up target lists for Matterhorn anyway. When the subject was again presented before the joint planners on 9 November 1943, they were not prepared to accept it without further study. They instructed Hansell to request that the joint chiefs secure approval of the construction of the desired bases in the event the plan became a reality. That decision would be made in a matter of days at the Cairo Conference in Egypt.[19]

On 11 November 1943, Hansell began a circumnavigation of the globe, a voyage that would bring him into contact with world leaders at the highest level. On that day the JCS—Admiral King, General Marshall, and General Arnold—boarded the USS *Iowa*. Along with Arnold came Generals Kuter, Hansell, and Emmett "Rosie" O'Donnell. That evening this most illustrious company enjoyed the movie *Stage Door Canteen*, but their thoughts were certainly on much weightier matters. The next day, 12 November, the presidential yacht delivered President

Roosevelt, Adm William D. Leahy, Harry Hopkins, and others to the *Iowa*. The trip would take them to the Cairo and Tehran Conferences. After the initial excitement died down concerning the near torpedoing of the president's battleship by one of the US Navy's own destroyers, this group had the opportunity to engage in serious discussions about Matterhorn in a more informal setting. (Hansell later recalled his satisfaction in learning that Marshall was actually an advocate of airpower.) On 20 November they arrived at Oran, Algeria, and then went on to Tunis, Tunisia, and Cairo, arriving on 22 November.[20]

Rear Adm Bernhard H. Bieri chaired the meeting of the joint planners during the Cairo Conference. Brig Gen Frank N. Roberts was the Army representative, and since the air force was part of the Army, Bieri did not consider Hansell to be an equal. Nevertheless, Hansell put forth three important proposals: (1) the consolidation of the strategic air forces in Europe and in the Pacific; (2) recognizing strategic air war as the principal war-winning strategy and utilizing it against Japan; (3) obtaining sites from which Japan could be bombed. General Roberts was helpful, and the Joint Plans Committee agreed to all the important proposals affecting the air force.[21] Hansell was, in effect, supporting the Navy's position, because the capture of the Marianas by naval forces was the cornerstone of both the Navy's and air force's strategy in the Pacific. Hansell counted it a great victory when the combined chiefs of staff agreed "to obtain objectives from which we can conduct intensive air bombardment and establish a sea and air blockade against Japan and from which to invade Japan proper if this should be necessary."[22]

The plan for Matterhorn saw much more resistance. Neither the joint nor the combined planners showed much enthusiasm for operating B-29s from China. Practically every member showed some objection or at least some uncertainty. Hansell seems to have been the only optimist among the planners. He felt that it was up to him "to carry the ball" on Matterhorn. As historian Grace Person Hayes observed, "At the JPS meeting, Brig Gen Haywood S. Hansell said he thought the problem of maintaining B-29s in China could be solved and he was not sure that invasion was necessary to accomplish Japan's defeat."[23] Political considerations, perhaps more than any other factor, caused the approval of Matterhorn at Cairo. President Roosevelt was adamant in his determination to aid China in some way, and the Chinese wanted to expand operations in their theater. The British agreed to build bases in India, and the Chinese agreed to provide bases in China.[24]

Hansell was indeed busy at Cairo. He was not only responsible for his planning meetings but also for keeping General Arnold informed and for working with the Allies. His meetings with Arnold, Kuter, Vandenberg, and O'Donnell were often followed by tea with Air Chief Marshal Sir Charles Portal and Adm Lord Louis Mountbatten, where they discussed the potential problems of the B-29 in India and China. While the president and most of the military staff traveled on to Tehran, Iran, for the meeting with Stalin, Hansell remained behind to work on plans for the strategic air war against Japan. When Arnold returned on 2 December, Hansell reported his progress, and when the official portrait of the Air Staff was made, Hansell was seated in a place of prominence.[25]

After the Cairo and Tehran Conferences, General Marshall learned that General Eisenhower would command Overlord. Even though his command concerns were still global, General Marshall did not want to face the British, who were still trying to get him to support the diversion of precious resources to the island of Rhodes, which was held by Italy. In order to avoid the issue, he chose to fly home via the Far East. Hansell was selected to make the trip with him. A C-54 took them from Cairo to Karachi, Pakistan, then to Ceylon, where they fueled up for the long flight across the Indian Ocean to Exmouth Bay, Australia. From there they flew to Darwin, Australia; Lt Gen George C. Kenney, MacArthur's air commander, met them. Kenney escorted them to Port Moresby, New Guinea, and then to Goodenough Island, New Guinea, where General MacArthur was conferring with Gen Walter E. Krueger, commander of the Sixth Army, who was about to commence operations on the island of New Britain.[26]

This was the first meeting between Marshall and MacArthur in eight years and the only time the two met during the war. According to MacArthur's biographer, D. Clayton James, MacArthur considered conducting the Cape Gloucester operations in person, "thus relieving Marshall of his presence." Hansell's account of the meeting claims that if there was embarrassment on MacArthur's part he did not reveal it.

After an inspection tour with General Krueger, Generals Marshall, MacArthur, Kenney, and Hansell met privately for what has been described as a "long, frank discussion." The subject of the meeting was future strategy. Obviously, MacArthur and Kenney saw no need to capture the central Pacific islands and favored taking the Philippines instead. MacArthur also complained about the small number of men and limited resources he was getting. According to MacArthur, Marshall placed the blame on Admirals King and Leahy. No decisions were reached, but MacArthur had made his position clear. MacArthur was careful not to meet with Marshall alone, and this was their only meeting of the trip.[27]

As junior member of the group, Hansell was clearly in awe of this select, august gathering. Hansell later described his impression of the meeting: "Throughout the presentation [MacArthur] employed wit and charm with devastating persuasiveness. Although I had from the first been an advocate of a 'Europe first' strategy, with attendant delay against Japan, I simply melted under the persuasive logic and the delightful charm of the great MacArthur. By the time he had finished, I was anxious to give him what he had asked for."[28] Marshall, however, was of "far sterner stuff" and maintained the strategic course that had been set at the beginning of the war. On 16 December Marshall and his party returned to Port Moresby and the next day departed for Hawaii via Guadalcanal. After a weather delay in California, Marshall and his party arrived back in Washington on 22 December.[29]

Upon his return, Hansell was appointed deputy chief of the Air Staff. Hansell had been long associated with General Arnold, but this new position placed him in daily contact with the hard-driving commanding general of the Army Air Forces. Arnold's nickname was "Hap" because of his perpetual smile, but this permanent facial fixture belied his true temperament. He has been described as ruthless and capricious, and drove himself so hard that he suffered four heart attacks during the war. He met with his staff every morning, seven days a week. One Sunday morning he lashed out at a staff officer so harshly that the man's face reddened, the veins in his neck expanded, and, just as he opened his mouth to speak, he fell dead of a massive heart attack in front of Arnold's desk. Arnold gave his staff the rest of the day off. General Kuter knew of at least one officer who was in the "psychopathic ward at Walter Reed" as a result of overwork in Arnold's service.[30]

Arnold's rash actions were legendary. It was not uncommon for him to have a sudden idea, literally grab the first staff officer he saw, and send him on this urgent errand across the country without allowing the man to cut orders for the mission. He also remembered those who had been opposed to him or the air force in the past. Generals who had not supported the air arm before the war could not expect to have their own private airplane during the war.[31]

Now Hansell was in daily contact with Arnold and, moreover, had the misfortune to be directing Arnold's pet project. The new assignment certainly placed Hansell in a better position to promote daylight strategic bombing, but it also placed a great deal of pressure on him to perform for Arnold. Lauris Norstad recalled, "The Old Man used to keep the button on Possum Hansell's box going constantly. Arnold was into every damn detail . . . you know his life was that B-29."[32] It would be up to Hansell to see that the planning phase of the B-29 operations went smoothly—a task which would be nothing less than Herculean.

Even before Matterhorn had been approved at the Cairo Conference, Arnold had appointed Brig Gen Kenneth Wolfe commander of the XX Bomber Command because Wolfe knew more about the technical aspects of the B-29 than anyone else in the air force. On 15 December 1943, Arnold had the Army construction units alerted for shipment to India.[33] Arnold's expectations of Wolfe were made clear in a memo: "I have told the President that this [the departure of B-29s for China] will be started on March 1. See that it is done."[34] Yet by January 1944 only 97 B-29s had come off the assembly line, and of that number only 16 were flyable. The shortage of planes meant that the training of crews had been delayed. Arnold was not happy.[35]

The Chinese were scheduled to have the airfields ready by 15 April 1944, but there were still 54 major modifications to be made on the B-29, and they were sitting in the snow outside the aircraft factories in Kansas. Arnold suddenly appeared on the scene in Kansas, surveyed the situation, and placed Maj Gen Bennett E. "Benney" Meyers, the chief of Army Air Forces procurement, in command of what has come to be known as the "Battle of Kansas." Knowing that Arnold meant business, Meyers spent five weeks working with the aircraft firms, begging, threatening, sweet-talking, and doing whatever else would get the job done. Work went on day and night until the first B-29 unit was ready to depart for India on 26 March.[36]

General Arnold's reasons for placing such a high priority on B-29 operations from China were political. First of all, President Roosevelt expected bombing operations from China, and the B-29 was the only aircraft capable of such a mission. Second, Arnold had staked his reputation and the possible future of an independent air force on this "three-billion-dollar gamble." A bomber force that was not operational was useless, and the last thing he wanted was for the war to end before the B-29 could prove its worth and the value of an independent air arm. So in spite of the mechanical, logistical, and geographical problems associated with operating the untried B-29s out of China, Arnold expected B-29 operations to commence on schedule.

Hansell, on the other hand, saw B-29 operations against Japan as a second chance to prove the strategic air war theory that he and his colleagues had formulated at the Air Corps Tactical School in the 1930s. Here was an opportunity to use a much-improved bombing aircraft in a theater where he had the opportunity to avoid the administrative red tape that existed in Europe and against an island nation that he felt offered the kind of targets suited for daylight precision bombing. His only concern with politics was using his contacts to ensure that his plan for the strategic air war against Japan was adopted. While Arnold was using his influence and authority to get the B-29 operational, he trusted Hansell to see that the appropriate war plan was adopted and a command organization created to make his B-29 operations a reality. This was indeed Hansell's greatest opportunity to influence the course of American airpower, because, while Arnold wanted his B-29s in action as soon as possible, he left most decisions concerning the actual operations up to Hansell.

Hansell knew that the only appropriate targets for the B-29 were to be found in Japan and that if they were going to be successful, the bombers would have to be concentrated against strategic targets in the Japanese home islands. Yet as early as July 1943, General Kenney had requested B-29s for the southwest Pacific, and by January MacArthur and the Navy were in rare agreement that B-29s should be based at Darwin, Australia, to attack Japanese shipping and oil targets in the Dutch East Indies. In fact, the Joint War Plan document JWP2 recommended placing the first four B-29 groups in the southwest Pacific. Hansell alone opposed any deployment except against Japan proper. He suggested that the Joint War Plans Committee report had made insufficient use of the COA report concerning Japanese targets and had neglected to consider that bases in India and Ceylon could strike the same targets as aircraft based in Australia. At Hansell's request the Joint Planning Staff sent the report back to the Joint War Plans Committee for revision; when it was returned on 15 February 1944, the committee still maintained that Australia was a better choice than China. In the final analysis, it was President Roosevelt's decision to proceed with Matterhorn, but Hansell fought for a project in which he believed deeply and emerged from the first round on the winning side.[37]

Also on 15 February, Hansell presented to the joint chiefs the Army Air Forces' concept of the Pacific war. He stressed the importance of obtaining the Marianas as a base for operations against Japan. With the role of the B-29 still under much discussion, a great deal was at stake. Hansell was even willing, as an Army officer, to side with Admiral Nimitz over MacArthur concerning Pacific strategy. On 12 March the JCS decided to bypass Truk Island and launch an amphibious attack on the Marianas, with D day on Saipan set for 15 June 1944. Since the B-29s could reach Sumatra via Ceylon, even a scaled-down request for the aircraft in the southwest Pacific was rejected. After a struggle Hansell achieved concentration of force against the only target systems that mattered to strategic bombers—those located on the Japanese islands themselves.[38]

By March 1944 the joint chiefs finalized the Matterhorn plan. On 2 March the JCS cut the Matterhorn force to one bomb wing (four groups or 280 aircraft), the 58th; the 73d would later operate from the Marianas. Since there would only be one wing operating out of China, the Matterhorn plan could not be fully implemented, but Hansell made the most of what he had. As Craven and Cate observe, "The Joint Planners adhered more closely to Hansell's ideas in the report they sent to the JCS on March 2."[39] The original plan recommended that the first eight groups (560 aircraft) would operate from China and India and would attack coke ovens in Manchuria; petroleum, oil, and lubricant targets in the Dutch East Indies; and industrial targets in Japan. Twelve groups (840 aircraft) would be assigned to the Marianas, then perhaps other groups would be stationed in the Aleutians, Luzon, Formosa, or Siberia, depending on the course of the war.[40]

On 6 March 1944, Hansell's plan was placed before the JCS, and he was to present the case personally before them on 9 March. When he went to General Arnold for last-minute advice, he found that Arnold had left for the West Coast and would not be in attendance at the JCS meeting. Hansell later learned that Arnold had never been accepted as full partner on the JCS, and that whenever his presence at a meeting might cause friction he would be conveniently absent. Since the Navy's plan to capture the Marianas was in the best interest of the air force, and the Army supported the reconquest of the Philippines, Arnold did not want to be in a position to disagree with General Marshall. Hansell was anxious about giving the presentation with Arnold absent, but, as it turned out, Marshall was in favor of operations in the central Pacific as well as the liberation of the Philippines. Thus as was so often the case in the Pacific, the two rival strategies were both endorsed and Hansell would have his Marianas bases.[41]

Hansell's next major objective was to establish the command structure of this new strategic air force. He and his colleagues at ACTS had long held that an independent air force was essential to strategic operations. By "independent" they meant that the bomber force would be independent of the surface forces and would be free to launch an uninterrupted bombing campaign against strategic targets in the enemy's hinterland. Since the Eighth Air Force had been under theater command, it was often diverted to such tactical operations as the invasion of North Africa and the interdiction missions prior to Overlord. Hansell had always viewed such diversions as counterproductive to the true purpose of a bombing force. At Cairo, Hansell was successful in carrying out Arnold's wishes in creating the United States Strategic Air Force (USSTAF), consisting of the Eighth and Fifteenth Air Forces. Yet, even Spaatz's USSTAF was under the theater commander and liable to be used for tactical missions.[42]

Every theater commander had a vested interest in being able to use the B-29 for his own particular purposes. Admiral Mountbatten recommended that the JCS retain control over the very long range (VLR) bomber force, but that the local theater commander be treated as an equal of the bomber commander. In short, Mountbatten wanted Gen Joseph W. Stilwell to have control of the bombers in China so he could utilize their services when he wanted them. Since there was no unity of command in the Asiatic-Pacific theater as there was in the European theater, Mountbatten's plan would have meant that he, MacArthur, and Nimitz would be in a continual tug-of-war over the allocation and use of the aircraft. The British wanted the combined chiefs of staff to retain control over the bomber force because they eventually planned to commit RAF heavy bombers to the attack on Japan. Since Matterhorn and the planned operations from the Marianas were American enterprises, the British did not press the issue.[43]

Hansell realized that he must act quickly and at the highest levels in order to secure the command system he desired for the new Twentieth Air Force. Hansell proposed the establishment of the headquarters of the Twentieth Air Force in Washington under the command of General Arnold and under the direction of the JCS. He wanted it to be free from local theater control (except in emergencies), and he wanted the air force to be totally dedicated to the strategic bombing of Japan. General Arnold had an idea of how he wanted the command structure set up, but he left the details to Hansell. Thus it was Haywood Hansell who designed the command structure of the world's first truly independent bombing force and gained acceptance from the heretofore skeptical joint chiefs. In later years historian Murray Green asked Hansell how much of the plan for the command setup of the Twentieth Air Force was his, and after initial modesty, Hansell admitted that, even though Arnold approved, the plan had been his. It is clear that Hansell had the unique responsibility of establishing new directions for the Air Force, directions that he and his colleagues at ACTS had only dreamed of less than a decade before.[44]

It was important to establish underlying principles that could justify in the eyes of the JCS the creation of an independent strategic air force. Unity of command was a cherished concept in the American military. The Army utilized geographic control over its units, while the Navy utilized a control over major naval units that transcended geography. Hansell realized that his concept more closely resembled the Navy's version. This was a fortunate circumstance since Admiral King would probably be the most difficult to convince.[45]

Hansell hurried to see Admiral King, because he knew that if a decision was not reached soon, his plan could be replaced by one that would destroy all he had worked for. Even with General Arnold's approval, it took courage for a brigadier general from a rival branch of the service to approach the chief of naval operations with such a far-reaching proposal. Hansell later gave his account of the meeting:

> The manner in which this important agreement was reached seems almost trivial. I secured General Arnold's permission to discuss the subject with Admiral King. I found Admiral King and General Arnold walking down a corridor leading to the JCS conference room. I asked Admiral King if I might have a word with him. I described briefly the problem of concentrated command and control of the long-range bombers, which would be attacking common targets in Japan but would be operating from bases under the command of several separate theater commanders. I suggested a similarity with the problems attendant on control of the US Fleet. . . . Would it not be sensible to concentrate the very long-range bombers in a strategic air force under General Arnold? Under this arrangement, the B-29s would actually fall under the control of the joint chiefs of staff, with General Arnold serving not only as commanding general, but also as executive agent for the joint chiefs. The joint chiefs would provide unified strategic air objectives. Like fleet units of the Navy, logistic support could be provided through directives to appropriate area and theater commanders. Admiral King reflected for a moment and then said, "I could find such an arrangement acceptable."[46]

This was one of the few times during the war that Admiral King readily agreed to an Army proposal. Hansell's success was something of a coup. As Craven and Cate observed, "In view of the Navy's attitude toward strategic bombardment in general and the Matterhorn project in particular, Admiral King's advocacy of the AAF view in this issue is difficult to explain; but the record is as precise as his motives are uncertain."[47]

Hansell then prepared to bring the issue before General Marshall. After a meeting with Generals Fairchild and Kuter, he took the proposal over to the War Department Operations Division and presented it to Maj Gen Thomas T. Handy, Marshall's deputy for plans and operations. Handy's response was at first disappointing: "I'll tell you the truth, Hansell, I don't like any part of this paper. It violates the principle of unity of command in a theater of war. It inserts operational forces into a commander's area of responsibility but gives him no control of those forces. At the same time, the theater commander is expected to defend and supply and support those forces in competition with his own requirements. I don't like it." Then he grinned and said, "But I don't have a better solution. I'll buy it." General Marshall was not in his office, but Handy was sure that he would go along, since Admiral King and General Marshall were in agreement. Handy agreed to approve the plan in Marshall's name.[48]

After the Navy staff won a small battle by rewording the provision that would give theater commanders temporary control of the VLR bomber force in an emergency, the Twentieth Air Force was created by order of the JCS on 4 April 1944. It reflected both the theories put forth at ACTS in the 1930s and the recent experiences of strategic air war in Europe. Hansell had reason to be proud of his creation. The Twentieth Air Force would be under the JCS and the commanding general of the Army Air Forces. Major decisions concerning deployment, missions, and target objectives would be made by these agencies. In an emergency situation the theater commander might take control of the B-29 force. Area commanders would be responsible for providing bases, while the theater air commander would provide the administration of the force. Directives would be formed with a minimum of friction, and General Arnold would have direct command through his commander in the field.[49]

The world's first global bomber force had just been created. The significance of this event cannot be lost on a world that saw the cold war dominated by the Strategic Air Command, the logical successor to the Twentieth Air Force. Also, according to Michael Sherry, the creation of the Twentieth Air Force signaled the end of President Roosevelt's direct involvement in the formulation of strategy. From that point on his involvement was more indirect or secret. The instrument that would end the war with Japan would soon be unleashed.[50]

Arnold assigned Hansell to be chief of staff of the Twentieth Air Force in addition to being deputy chief of the Air Staff. Hansell was opposed to the idea of creating yet another staff organization for Arnold at the Pentagon, so he suggested that the Air Staff also fulfill the function of the staff of the Twentieth Air Force. Each of the assistant chiefs was instructed to "wear two hats," working both for the headquarters of the Army Air Forces and the Twentieth Air Force. Arnold agreed "somewhat reluctantly" to Hansell's plan to dovetail the two organizations. Although Arnold selected the top commanders himself, Hansell drew up the tables of organization and established the tactical doctrine and standing operational procedures. His other immediate concerns included the handling, control, and coordination of many aircraft and units literally scattered over the globe. He was also responsible for establishing a basis for uniform training. From the very beginning Hansell in reality served more as commander of the Twentieth Air Force than as chief of staff. With Arnold's wide-ranging commitments all over the globe and his poor health, Hansell was given nearly a free hand to do as he saw fit with the new global strategic air force as long as the end results met Arnold's expectations.[51]

This was a time of unusually high tension between Arnold and his staff. Arnold met every morning at seven thirty with Generals White, Kuter, and Hansell in his inner office. Armed with top secret dispatches to which his staff was not privy, Arnold would demand to know what they were doing about a given situation and castigate them with what Hansell later called "withering comments about our competence." "General Arnold enjoyed this game, but it was pretty rough business to be on the receiving end."[52] In spite of this "game," Arnold certainly had every confidence that the Twentieth Air Force was in good hands. Hansell conducted the first staff meeting of the Twentieth Air Force on 12 April 1944, in which he explained the peculiar nature of the new organization and introduced the administrative procedures to be followed. There was much to be done.[53]

Hansell employed a host of troubleshooters on the Twentieth Air Force staff. General Kuter served as A-5 (plans) by virtue of the fact that this was also his function on Arnold's staff. Col Cecil E. Combs served as A-3 (combat operations) and Col Guido Perera served as the intelligence representative from the Committee of Operations Analysts. Brig Gen Harold McClelland served as communications officer. Arnold ordered McClelland to report to his office and instructed him to create a communications net to "include Washington, Hawaii, the Marianas (which had not yet been captured), Calcutta, India, and Chengtu, China, with provision for extension to somewhere in the Aleutian chain and somewhere in the Philippines (when they were captured). He wanted TOP SECRET Security with instantaneous coding and read-out by teleprinters. He wanted the net in operation twenty-four hours a day." Hansell thought that this was impossible, but McClelland simply said, "Yes, sir," saluted and departed, much to the surprise of both Hansell and Arnold. The communications net worked so well that, when Hansell was in command of the XXI Bomber Command in the Marianas, he grew sick of the click of the teleprinters.[54]

Col Sol Rosenblatt, a temporary wartime officer, was A-4 (supply). One day, early in the development of the Twentieth Air Force, Hansell called Rosenblatt into his office and complained that the Navy always got the best of everything and the XX Bomber Command was operating on a shoestring. Hansell said that since the Twentieth Air Force was on its way to becoming the most powerful fighting force in the world, it deserved the best; Rosenblatt and his staff could provide it. Colonel Rosenblatt took him seriously and used Hansell's and (more importantly) Arnold's names to obtain supplies.[55]

Hansell also had the thorny problem of dealing with the press. His public relations officer, Col Rex Smith, a veteran newsman and former *Newsweek* editor, made a bold suggestion. He proposed that the Twentieth Air Force headquarters reveal all information about a given operation to the members of the press and allow them to write their stories. When they were completed, the stories would be turned in to headquarters, which would release them all simultaneously at the earliest time that would not jeopardize the mission. Hansell was uncertain about the idea at first, but Smith won him over and Arnold agreed. The plan worked and became the policy of the Twentieth Air Force during the war.[56]

While Hansell was working out the administrative problems in Washington, Gen Kenneth Wolfe was wrestling with the operational challenges in India and China. He had arrived at New Delhi on 13 January 1944 to set up the advanced echelon of the XX Bomber Command staff. Since he reported directly to Arnold in Washington and was technically not a part of the China-Burma-India theater of operations, his difficulties were compounded. The plan for Matterhorn called for the B-29s to be based in India and to conduct combat missions against Japan from bases in China. The bases were being built even as Wolfe arrived in India. Each concrete bomber strip had to be 8,500 feet long and 19 inches thick. In addition each base had to include 52 hardstands—one for each airplane. The construction of the bases in China required the labor of hundreds of thousands of Chinese workers, employing so much manual labor that their construction has been compared to the building of the Egyptian pyramids.[57]

On 24 April 1944, three months from the day that construction on the airfield began, Brig Gen LaVerne G. Saunders landed the first B-29 at Kwanghan, China. By 1 May all the B-29 bases in China were open to traffic. The next step was to transport the necessary supplies over the Himalaya mountains—the "Hump." Crossing the mountains was quite treacherous because of the weather and the fact that the B-29 was still prone to engine failure. Of the 150 B-29s that began the journey on 24 April, five were lost and four were seriously damaged. Amid such difficulties, Wolfe and Saunders had to supply and operate the 58th Bombardment Wing, which consisted of 112 aircraft. There was a shortage of transport aircraft, so the B-29s had to transport their own gas and bombs from India to the Chinese bases before they could fly a combat mission. This amounted to four transport missions for every single combat sortie a B-29 flew. The XX Bomber Command was not self-sufficient until July 1944, when it was able to haul 3,000 tons of supplies on its own airplanes, thus allowing for 115 sorties or about one mission involving the entire wing.[58]

Arnold was anxious for Matterhorn operations to begin. And, in spite of McClelland's excellent communications system, the twelve thousand miles that separated the headquarters in Washington from the field headquarters in India and China only frustrated Arnold more. On 10 May 1944, Arnold suffered his third heart attack in 14 months. This attack was not as severe as those that had preceded it, but his doctor sent him to Coral Gables, Florida, to rest and recuperate. Arnold's absence placed Hansell in active control of the Twentieth Air Force. This was nothing new, because Arnold was constantly away from Washington and Hansell had matters well in hand even when Arnold was present. As combat operations commenced, it was obvious that Hansell had Arnold's ear and that operations would clearly reflect Hansell's beliefs concerning daylight precision bombardment.[59]

The first combat mission of the XX Bomber Command was conducted from Kharagpur, India, against Bangkok, Thailand, on 5 June 1944. The lack of training was evident in this daylight precision-bombing attack. There was an extreme need for high-altitude formation practice, and the rendezvous, gunnery, and bombing (visual and radar) were deficient. Four of the 97 B-29s were lost on the way home and others were scattered all over Asia. Wolfe was probably thankful that credit for the raid was mistakenly given to the B-24s.[60]

On 6 June 1944, Arnold's headquarters (Hansell) requested a maximum effort raid against Japan on or before 15 June, D day for the Saipan invasion. Wolfe replied that he could deploy approximately 50 aircraft on 15 June. Arnold wanted at least 70 aircraft airborne and would not accept a smaller number. Hansell had preferred a daylight attack on the coke facilities at Anshan in Manchuria because he believed it to be more vulnerable, but the Imperial Iron and Steel Works at Yawata, Japan, was selected as the target. Following the poor performance in daylight over Bangkok, Wolfe wanted a night mission to provide protection from Japanese fighters and antiaircraft fire. Hansell agreed but would continue to insist on daylight attacks.[61]

Yawata, on the island of Kyushu, was attacked on the evenings of 14 and 15 June 1944. Seventy-five B-29s were dispatched, 68 were airborne, and 47 made it over the target. Japanese resistance was light, but six aircraft were confirmed lost. Two were lost due to enemy action; two crashed on take-off; two crashed in unoccupied China; and two were unaccounted for. The bomb damage had been unimportant, but the world finally knew of the existence of the Twentieth Air Force. Wolfe and Hansell got substantial press coverage following the first bomber attack on Japan since the famous Doolittle Raid. What the public did not know was that Wolfe's planes could not reach Tokyo from China. Only B-29s launched from the Marianas could attack the Japanese capital.[62]

With the first raid on Japan behind him, Wolfe found himself trying to please both Arnold and Hansell. On 17 June Arnold informed Wolfe that he wanted him to increase the pressure on Japan and prepare for a daylight attack on Anshan. In addition to this he requested "small harassing raids on the home islands" and a strike on Palembang in the Dutch East Indies. Wolfe replied that he was low on fuel and could not possibly hit Anshan before 10 August. Arnold was clearly seeking the political advantage of showing how effective and versatile the global bomber force could be. Hansell, on the other hand, wanted to make sure that Wolfe did not stray from daylight strategic bombing. Hansell was not pleased with the progress the XX Bomber Command was making and, as he later recalled, "As Chief of Staff of the Twentieth Air Force, I prodded General Wolfe to improve bombing results. I requested that daylight bombing attacks be conducted against the coke ovens in the Mukden area in Manchuria, where Japanese fighter planes were not considered to be very effective. . . . General Wolfe vigorously denied that his B-29s were capable of flying in formations in daylight to these targets and added the categorical statement that they would be incapable of reaching their targets in daylight operations in formation from the Marianas also."[63]

From a distance of twelve thousand miles, Hansell continued to charge that Wolfe was dragging his feet. In a 5 July 1944 memo to General Arnold, Hansell accused Wolfe of underestimating his effective strength and took exception to

Wolfe's argument that he could not bomb Palembang in formation in daylight. Arnold scribbled a note at the bottom of the memo, agreeing with Hansell's charges. On 7 July a small night mission involving only 14 B-29s attacked Sasebo, Japan. The actual intent of the mission was to run night reconnaissance missions on probable targets during the favorable moon, but it appeared that Wolfe was not using his force to its fullest potential. Arnold and Hansell, however, wanted Anshan attacked in force, and Wolfe sought to please them as soon as possible.[64]

Even though General Saunders, commander of the 58th Wing, would have preferred a night raid, Wolfe planned a daylight precision attack. Arnold had wanted a hundred-plane raid on Anshan, but only 76 B-29s participated in the mission. Sixty of them bombed the primary target, which was the Showa Steel Works. One was lost in combat, even though opposition was characterized as "light." Bombing conditions were near perfect, and substantial damage was done to the Anshan plant and by-products facility, just off the aiming point. Sixteen aircraft from the 444th Bomb Group bombed secondary targets. The total loss for the day was five B-29s.[65]

On 4 August, XX Bomber Command asked permission to make a second attack on the Imperial Iron and Steel Works at Yawata—this time using daylight precision bombing. Hansell was delighted with the change of heart, having sent Wolfe a cable the same day reminding him that attacks on shipping, storage facilities, and rail facilities in China were tactical missions reserved for the Fourteenth Air Force. Hansell insisted on strategic attacks on Palembang, Nagasaki, Yawata, and Penchihu. Wolfe responded by launching a simultaneous double strike on Nagasaki and Palembang on 10 August. Thirty-three B-29s were detailed for the night attack on Nagasaki, but only 24 succeeded in dropping their payloads of incendiaries and fragmentation bombs. The attack on Palembang, in spite of Washington's insistence on a daylight precision attack in formation, was conducted in the early evening by 31 bombers flying individually. Much to Wolfe's delight not a plane was scratched in combat, although high casualties had been expected. However, bomb damage to Japanese targets also was slight.[66]

On 20 August 1944, the XX Bomber Command launched its second attack on Yawata. Seventy-five B-29s attacked in this daylight effort. Sixty-one planes dropped 96 tons of high explosives over the target. One B-29 was brought down by flak, but enemy fighter opposition was termed "moderate," even though two bombers were downed by ramming. The American gunners claimed 17 kills. That night 10 additional B-29s followed up with a night attack. Bomb damage was not serious, but Wolfe showed that, in the face of tremendous logistical problems, he could carry out the kind of mission Hansell wanted. But by this time it was too late.[67]

Hansell had been relieved from duty as the deputy chief of the Air Staff and chief of staff of the Twentieth Air Force on 10 August. He was to take command on 20 August of the XXI Bomber Command, which was destined to operate from the Marianas. At the same time, General Arnold decided that Wolfe would be relieved of command. He had set up the initial B-29 operations, as Michael Sherry observed, "almost in defiance of operational constraints."[68] Considering the fact that the B-29 was a new, untried aircraft and that the physical restraints of operating in the China-Burma-India theater were overwhelming, Wolfe had done the impossible. Months later in a letter to General Spaatz, Arnold admitted, "With due respect to Wolfe he did his best, and he did a grand job, but LeMay's operations make Wolfe's very amateurish."[69] LeMay, fresh from the Eighth Air Force in England, arrived to take command of the XX Bomber Command on 29 August 1944. Gen Lauris Norstad would assume Hansell's position as chief of staff. This was an ominous development because Norstad did not share Hansell's belief in daylight precision bombardment, and he would have tremendous influence on Arnold.[70]

Hansell now stood at the pinnacle of his career. He had created and was to command the strategic instrument that could force Japan to surrender without an invasion and thus prove what he and his colleagues had maintained since their days at ACTS: daylight precision bombing, when correctly applied, could bring enemies to their knees. Hal George and Larry Kuter were out of the picture because of other military assignments; Ken Walker had been killed while on a bombing attack on Rabaul. It was up to Possum Hansell to make their bombing theory work, and he was eager to get started.

Notes

1. Wesley Frank Craven and James Lea Cate, *The Army Air Forces in World War II*, vol. 2, *Europe: Torch to Pointblank, August 1942 to December 1943* (1949; new imprint, Washington, D.C.: Office of Air Force History, 1983), 635; and Charles Carrington, *Soldier at Bomber Command* (London: Leo Cooper, 1987), 133.

2. Henry H. Arnold to Ira C. Eaker, letter, 19 June 1943, Ira C. Eaker Papers, Box 18, Library of Congress, Washington, D.C.

3. Ira C. Eaker to commanding general, ETOUSA, 20 June 1943, Ira C. Eaker Papers, Box 18, Library of Congress, Washington, D.C.

4. Ira C. Eaker to AGWAR, 22 June 1943, Ira C. Eaker Papers, Box 18, Library of Congress, Washington, D.C.

5. DeWitt S. Copp, *Forged in Fire: Strategy and Decisions in the War over Europe, 1940–1945* (New York: Doubleday & Co., 1982), 419, 425–426.

6. Mrs. Haywood S. Hansell Jr., interviewed by author, 21 March 1992.

7. Ibid.; Haywood Hansell III, interviewed by author, 16 February 1992; and *Atlanta Constitution*, 29 July 1943.

8. Mrs. Hansell.

9. Grace Person Hayes, *The History of the Joint Chiefs of Staff in World War II: The War against Japan* (Annapolis: Naval Institute Press, 1982), 321.

10. Haywood S. Hansell Jr. to Ira C. Eaker, letter, 24 July 1943, Chief of Staff, Supreme Allied Commander File (COSSAC), AFHRA, Maxwell AFB, Ala.

11. James MacGregor Burns, *Roosevelt: The Soldier of Freedom* (New York: Harcourt Brace Jovanovich, 1970), 392–93; and Craven and Cate, 13.

12. Hansell to Eaker.

13. Ibid.

14. Brig Gen Haywood Hansell Jr., interviewed by Bruce C. Hopper, 5 October 1943, Carl A. Spaatz Papers, Library of Congress, Washington, D.C.

15. Thomas A. Coffey, *Hap: The Story of the U.S. Air Force and the Man Who Built It, General Henry "Hap" Arnold* (New York: Viking Press, 1982), 334–35; and Robert Frank Futrell, *Ideas, Concepts, Doctrine: A History of Basic Thinking in the United States Air Force, 1907–1964* (Maxwell AFB, Ala.: Aerospace Studies Institute, 1971), 145.

16. Haywood S. Hansell Jr., *Strategic Air War against Japan* (Maxwell AFB, Ala.: Air War College, Airpower Research Institute, 1980), 18.

17. Ibid., 19.

18. Wesley Frank Craven and James Lea Cate, *The Army Air Forces in World War II*, vol. 5, *The Pacific: Matterhorn to Nagaski, June 1944 to August 1945* (1953; new imprint, Washington, D.C.: Office of Air Force History, 1983), 7–9; and Hansell, *Strategic Air War against Japan*, 21.

19. Hansell, *Strategic Air War against Japan*, 21; and Army Air Force Historical Office, *History of the Twentieth Air Force: Genesis* (Headquarters Army Air Forces, October 1945), 139; and Curtis E. LeMay Papers, Box B-39, Library of Congress, Washington, D.C.

20. Coffey, 325–26; Diary of Henry H. Arnold, Henry H. Arnold Papers, Container 272, Library of Congress, Washington, D.C.; Thomas B. Buell,

Master of Sea Power: A Biography of Fleet Admiral Ernest J. King (Boston: Little, Brown & Co., 1980), 419; Burns, 402–3; and Haywood Hansell Jr., "The Military in American Society Today: The Questions an Old-Timer Might Raise," in *The Military and Society: The Proceedings of the Fifth Military History Symposium*, ed. David MacIsaac (Colorado Springs: US Air Force Academy, 5–6 October 1972), 73.

21. Haywood S. Hansell Jr., *Strategic Air War against Germany and Japan: A Memoir* (Washington, D.C.: Government Printing Office, 1986), 136–41.

22. Ibid., 141.

23. Hayes, 501; and Haywood S. Hansell Jr., interviewed by Murray Green, 2 January 1970, Murray Green Collection, US Air Force Academy Library, Colorado Springs, Colo.

24. Hansell, *Strategic Air War against Germany and Japan*, 147–48; Eric Larrabee, *Commander in Chief: Franklin Delano Roosevelt, His Lieutenants, and Their War* (New York: Harper & Row, 1987), 611.

25. Arnold diary; and Hansell, *Strategic Air War against Germany and Japan*, 140.

26. David Eisenhower, *Eisenhower at War, 1943–1945* (New York: Random House, 1986), 49; Hansell, *Strategic Air War against Japan*, 21; Hansell, *Strategic Air War against Germany and Japan*, 148; and George C. Kenney, *General Kenney Reports: A Personal History of the Pacific War* (New York: Duel, Sloan & Pearce, 1949), 332.

27. D. Clayton James, *The Years of MacArthur*, vol. 2, *1941–1945*, (Boston: Houghton Mifflin Co., 1975), 370; Hansell, *Strategic Air War against Germany and Japan*, 150; Forrest C. Pogue, *George C. Marshall*, vol. 3, *Organizer of Victory, 1943–1945* (New York: Viking Press, 1973), 323–24; and Kenney, 332–34.

28. Hansell, *Strategic Air War against Germany and Japan*, 149.

29. Ibid.; Kenney, 334; and Pogue, 324.

30. Michael S. Sherry, *The Rise of American Air Power: The Creation of Armageddon* (New Haven: Yale University Press, 1987), 181–82; and Coffey, 256.

31. Coffey, 256, 271.

32. Lauris Norstad, interviewed by Murray Green, 15 July 1969, Murray Green Collection, US Air Force Academy, Colorado Springs, Colo.

33. Craven and Cate, *The Pacific: Matterhorn to Nagaski, June 1944 to August 1945*, 23; and Coffey, 336.

34. Coffey, 335.

35. Ibid.

36. Gen Curtis E. LeMay and Bill Yenne, *Superfortress: The Story of the B-29 and American Air Power* (New York: Berkley Books, 1988), 70–71.

37. Craven and Cate, *The Pacific: Matterhorn to Nagaski, June 1944 to August 1945*, 5, 12, 29; and Sherry, 166.

38. Ibid., 31.

39. Ibid., 29.

40. Ibid.

41. Hansell, *Strategic Air War against Germany and Japan,* 22–24; and Hayes, 593.

42. Hansell, *Strategic Air War against Japan,* 18.

43. Hayes, 591; Craven and Cate, *The Pacific: Matterhorn to Nagaski, June 1944 to August 1945,* 5, 348; and Hansell, *Strategic Air War against Japan,* 27.

44. Hansell, Green interview.

45. Hansell, *Strategic Air War against Japan,* 153.

46. Ibid., 26.

47. Craven and Cate, *The Pacific: Matterhorn to Nagaski, June 1944 to August 1945,* 5, 38.

48. Hansell, *Strategic Air War against Germany and Japan,* 158.

49. Hayes, 594–95; and Craven and Cate, *The Pacific: Matterhorn to Nagaski, June 1944 to August 1945,* 5, 38.

50. Sherry, 219.

51. Hansell, *Strategic Air War against Germany and Japan,* 161.

52. Ibid., 181.

53. *Genesis,* 108.

54. Hansell, *Strategic Air War against Japan,* 28.

55. Ibid.

56. Ibid.

57. Craven and Cate, *The Pacific: Matterhorn to Nagaski, June 1944 to August 1945,* 42, 45, 49, 58–59, 71.

58. Ibid., 71, 87, 91.

59. Coffey, 343.

60. Craven and Cate, *The Pacific: Matterhorn to Nagaski, June 1944 to August 1945,* 95.

61. Ibid., 98–99; and Wilbur H. Morrison, *Point of No Return: The Story of the Twentieth Air Force* (New York: Times Books, 1979), 66.

62. Craven and Cate, *The Pacific: Matterhorn to Nagaski, June 1944 to August 1945,* 100–102; and Haywood S. Hansell to Henry H. Arnold, letter, Record Group 18, File 273.2, National Archives, Washington, D.C.

63. Hansell, *Strategic Air War against Japan,* 30.

64. Haywood S. Hansell to Henry H. Arnold, letter, Record Group 18, 373.2, National Archives, Washington, D.C.; Craven and Cate, *The Pacific: Matterhorn to Nagaski, June 1944 to August 1945,* 104; and LeMay and Yenne, 184.

65. Craven and Cate, *The Pacific: Matterhorn to Nagaski, June 1944 to August 1945,* 107; and LeMay and Yenne, 184.

66. Haywood S. Hansell to Kenneth Wolfe, 4 August 1944, Record Group 18, 373.2, National Archives, Washington, D.C.; and Craven and Cate, *The Pacific: Matterhorn to Nagaski, June 1944 to August 1945,* 111–13.

67. Craven and Cate, *The Pacific: Matterhorn to Nagaski, June 1944 to August 1945,* 114.

68. Sherry, 176.

69. Craven and Cate, *The Pacific: Matterhorn to Nagaski, June 1944 to August 1945,* 104.

70. Ibid., 115.

Chapter 6

Triumph

General LeMay had originally been slated to command XXI Bomber Command and Hansell the XXII, but Arnold's decision to send LeMay to China meant that Hansell would move to the Marianas to command the XXI. The decision was not without controversy. Gen Barney Giles, deputy commander of the Army Air Forces and chief of the Air Staff, disagreed with Arnold about Hansell's selection. "I begged him not to do it—to keep him in Washington," Giles recalled. He told Arnold that Hansell was a brilliant staff officer, but that he was not a tactical commander. Still, Arnold was insistent on naming Hansell. Giles then asked Arnold to promise him that he would not relieve Hansell in the first two to three months, "Because he is going to be involved in deals out there, getting stuff started, opening bases, and getting the bombs, the ammunition, the crews all trained." Arnold's reply was, "No, I won't! No, I won't!"[1]

Before Hansell left for the Pacific, Giles offered his support: "Possum, I hope everything works fine for you. You have an awfully tough job to do. General Arnold is going to be very impatient." Hansell replied, "Barney," then snapped his fingers, "I can do the job." But Giles did not think he could. Neither, according to Giles, did Kuter. Giles certainly considered Hansell to be an excellent staff officer, but he did not think he had the temperament to be an operational commander. Yet Giles's biggest concern was that Hansell would not set up successful operations fast enough to please Arnold.[2]

Hansell assumed command of XXI Bomber Command at Colorado Springs, Colorado, on 28 August 1944. Ultimately, the command was to consist of the 73d, 313th, 314th, and 315th Bombardment Wings. For initial operations from the Marianas, however, Hansell had only the 73d Wing, with the others to follow as soon as facilities were available. The commander of the 73d was Gen Emmett O'Donnell, a veteran of the Far Eastern air force during the discouraging battles in the Philippines immediately following Pearl Harbor. He was a tough, Brooklyn-born graduate of West Point, where he had coached football. O'Donnell was also one of the few air force officers who felt free to speak his mind to General Arnold.[3]

When Hansell took command of the 73d Wing, he found that O'Donnell was preparing for area bombing attacks at night. As it turned out, O'Donnell had encouraged Arnold to shift to night missions in a memo dated 7 February 1944. Citing the B-29's advantage in speed, O'Donnell suggested stripping the armament from the Superfortress. "For use in the specific task of attacking Japanese cities from Chinese bases with incendiary bombs, I believe this airplane could be used with great effect without any armament by dispatching them singly at night and bombing by radar."[4] Arnold submitted O'Donnell's idea to the Army Air Forces Proving Ground Command at Eglin Field, Florida, which responded favorably by recommending that B-29 operations be initially conducted at night but that the armament be retained. In May 1944 the tactical doctrine for the 73d Wing included detailed procedures for night missions at nine separate altitudes and at different spacing intervals. It is clear that, as far as O'Donnell was concerned, the 73d Wing would conduct night operations. Upon assuming command, Hansell ordered the conversion to daylight tactics and established a new tactical doctrine, including standard formation. Opposition from O'Donnell and the men of the 73d was (in Hansell's words) severe, but Hansell insisted on intensive training. The pressure to commit the XXI Bomber Command was already becoming intense, but Hansell refused to budge from his insistence on daylight precision bombing.[5]

The B-29s were still subject to mechanical failures since the aircraft was so new, complex, and untested. Engine problems were solved by making modifications to the exhaust valves. The gunners' bubbles iced over at altitude, but this problem was solved by fitting the bubbles with hot air hoses. Most of the mechanical problems demanded the attention of Hansell, and work went on at a furious pace, with most of the problems solved only at the 11th hour.[6]

The bombers had no practice in formation flying. Hansell directed that tests be conducted in which the B-29s fly from their bases in Kansas to Havana, Cuba, roughly the distance from the Marianas to Tokyo. The training stressed takeoff, assembly, rendezvous, formation flying, and simulated frontal weather penetration. The main result of the training missions was that downed B-29s were scattered all over the Gulf states. It was clear that the bomber crews would have to complete their training in the Marianas, because there simply was not enough time to do it anywhere else, and the pressure to deploy the XXI Bomber Command increased.[7]

In September 1944 Hansell reported to Washington for final instructions before departing for the Marianas. Arnold was clear in his expectations of Hansell's command: "I know that you, in your position as commander of one of our great striking forces, will do your utmost to help accomplish the earliest possible defeat of Japan. This can only be done by making the best possible use of the weapon at your disposal."[8] Hansell later recalled a brief courtesy call on General Marshall: "We had a very brief conversation of 15 minutes or so, [he was] as cordial as he ever was. He's very aloof. And he asked me how long it was going to take to get this operation going, and I said, 'I hope to launch the first operation by six weeks after we get there.' He said, 'What's going to take so long?' And I said, 'Green outfit, and we [have] got brand new airplanes, have to learn how to do this.'"[9]

The pressure was certainly on for Hansell to produce a successful bombing offensive in the shortest amount of time and with a new, untried weapon. Before he left Washington, the British government honored him for his service in England with the Eighth Air Force. The earl of Halifax presented Hansell with the Order of the British Empire at the British embassy in Washington "in recognition of distinguished services as commanding officer, First Bombardment Wing, Eighth Air Force." Hansell had been a pioneer in American heavy bomber operations in Europe, and now his greatest challenge lay before him—to pioneer American very heavy bomber operations in the Pacific. The eyes of the world would soon be upon him.[10]

Mrs. Hansell and the three children were in San Antonio, where they had bought a house to be near the Hansell family. Dotta was busy enough taking care of the family, and especially keeping Tony out of trouble. While she was at San Antonio she was asked to speak on the radio in connection with the activities of Possum. She did so well that the manager of the radio station asked her to do a regular radio program for air force "widows" living in the area. She was able to do only one show, however, because, like many women during the war, she could not find anyone to keep the children.[11]

When Possum said his good-byes, he told her he was going overseas, but did not specify exactly where he was going. After his departure, Mrs. Hansell took the children to Eugene, Oregon, where her younger brother was in college. She was able to rent the home of a professor on sabbatical leave and take care of her brother, who suffered from asthma. She remained in Eugene until Possum returned from the Pacific.[12]

Concerned that the crews of the 73d Wing had not had enough training in long-distance formation flying, Hansell requested that the Air Transport Command allow the squadrons to fly from California to Hawaii in formation. Permission was denied on the grounds that the aircraft lacked sufficient range to fly that distance in formation. The flight would have been without bomb load and would encounter no opposition, as they would in a few weeks on a similar flight from Saipan to Tokyo. Still, Hal George, commander of the Air Transport Command and Hansell's long-time friend and mentor, flatly refused to agree to Hansell's plan.[13]

On 5 October 1944, Hansell departed from Mather Field near Sacramento, California, on Maj Jack J. Catton's *Joltin' Josie: the Pacific Pioneer*. Catton had named his airplane after his wife, but Hansell added *Pacific Pioneer* to the name. With Hansell at the controls, the B-29 lumbered down the runway and lifted up toward the Pacific. Hansell had mistakenly hit the brake pedals before the airplane was airborne, but after an initial jolt they were on their way. Each B-29 that headed for the Marianas carried a spare engine in the bomb bay, a load that placed the weight of the airplane at 130,000 pounds—ten thousand pounds over the original design weight.[14]

Upon arrival in Hawaii, Hansell met with Lt Gen Millard F. "Miff" Harmon, deputy commanding general for administration and logistics, Twentieth Air Force. They discussed Hansell's mission and requirements. Even though Harmon was responsible for administering the XXI Bomber Command, he exercised no operational control of it. The next day Hansell met with Admiral Nimitz. Nimitz had been briefed by Laurence Kuter and a bit later by Maj Gen Tony Frank concerning the unique command relationships. Much to his surprise, Hansell found Nimitz very much opposed to the command structure. Nimitz indicated that he did not understand that he was to have no operational control over a unit he was to supply with airfields. Yet, he gave Hansell his best wishes and warned him to watch out for the commander in the forward area, Vice Adm John Hoover. Nimitz warned Hansell that Hoover "breaks my admirals and throws them overboard without the slightest compunction, God knows what he is going to do to you."[15]

From Hawaii the *Joltin' Josie* flew to Kwajalein and then to Saipan, arriving on Columbus Day, 12 October 1944. The arrival of the first B-29 on Saipan was a big event. "A group historical officer reported that as the huge bomber swept in with its fighter escort, 'a great cheer went up, and all work stopped as men shaded their eyes to watch the plane pass over. . . . The thrill that went through all was almost electric in effect.'"[16] When the *Joltin' Josie* came to a halt and the crew was welcomed by the crowd, Hansell was asked to say a few words for the newsreel camera. Taken by surprise, he said, "The first elements of the XXI Bomber Command have arrived and when we've done some more fighting we do some more talking." When he realized that he had stolen those words from Ira Eaker, Hansell sent a cable to Eaker's headquarters in Europe to apologize.[17]

Hansell was welcomed not only by the military personnel on the island but also by "Tokyo Rose," who broadcast a welcome to "General Possum Hansell" over the Japanese radio network. Hansell had not even told his wife where he was going and wondered how the Japanese had found out so quickly. The Japanese, of course, had a serious interest in Hansell and his bomber force. Col Richard H. Carmichael, a B-29 group commander from the XX Bomber Command in China, had been shot down and captured by the Japanese. Carmichael did not know Hansell personally and knew very little about the general, but the Japanese beat and interrogated him for days in order to find out why Hansell was called "Possum." Fortunately, the Japanese finally decided that he knew nothing about Hansell and halted the torture.[18]

One of Hansell's first tasks was to secure an aide. When asked the qualifications, Hansell listed "intelligent, alert, hard-working, good humored, tolerant, and courteous." Lt Ray Milne was the perfect officer for the job and became a cherished friend. This was one of Hansell's easier tasks. Even though advanced echelons of the XXI Bomber Command and 73d Wing headquarters had arrived before Hansell, it would take weeks for all the headquarters personnel to arrive. General O'Donnell arrived on 20 October, and Superfortresses were promised to arrive at a rate of five a day. Yet, in spite of General Harmon's best efforts, they were arriving at the rate of two per day. Time was running out and there was much to do.[19]

As a student and instructor at Air Corps Tactical School and as a planner writing AWPD-1, Hansell had dealt with combat operations in the abstract, where he was not confronted with Clausewitzian frictions. To be sure, Hansell had always been aware of them and had made an effort to factor them into his lectures and war plans, but it was the experience of war in Europe that drove home their importance in military operations. As a pioneer of heavy bomber operations in Europe, Hansell had been confronted with supply problems, inadequate training, difficulties in putting the bombs on target, problems with the weather, difficulties in the command structure, and a myriad of other frictions, not to mention enemy opposition. In the Marianas Hansell found himself confronted by a whole new set of frictions which were far more daunting than those he or any other bomber commander had confronted in England.

When Hansell arrived at Brampton Grange as commander of the 1st Bomb Wing in England, he described his quarters as "the most uncomfortable living accommodation in England." Now he was living in a tent, dressed in shorts because of the heat, and eating food that probably made him homesick even for English cooking. When a group of congressmen arrived on Saipan early in the operation, Hansell entertained them with the best he had. He housed them in his tent and then took them through the chow line and instructed them in how to wash their own eating utensils. When they returned to Washington they wrote an unfavorable report of Hansell's command, but it was probably the living conditions they objected to most.[20]

When the first American heavy bomber groups had arrived in England, fully equipped Royal Air Force bases were, in many cases, turned over to the fledgling bomber groups. There was no such luxury in the Marianas. Engineers had begun work soon after Saipan was secured from the Japanese, but all through July and August they were beset with tropical rains that made roads virtually impassable. So many trucks broke down that men had to be diverted from runway construction to make passable roads. Enemy air raids and unexpectedly hard coral formations had slowed the work down considerably. Isley Field was not even completed on 12 October when Hansell arrived in the first B-29. Maj Gen Sanderford Jarman had four aviation engineer battalions working around the clock. Many of these workers even slept under their trucks.[21]

Only one runway could be used, with only 5,000 feet of the 7,000-foot runway actually paved. Only 40 hardstands were ready, thus causing the B-29s to double park—a tempting target for Japanese bombers. All other facilities were woefully behind schedule, and Isley Field was not substantially completed until April of 1945. It was obvious to Hansell that Saipan was not ready to receive the 12,000 men and 180 aircraft of the 73d Wing. There were similar delays on the islands of Tinian and Guam.[22]

Hansell's supply problems were overwhelming. Craven and Cate describe the situation: "The XXI Bomber Command was unique in that it carried out its operations without an air service command, without control of an air depot, without aviation engineer battalions or ordnance companies, and with the barest minimum of work and service troops."[23] The first troops and supplies for the depot on Guam did not arrive until 9 November 1944. The depot itself was combat loaded so it could be unloaded quickly and assembled. When the ship carrying the depot arrived at Guam, the harbor master allowed only 24 hours to unload the ship. It was unloaded in such a hurry that supplies were scattered all over the jungle and never recovered. Aircraft supplies then had to be flown in from Sacramento, over four thousand miles away. The XXI

Bomber Command did not possess a working aircraft depot until February 1945.[24]

Even though Hansell was pleased with the cooperation he received from the Navy, supplies were still slow in arriving. His supply officer, Col Sol Rosenblatt, came up with a very creative and surprising solution to the problem. One day early in the operation, Rosenblatt appeared at Hansell's headquarters and requested that the general accompany him to the dock. When they arrived Hansell discovered that he was in command of a small fleet of supply ships, one of which was unloading. Rosenblatt had used his connections to acquire six supply ships in the name of the Twentieth Air Force. When the Navy realized what was happening, it commandeered the vessels.[25]

Obviously Rosenblatt's fleet was not going to solve Hansell's supply problems. By early November Hansell took measures to adapt the supply and maintenance procedures to meet existing conditions. He centralized the activities of supply and maintenance under his chief of staff for supply and maintenance, Col Clarence S. Irvine. Irvine's efforts served to keep the command operating and the B-29s flying even though the most important aircraft parts had to be flown in directly from Sacramento over thousands of miles of ocean. Unlike the Eighth Air Force in England during its early days, the XXI Bomber Command was operating on a very long and uncertain shoestring.[26]

When the B-17 arrived in Europe it had already gone through a number of versions and most of the imperfections had been corrected. The B-29 was a much more complicated aircraft, and, since it was fresh off the assembly line (not to mention the drawing board), its technical problems were numerous. Hansell was very much involved in making the Superfortress ready to fly in combat. He was concerned over the rate of engine failures, flawed weapons systems, and the rate of aborts, all of which would be a problem once the bombing campaign began. He had the ground crews lighten the aircraft as much as possible to extend the range. In spite of all his efforts, the fact remains that the B-29 had been rushed into combat before it was entirely ready, and only time and experience could correct the problems. Time was one thing Hansell did not have.[27]

Hansell had found both the 3d and 1st Bomb Wings, which he commanded in England, to be lacking in training, and he had set up programs to iron out such deficiencies as gunnery and formation flying. One major difference is that the crews in England had been trained in daylight precision bombardment from the beginning; the 73d Wing had been trained in night radar bombardment. Most of the 73d's crews had less than one hundred hours of flying time in the B-29, only 12 hours of which was at high altitude. Hansell sent the bombers on practice missions to bomb Japanese-held islands in the Carolines. Technical problems multiplied with each mission. Hansell had less than a month to get the bombers ready to strike the home islands of Japan.[28]

Hansell's decision to switch the 73d Wing to daylight operations was not popular because many "seasoned experts" believed that the B-29s would be shot out of the air over Japan. But the targets which XXI Bomber Command had been assigned to bomb simply could not be hit using the existing radar. Radar had been used in Europe to bomb in adverse weather, but the results were far from what Hansell had expected. The air force was in the process of improving its radar, but the improved AN/APG-3 and AN/APG-15 radars were not ready for operations and would not be until the last quarter of 1945. To make matters worse, Hansell did not have a single target folder. Unlike his days in England when he could rely upon the RAF for targeting assistance, he found Japan to be virgin territory that had to be mapped out by F-13 photoreconnaissance aircraft.[29]

Weather had always been a problem for the Eighth Air Force in England, but at least they had weather stations to the west to help them make a forecast. In the Pacific, Hansell had to rely upon nightly flights of B-29s over Japan for his weather predictions. Even though intelligence sources had decoded Japanese weather reports, those reports had not been made available to the XXI Bomber Command. Hansell gave his weather officer, Col James Seaver, qualified praise by saying, "Often he was right." Japan was almost constantly covered by clouds, and cloud formations arose from 1,500 to 30,000 feet over the ocean, thus standing between the assembly points and the targets. The winds often reached 200 knots over the targets, causing the bombers to drift 45 degrees, but the bomb sights could correct for only 35 degrees. To further complicate matters, winds at lower altitudes often changed in direction and velocity, forcing the bombardier to make any number of corrections.[30]

When a bomber of the Eighth Air Force was shot down over Europe, the crew had reasonable hope for survival. If they survived the ordeal, they would be either captured by the Germans or aided by civilians in the occupied countries. If the plane ditched in the English Channel, they stood a chance of being rescued by either the British or Germans. It was a thousand miles from Japan to Saipan, and Iwo Jima was still in Japanese hands. Falling into the hands of the Japanese military most often meant death, and ditching in the vast Pacific so far from friendly territory offered little comfort. Hansell was very concerned for the safety of the crews that were forced to ditch in the Pacific. Through his naval liaison officer, Comdr George C. McGhee, Hansell worked out a plan with the Navy in which US submarines were stationed at intervals along the route. In addition, the Navy sent flying boats, Dumbos (B-17s carrying droppable lifeboats), and Super Dumbos (B-29s with droppable lifeboats) over the route to spot downed airmen. Destroyers were also stationed along the route. The rescue system was responsible for saving over 600 bomber crewmen in open-sea rescues. One submarine even rescued a B-29 crew in Tokyo Bay in broad daylight.[31]

The technical and operational problems were not all that plagued Hansell. Though he was happy to be free from the control of the theater commander, the new command relationship brought on by the Twentieth Air Force had its own unique problems. In Europe the command structure had been more traditional. The commander of the Eighth Air Force was ultimately under the command of Supreme Headquarters Allied Expeditionary Force (SHAEF). Even when Spaatz set up the United States Strategic Air Forces, it fell ultimately under the command of Eisenhower. In Europe the theater commander could direct the strategic air forces to fulfill the tactical missions he deemed necessary, but Hansell theoretically answered to no one but General Arnold.

In reality, Hansell was very much dependent upon the Navy for logistic support. He found his relationship with the Navy to be most agreeable. Admirals Nimitz and Hoover were very helpful and actually went to bat for Hansell on a number of occasions. Hansell, however, feared that the Navy would take command of his bomber force in "emergencies." This fear was so deep that at the first sign of trouble during the Battle of Leyte Gulf, Hansell offered his services to the Navy before they asked for them. Hansell's offer was refused, much to his relief. On the other hand, when asked to participate in aerial mining of Japan's harbors, Hansell refused to do so until his force was larger. He remembered the diversion of his forces for antisubmarine operations in 1943 and was not about to repeat that mistake. Later, he recognized the wisdom of the mining operations, but at the time he would not allow the Navy any control of his B-29s.[32]

Hansell found that it was the other air force generals who gave him the most trouble. General Harmon had always believed that he should share in operational control as deputy commander of the Twentieth Air Force although he was very supportive of Hansell's activities. Hansell's most serious confrontation was with Maj Gen Willis H. Hale, commander of the Seventh Air Force. When Hansell arrived on Saipan he found a number of Hale's aircraft parked on Isley Field. Hale agreed to remove them but failed to do so. Admiral Hoover offered to intervene, but to Hansell this was an air force matter. Hansell and Hale had a showdown, after which Hale removed the aircraft but complained to Washington about Hansell's "arrogant" attitude. Arnold backed Hansell up, but Hansell feared that the incident did him no good.[33]

The headquarters of the Twentieth Air Force was over six thousand miles away in Washington. Hansell could select the size of the force he was going to use, the dates he was going to strike, the sequence of targets on the priority list, and the method in which he would attack the targets. This was no more or less control than Eaker or Spaatz enjoyed in Europe. The main difference lay in the fact that this operation had General Arnold's personal attention and was under his direct command. There was no Eaker or Spaatz in the Twentieth Air Force to reason with Arnold, and Arnold was too far away to really know what was going on. Norstad contended in September 1945 that Washington had run the air war in the Pacific, and Michael Sherry also maintains that LeMay and Hansell were subject to tight control from the Pentagon. This is true, but that control was mainly in the form of "suggestions" complicated with assurances that the field commander had Arnold's and Norstad's full support, while they were trying subtly to nudge the commander to go in the direction they wanted him to go. In the end the only way Arnold could control XXI Bomber Command operations was to place a commander in the field who would do what he wanted without having to spell out his wishes.[34]

One of the main problems with the Twentieth Air Force was its command structure. Arnold could not possibly run an air campaign from a distance of six thousand miles, and the field commander could not discern the difference between a suggestion and a subtle imperative to get on with the show in a particular way. Since Hansell had created the command structure, he had sewn the seeds of his own downfall. Before his experience in the Marianas was over, he undoubtedly understood how Wolfe must have felt when he received Hansell's demands from Washington. The solution to the problem would not come until the summer of 1945 when Spaatz arrived to command the US Army Strategic Air Forces in the Pacific, which would include both the Eighth and Twentieth Air Forces.[35]

Another important problem with the command structure was the fact that Hansell was only a brigadier general. As commander of the most important bomber command in the air force, he potentially had to deal with Fleet Admiral Nimitz and General of the Army MacArthur, both of whom wore five stars. At the local level, he had to deal with major and lieutenant generals who, even though they outranked him, were supposed to support him. It is true that the Twentieth Air Force was commanded by General of the Army Arnold, but he was in Washington and Hansell was seen as only his proxy. As Conrad Crane points out, "One can only wonder what would have happened if another leader, such as Spaatz, had commanded the B-29s, someone more committed [than LeMay] to precision and perhaps more experienced and secure in his own position."[36] As it was, Hansell was far away from the center of

166

power and tied to Washington by a teleprinter which clicked out often confusing and conflicting information.[37]

When Hansell departed for the Marianas the task before him was clear. He would command the force that would defeat Japan with selective bombing. The technology of the day dictated that all precision bombing be done by daylight. The new radars were not ready, and Hansell had to operate within the existing technology and proven operational methods. To Hansell, his mission was to carry the air war against Japan just as he had against Germany, using the lessons learned in combat over Europe. There had never been any question among air force officers in Europe about daylight precision bombing. Eaker had defended it at Casablanca, and the bomber crews risked their lives to prove it on each mission.

When Hansell left Washington, the plan for the defeat of Japan seemed to be firm. The strategic objective was to force Japan to acknowledge defeat and accept Allied terms for surrender. To achieve the strategic objective, the primary air strategy was to (1) destroy the effectiveness of the Japanese air force by destroying Japan's aircraft production facilities; (2) destroy the war-making industrial structure through precision bombing; (3) destroy and undermine the social and economic structure of the Japanese state through precision bombing; and (4) prepare for, and, if necessary, carry out urban incendiary attacks as a last resort. The secondary air strategy was to support a surface invasion of the home islands "if the air offensive failed to achieve its purpose."[38]

Hansell had been at the very center of the effort to plan the air war against Japan and was thus quite familiar with it. The original plan had been changed, however, even before Hansell could make the trip from Sacramento to Saipan. On 11 October 1944, the Committee of Operations Analysts issued its final report in which it recommended that precision bombing continue only until the Twentieth Air Force was ready to "obliterate the Honshu cities" of Tokyo, Yokohama, Nagoya, Kobe, Kawasaki, and Osaka. The proposed results of the attacks would be (1) direct physical damage; (2) destruction of finished items and materials plants; (3) disruption of internal transportation; and (4) reduced labor efficiency. There was neither direct mention of the killing of civilians nor any attempt to show how such raids would help secure final victory.[39] Hansell was aware of the report, but as he later explained, "Since I had not yet accomplished my first priority task, destruction of Japanese aircraft and engine plants, I was not immediately affected by this change and I continued my emphasis on selective bombing."[40]

The previous year, on 11 November 1943, the COA had issued a report in which it stated its belief that a series of massive firebomb attacks on urban areas would produce a major disaster for Japan. The potential for the rapid destruction of Japan's cities was soon to be seriously reconsidered, because on 1 December 1944, the joint chiefs of staff decided that the invasion of Japan was JCS policy and that aerial bombardment would be a preliminary to invasion. These decisions fundamentally changed air strategy in the Pacific. The COA had given the air force the reasons for an incendiary campaign against Japan, and the JCS had set the date for the invasion of Kyushu (1 November 1945), thus giving the air force the incentive to act quickly to bring about victory before the invasion.[41]

The idea of launching incendiary attacks on Japanese cities was not new or secret. The Tokyo earthquake of 1923 had alerted the world to the vulnerability of Japanese cities. In 1939 Maj Charles E. Thomas had delivered a lecture at ACTS on aerial operations against Japan using the 1923 earthquake as a model, and popular magazines had explored the possibility of burning Japanese cities even before Pearl Harbor. "Little Tokyos" had been erected at Eglin Field to test incendiary bombs against simulated Japanese cities. Colonel Perera, of the COA and Twentieth Air Force staff, had again raised the issue of incendiary bombing in May 1944, recommending that an incendiary campaign begin in the spring of 1945 when weather conditions could maximize the effect.[42] Michael Sherry contends that "by September the air staff apparently had committed itself to a major incendiary campaign" and that "the shift in emphasis may have been hastened by the replacement on 20 August of Hansell . . . with Norstad, an eager advocate of incendiaries."[43]

General Arnold tended to measure success in terms of tons of bombs dropped over a target—not in how many bombs actually destroyed a target that was part of the strategic plan. Hansell was apparently concerned about his chief's attitude, because on 26 July 1944 he hand-delivered a memorandum to General Arnold: "Mere tonnage of explosives is a fallacious criterion. In the final analysis, the victories are achieved because of the effect produced, not simply because of the effort expended."[44] Yet Arnold reminded Hansell two months later: "Every bomb that is added to each airplane that takes off for Japan will directly affect the length of the war."[45] Arnold wanted quantifiable results, the kind which would be more readily discernable through fire bombing.

The kind of bombing advocated in Washington in the fall of 1944 was closer to the Douhetian vision than anything the Army Air Forces had considered before. This was, in effect, a complete reversal of policy. In a lecture in the late 1930s entitled "The Aim in War," Hansell expressed the prevailing American attitude: "Let us make it emphatically clear that that [strategic bombing] does *not* mean the indiscriminate bombing of women and children."[46] The American public, after three years of brutal war in the Pacific, had come to see the Japanese as inhuman monsters worthy of extermination. At the highest level of decision making, the perception was much the same. In justification of his proposal for incendiary attacks, Colonel Perera stated that the United States was at war "with a fanatic enemy whose record of brutality was notorious, and if his cities were indeed honeycombed with small warmaking plants . . . there were logical grounds for attacking them."[47] It is most significant that the interest in incendiary attacks came before Hansell actually began operations against Japan. The case has been made that the air force resorted to incendiaries in response to the failure of the XXI Bomber Command to hit the assigned targets. But since the case for the attacks predates Hansell's efforts, it is apparent that the fire bombing of Japanese cities was ultimately the result of the technology that made the fire bombing possible, the desire on the part of the air force to end the war before an invasion, and the perceived desire for vengeance by the American public.

Daylight precision bombing had become the American air doctrine through the efforts of ACTS. Hansell and his fellow instructors had taught hundreds of officers the principles behind selective bombing. They had given the doctrine a permanent place in American war plans in AWPD-1, and Hansell had ensured its predominance in AWPD-42 and the plan for the Combined Bomber Offensive. There was no reason for Hansell to suspect that daylight precision bombing was in danger of being dropped as the preferred method of bombing Japan.

As war approached in 1939, General Arnold had been concerned that not all eligible officers could attend the nine-month course offered by ACTS. He, therefore, shortened the course to 12 weeks. This so-called short course reflected the same curriculum, but in a more abbreviated form. Also, by this time the "bomber radicals" such as George, Walker, Hansell, and Kuter were no longer instructors. Those who attended the short course in the 1939–40 session later spoke of only having 90 days at ACTS, LeMay flatly admitting that he learned "not much" at ACTS. Arnold naturally did not attend ACTS, but the officers who advocated and ultimately carried out the incendiary raids on Japan were graduates of the short course. LeMay, Norstad, and O'Donnell all attended ACTS during the 1939–40 session and thus had missed the experience (and indoctrination) of the full nine-month course. It seems likely that they were therefore more pragmatic in their approach to the application of airpower and were more willing to try methods other than selective bombing.[48] Arnold's experiences predated ACTS, but even with his varied experiences he was not committed to a particular air doctrine. Michael Sherry observes, "Though a veteran of battles over air power and a defender of the AAF's interests, he was never an articulate or visionary exponent of air power on a doctrinal level."[49] General Kuter was at Arnold's side at the time the idea of shifting to incendiaries arose. In fact, as early as April 1944 he had called the Twentieth Air Force's attention to incendiary tests; but Ronald Schaffer contends that "General Kuter disliked shedding civilian blood in terror attacks, but he analyzed ways of employing terror raids because Arnold wanted the subject investigated."[50] Perhaps the fact that he was so close to Arnold prevented Kuter from speaking against the incendiaries. At any rate Hansell felt that the continuing interest in selective targeting in Washington came from Kuter.[51]

It was not only Hansell's superiors in Washington who had taken up the idea of area bombing. At an 8 August 1944 meeting with Arnold, General O'Donnell took issue with the bombing strategy. He maintained that his force was too small for selective bombing attacks and that, until the force was built up, they should bomb "singly and at night using radar to destroy and burn down the several large cosmopolitan centers . . . thereby striking a tremendous blow at civilian morale."[52] This difference of opinion obviously caused friction between Hansell and his wing commander. When they arrived at Saipan, Col John B. Montgomery, XXI Bomber Command operations officer, reported that O'Donnell was "very unhappy" with the fact that Hansell's staff exercised so much control over the 73d Wing.[53] Hansell had to contend with commanders and staff in Washington who did not share his belief in daylight precision bombing. In addition to this, Hansell's senior wing commander advocated a method of bombing totally different from his.

Considering all the difficulties facing Hansell in the operation of the XXI Bomber Command, the subject of public relations seems rather secondary. But Hansell's handling of this aspect of his command was actually crucial to its prospects of success. Lt Col St. Clair McKelway, a former writer for *The New Yorker*, served as his public relations officer. Hansell had earlier set up the public relations procedure used by the Twentieth Air Force, and his policy for the XXI Bomber Command was little different. Arnold had advised Hansell to "emphasize accuracy rather than press-agentry" because he did not want the B-29 to be "over-evaluated in the public mind."[54] Hansell shared Arnold's concern and issued his press releases accordingly: "Reports of effectiveness were deliberately played down by the XXIst Bomber Command headquarters. I wanted to build a reputation for credibility in XXIst Bomber Command reports to counterbalance the known tendency to exaggerate. Our whole energy was devoted to efforts to improve effectiveness and accuracy."[55] As it turned out, Hansell's press releases would be too accurate and modest to please Arnold and Norstad.

Hansell was confronted with so many command problems that one commander could not possibly have dealt with all of them. The most serious was lack of support both from Washington and the 73d Wing headquarters for selective bombing.

Arnold was impatient, and the time for combat operations against Japan was fast approaching. There was no time to take stock of the problems, only time to act.

Hansell's initial missions were to be training runs to Truk Atoll in the Caroline Islands. The first one was to take place on 26 October, but the Battle of Leyte Gulf prompted Hansell to cancel that mission and order the B-29s to be on two-hour notice. The Navy, however, did not need Hansell this time, and General Harmon informed him that he could proceed with the Truk mission.[56]

On 27 October 1944, the 869th Squadron of the 497th Bomb Group struck Dublon Island in the Carolines. Results were discouraging, but opposition was light, with the antiaircraft fire labeled "inaccurate." Only one Japanese fighter plane made a feeble attempt to defend the island. The 73d Wing conducted similar strikes on 30 October and 2, 5, and 11 November. In each case the bombing was poor and the enemy defense was just evident enough for the crews to say they had been under enemy fire. Yet the missions served the purpose of giving the crews some experience under "combat" conditions.[57]

As Hansell looked toward the XXI Bomber Command's first attack on Japan, he intended to lead the mission himself. Soon after, he accompanied one of the training missions to Truk; however, he was ordered to fly no more missions. He complained in a letter to Norstad that he had been careful not to receive any information that would prevent him from flying combat missions and that he was surprised at the order. At first he had intended to ignore the order and lead the raid anyway. Before he could do so, a Navy lieutenant accompanied by a petty officer gave Hansell a written copy of the order and demanded acknowledgment of its receipt. In the meantime Hansell had received "certain information" which he had been careful not to accept up to that point. It is certain that he knew too much about the breaking of the Japanese codes and probably had slight familiarity with the atomic bomb.[58]

In his letter to Norstad on 1 November, Hansell had expressed concern that the Japanese were going to launch air attacks on his bombers as they sat double parked on the hardstands. The next day the Japanese struck. Although the Japanese bombers did no damage on this raid, the Marine air defense units had failed to protect Hansell's base. As a result of the bombing, General O'Donnell decided to attack the Japanese airfields on Iwo Jima, thus combining training with an effort to prevent future attacks. The bombing results from the B-29 "practice" attacks were poor, and the Japanese would be back.[59]

On 1 November 1944, an F-13 from the 3d Photo Reconnaissance Squadron piloted by Capt Ralph D. Steakley became the first American airplane over Tokyo since the Doolittle raid in April 1942. The photorecon version of the B-29 was appropriately named the *Tokyo Rose* and experienced a phenomenon over Japan—clear weather. Steakley's crew was able to take seven thousand photographs of the Tokyo area from 32,000 feet. From these Hansell compiled target folders on the important aircraft assembly and engine facilities in the Tokyo area. Hansell was excited about this development and sent copies to Arnold and Admiral Halsey. Instead of being impressed, Halsey complained that Hansell was simply stirring up the Japanese and requested that the reconnaissance be halted.[60]

Hansell had submitted his plan for San Antonio I, the first B-29 raid on Tokyo, to Washington on 30 October 1944. Intelligence estimates stated that the Japanese had 608 first-line fighters. Preliminary analysis of photos indicated at least 150 heavy antiaircraft guns, and intense accurate fire was predicted. Japanese radar capabilities were still unclear, but after a debate between Hansell and Harmon over countermeasures, O'Donnell decided to drop "window" (aluminum strips dropped by the bombers to confuse enemy radar) over Nagoya as a diversion. The target, in accordance with JCS directives concerning targeting, was the Nakajima-Musashino aircraft complex outside Tokyo. The plant was responsible for 27 percent of Japanese aircraft engines.[61]

As the date to execute San Antonio I approached, Hansell was confronted with three crises that presented difficulties far above the already perplexing operational frictions. In the original operational plan, Hansell's raid on Tokyo would be assisted by carrier-based Navy aircraft. This would confuse Japanese defenses and give fighter support for the Superfortresses. Because of obligations in the Philippines, Operation Hotfoot, as the Navy portion of the mission was called, was canceled. The Navy recommended that the entire mission be postponed until they could participate. With Arnold anxious for action, Hansell decided to continue with the mission without the Navy. Furthermore, if he waited for the Navy, it would appear that the XXI Bomber Command could not conduct the mission alone, and thus the separate chain of command of the Twentieth Air Force would be meaningless.[62]

The second crisis manifested itself in a message from General Arnold. Arnold had forwarded a copy of the plan for San Antonio I to General Kenney, commander of the Far Eastern air force. Kenney contended that the B-29s lacked sufficient range to carry out the mission and that Japanese fighters would shoot them out of the air in any case, and he was opposed to carrying out a daylight raid on Tokyo. Arnold professed his respect for the skeptics and said that he was inclined to agree with them. Hansell later recalled, "General Arnold did not direct me to abandon or modify the mission. Rather, he put me on record as having been warned. He left the decision up to me and said that if I chose to go ahead, then he wished me luck. The effect was chilling. The warning was coming from the very area in which I had expected the firmest support."[63] Arnold had cleared himself of culpability if the mission should fail—Hansell would bear full responsibility for any disaster. Four days before the mission was to proceed, Hansell received a message from Arnold reminding him how the success of the entire program of the Army Air Forces rested on the results of the Tokyo mission. He concluded the letter: "I know that you are doing everything within your power to make them highly successful. I am confident that because of your effort they will be successful."[64] Hansell was, however, still on his own.

The third crisis must have come as a shock for Hansell. General O'Donnell gave Hansell a hand-written note in which he suggested abandoning the daylight mission and conducting a night mission instead. Hansell explained that a night mission could not hit the target they had been directed to attack and then informed O'Donnell that if he was unwilling to lead the mission he would find someone who would. Hansell respected O'Donnell's right and obligation to write the letter and valued his honest opinion,[65] but later felt that he had made a mistake. "If I'd had a little more time, I think I would have tried to find somebody else to lead it. It's a very bad idea to give a dangerous mission to a guy who says he can't do it, but if I had put somebody else in his place, I think the effect on the 73d Bomb Wing would have been very bad. They liked Rosey O'Donnell and had confidence in him."[66] Hansell destroyed the letter and nothing more was said.

On the early morning of 17 November 1944, the 73d Wing prepared for its first raid on Japan. Hansell briefed the crews himself: "Stick together. Don't let fighter attacks break up the formations. *And put the bombs on the target.* If the bombers don't hit the target all our efforts and risks and worries and work will be for nothing. That's what we're here for. If we do our job, this is the beginning of the end for Japan. *Put the bombs on the target. You can do it*" (emphasis in original).[67] The crews took their stations in the early dawn. Twenty-four war correspondents, representing every major news outlet in the United States, made great fanfare. The flashing of camera bulbs made the scene resemble a Hollywood premier, not a bombing mission. Just as the fully loaded bombers were about to start down the single runway, the wind changed direction. For the mission to be flown, each airplane would have to be turned 180 degrees. Isley Field was so crowded that if that were accomplished, there would not have been sufficient time for the mission. Hansell was forced to scrub the operation—a painful anticlimax.[68]

Hansell's decision was quite fortunate, because a typhoon was hitting the island and if the bombers had been able to leave the field, they certainly would not have been able to land on it upon return. For seven agonizing days the B-29s sat in the mud, fully loaded as the typhoon moved north, obscuring the targets in Japan. Hansell wrote General Arnold on 22 November that for the fifth time he had called off the raid on Tokyo. The stress on Hansell was evident in the letter as he expressed his fears that the weather delays must sound like mere excuses to Arnold, and he later admitted being distressed over the loss of an F-13 the previous night. The delay was, however, beneficial because it gave Hansell a chance to build up his force with newly arrived B-29s.[69]

O'Donnell had requested some changes in the operational plan, and Hansell agreed. The original plan called for two initial points at opposite sides of the target with two bombing runs converging on the Musashino plant to confuse enemy defenses. O'Donnell's plan called for a single axis of attack. The primary objective was the Nakajima-Musashino aircraft complex; the secondary target was the docking facilities of Tokyo; and the target of last resort was the urban area of Tokyo. O'Donnell led the mission from the cockpit of *Dauntless Dottie* with Maj Robert K. Morgan (formerly of the *Memphis Belle*). O'Donnell flew the mission, but even though he did not spell it out, he let Morgan know that the plan was not his idea.[70]

In spite of the tension at the command level, the launching of the mission was quite an event. Large crowds of ground crews and engineers lined the runways with great enthusiasm. As the historian of the 497th Bomb Group described the scene, "Even the men who endlessly ran the bulldozers, and who were working on runway B, stopped work and joined the crowd as the engines on the big ships turned over. The planes commenced to taxi to the end of the runway. The sky was clear. It was the dawn of the Big Day." There was a near accident when a line of dump trucks blundered on to the runway with a B-29 clearing the obstruction by only three or four feet, but at exactly 2015 Zula time, General O'Donnell's B-29 led the first Superfortress assault on Tokyo.[71]

On the morning of 24 November 1944, 111 B-29s (representing 90 percent of those on Saipan) took off—each weighing 140,000 pounds and using nearly every inch of runway. Some crews had been on Saipan for only a week at the time of their first mission. Seventeen Superfortresses aborted and six failed to bomb because of mechanical problems, but 88 bombers made it to Tokyo, with 24 bombing the primary target and 64 bombing the secondary. They had encountered a 120-knot tailwind, which gave them a 445-mile-per-hour ground speed. Since only 7 percent of the bombs dropped were observed in the target area, the results were deemed "unsatisfactory." No attempt was made to determine the results of bombing the secondary target due to poor photographs. Antiaircraft fire was "meager to moderate" and generally inaccurate. Approximately 125 Japanese fighters attacked, but the opposition was much less fierce than feared. One B-29 was apparently rammed by a damaged Japanese fighter and went down with the entire crew. One other B-29 ditched at sea with the entire crew being rescued. Losses amounted to less than 2 percent of the attacking force.[72]

Hansell had "sweated out" the mission in the tower. The operation lasted 12 to 14 hours and the return was at night. There were no runway lights and only smudge pots illuminated the way. Two groups flew on to Guam because of the congestion and returned the next morning. The first communiqué to be released stated, "Fires in the target." "The first reconnaissance photographs showed fires still burning in central Tokyo after the attack, and smoke rising to great heights in the industrial areas that were bombed."[73] Hansell was displeased with the bombing because the targets, both primary and secondary, were far from the center of Tokyo where the fires were burning, but there would be time to improve bombing accuracy. Of the 88 bombers that attacked, only two were lost. The Japanese air force could not prevent B-29 operations over Japan. This was Hansell's moment of triumph.

World reactions were swift. Arnold sent his congratulations: "You have successfully engaged the enemy in the very heart of his empire. This marks the beginning of what I know will be a most distinguished career for the Twenty-First Bomber Command. We are proud of you. Good luck and God bless you."[74] Newspapers in America ran headlines announcing the attacks. The *Atlanta Constitution* exclaimed, "BIG FIRES RAGE IN TOKYO AFTER RAVAGING B-29 BLOW"; the *New York Times* announced, "TOKYO AIRPLANT SMASHED, FIRES RAGE IN CITY." The accounts were exaggerated, but the message was implicit—the Japanese were being paid back for Pearl Harbor. The Japanese responded by announcing that any B-29 crewmen who parachuted onto Japanese soil were "enemies of civilization and humanity" and would be killed on the spot.[75]

The hyperbole surrounding the attack was tempered by a story run by *Time* on 4 December 1944: "The Air Forces, sometimes criticized for a too sanguine view of air power's potency, took the whole Tokyo show with sober calm. . . . Possum Hansell, one of Arnold's keenest young strategists, might have been pardoned a little excess enthusiasm. Instead he waited a day, until reports and reconnaissance photographs were in, then coolly summed up: 'a good job, but not exactly up to expectations.'" O'Donnell characterized the experience as "one of the easiest missions I've been on."[76] In spite of Hansell's cautious assessment of the mission, O'Donnell's comment was perhaps the more significant of the two. The fact that there were so few losses and that Hansell had proven that a heavy bomber force could operate over Japan made this mission a personal triumph for Hansell. He best expressed the reason for that triumph:

> The decision to launch the offensive in the face of such adverse conditions and recommendations seems to reflect recklessness, and results stemmed more from good luck than sound judgment. But this first great gamble proved the feasibility of the assault. Momentum, confidence, and improved efficiency would come with experience and numbers. If the decision had been to "stand down" SAN ANTONIO I and substitute a night attack against some urban area, the result would have been catastrophic, in my opinion, particularly as regards confidence in and continuation of the Twentieth Air Force.[77]

Hansell's next concern was to keep the bombers in the air and attacking targets. On 27 November 1944, San Antonio II was launched against the Musashino plant for a second time. Eighty-one B-29s launched against Japan and 59 dropped bombs on Japan. The target was completely cloud covered, and the bombers were forced to bomb the dock and urban area by radar, with poor results. One B-29 ditched, but there were no other losses.

The Japanese attacked Isley Field twice that day, once at noon (an attack that sent Hansell and Montgomery under a jeep for protection) and again at midnight. In the second attack, Hansell and his deputy commander, Brig Gen Roger M. Ramey, witnessed a twin-engine Japanese plane strafe the runway and then crash in a violent explosion. A number of B-29s were destroyed, and Hansell saw two B-29s "burning like torches" as men worked to move the other 60-ton bombers, many of which were loaded with gas and bombs, out of harm's way. With 50-caliber ammunition going off like firecrackers, the attack reminded Hansell of a scene from Dante's *Inferno*. Nearby engineers came to the rescue, performing heroics which, according to Hansell, were "far beyond the call of duty."[78] Hansell had been concerned enough to take what measures he could by sending some B-29s to Guam, but the attacks still plagued his command.[79]

The next week brought even more disappointing results. Because of the poor weather, Hansell authorized a night radar mission against the dock and industrial areas of Tokyo to keep the pressure on the enemy. On the night of 29 November, 24 B-29s bombed the primary target with two aircraft bombing other targets. The results were negligible and one Superfortress was missing. On 3 December, 76 B-29s struck out for the Musashino plant, once again on a daylight mission code-named San Antonio III. Fifty-nine planes bombed the primary target with seven B-29s bombing undesignated targets. Only 1 percent of the bombs dropped over the primary target fell within one thousand feet of the aiming point, and six B-29s were lost and six damaged. On 8 December, 79 B-29s attacked Iwo Jima with no opposition and 7/10 to 10/10 cloud cover, which totally obscured the target. There were no casualties, but no positive results either.[80]

The pressure was on Hansell to produce results. On 2 December 1944, he wrote to Norstad: "I am not at all satisfied with the results of our precision bombing." Hansell proposed creating a Lead Crew School because, he continued, "I believe the best way to correct this problem is to reindoctrinate and reeducate the lead crews." Graduates of the school would wear distinctive insignia to boost their morale.[81]

On 7 December 1944, Norstad sent a supportive letter to Hansell: "You and Ramey have done a really professional job of your first operation and I am proud of you." In reference to General Arnold, Norstad knew Hansell's fears and addressed them: "I knew you would worry about the Chief's feelings at that time [SAN ANTONIO I] since you know him well enough to realize that he would be very much keyed up until the first show was over. He was impatient, but his impatience was directed against circumstances and not against you. You were not 'on the pan' at any time." After the fourth and fifth postponement Arnold was disturbed, but when Norstad had indicated that it was not a good idea to put the heat on Hansell under the circumstances, "He replied, 'Who said anything about putting the heat on Possum?,' in a rather irritated manner. I hope you will accept the fact that you had, and have, the full support of all us back here."[82]

Norstad then gave Hansell two important hints as to how he could please Arnold. First, Hansell had written a fairly detailed letter to Arnold explaining the delays in San Antonio I and many other detailed aspects of his operations. Norstad cautioned against sending such a letter in the future: "The Boss likes to get letters. Don't make them too long; don't talk about minor troubles or problems. I would suggest that you send him a personal letter at least once every two weeks and include therein one or two interesting points that he can get his teeth into and perhaps take up at the chief of staff's meeting." It was obvious that Arnold had been too involved in Hansell's initial operation and that, in the future, information from Hansell to Arnold should be somewhat limited.[83]

Another important point was public relations. Norstad praised Colonel McKelway for his excellent work: "The handling at your end of public relations on the first operation was excellent. It got very good play here, both in the press and on the radio, and the tone of it was very, very good. We are going to send you from time to time our 'party line.' We are doing this also for LeMay. My thought in this is that we will get General Arnold from time to time, in his public announcements, to set the keynotes and following that, all our public relations will be oriented to the points he makes. I hope you will see fit to follow this line and to give me any comments or recommendations you have on it." This letter is characteristic of the correspondence between Norstad and Hansell— praise and support, followed by subtle suggestions and hints that things could be better.[84]

This letter might have reassured Hansell, but the fact remains that he was fighting a losing battle, not against the Japanese, but against both his immediate superiors and his immediate subordinates. In a letter to Arnold dated 29 November 1944, Norstad suggested bombing the Imperial Palace in Tokyo on 7 December 1944 to commemorate the third anniversary of Pearl Harbor. This suggestion illustrates either a lack of understanding of what kind of bombing campaign Hansell was running or a lack of respect for it. Norstad's only problem with the proposed attack was that it might bring serious consequences to Allied prisoners of war. Arnold returned the letter, with a hand-written reply at the top, "Gen. Norstad[,] Not at this time—our position—bombing factories, docks, etc. is sound—later destroy the whole city." Norstad wanted to use Hansell's force to bomb a purely political target, while Arnold was just biding his time before the cities of Japan were laid waste by incendiary attack. Neither of these options was part of Hansell's plan.[85]

Hansell was still unaware of the attitude in Washington, but he was very much aware of the problems he was having with his wing and group commanders. In a critique of a mission that failed to hit the target, General O'Donnell praised his group commanders for carrying out a tough mission and told them he was proud of them and that they were doing well. When he turned the meeting over to Hansell they were all in for a shock. Hansell told them, "I don't agree with Rosie. I don't think you're earning your salt out here. And the mission, if it continues like it is [—] the operation will fail."[86] Colonel Montgomery, who witnessed the scene, remembered the negative impact the event had on the 73d Wing, because Rosie O'Donnell was a very popular commander and the bomber crews were just as frustrated as Hansell over the bombing results. Hansell obviously made an error in judgment, but by this time he was frustrated by the poor bombing results. The weather was certainly not cooperative, with either extensive cloud cover completely covering targets or the winds at high altitude making the bombardiers' job very difficult. But Hansell's outburst was caused by his belief that his wing commander and group commanders were not with him. Hansell felt that high-altitude precision bombing would work if O'Donnell and the others gave it time and effort.

On 13 December, 82 B-29s attacked the Mitsubishi Aircraft Engine Works plant at Nagoya. Opposition was heavy for one squadron, and total wing losses amounted to four Superfortresses lost and 31 damaged. Bombing results were, however, termed "good," with 16 percent of the bombs landing within a thousand feet of the aiming point. It was later learned that 264 workers were killed and capacity fell by 25 percent.[87] But the encouraging news came only after a near disaster. A tropical storm hit Saipan before the B-29s could return. Hansell sweated out much of the mission in the tower listening to calls from crews nearly out of fuel and nearing the field. McKelway recorded the scene: "This night, this unforgettable night, Possum and Rosy stood in the rain for twenty-five minutes in a silence that ached and groaned with agony, screamed with apprehension, and made no sound."[88] The weather broke just in time to avert disaster, as Hansell watched the air traffic control sergeant bring each plane in "without a hint of panic." Hansell later recalled, "I realized that I really was quite helpless. The real commander of the XXIst Bomber Command was a noncommissioned officer who was functioning superbly as tower operator."[89]

On 18 December, 63 B-29s bombed the Mitsubishi plant in Nagoya for a second time. Results were disappointing with most of the damage being caused by fires set in the city by bombs that missed the target. Four bombers were destroyed in the mission. This only convinced Hansell further that he needed to set up the Lead Crew School as soon as possible; the situation had to be salvaged—the bombs had to hit their targets.[90]

Norstad too felt that action must be taken to change the situation, but he had something more radical in mind. Bolstered by the results of LeMay's incendiary attack on a military storage area in Hankow, China, on 18 December and his own keen interest in incendiary attacks, Norstad sent Hansell a directive on 19 December (in Arnold's name) to launch a full-scale incendiary attack on Nagoya as soon as one hundred B-29s were ready to go. He indicated that it was an "urgent requirement for planning purposes."[91]

Hansell protested the directive directly to Arnold. He pointed out that with great difficulty he had implanted the principle that the mission of the XXI Bomber Command was the destruction of primary targets by sustained attacks using both visual and radar precision bombing methods. Hansell felt that incendiaries did not have the ballistic characteristics to hit precision targets. Norstad, of course, had no intention of attacking "precision" targets, at least not the way Hansell defined the term. Hansell further explained to Arnold that even though he could claim no great success as yet, any diversions from his plan for selective bombing would undermine his efforts and impede the progress that "was beginning to be encouraging for the future."[92]

Norstad replied immediately, assuring Hansell that the Japanese aircraft industry continued to carry an "overriding priority" and that the incendiary mission was for test purposes only. Hansell took Norstad at his word and promised to run the test mission as soon as his scheduled missions were flown. Hansell must have felt that the concept of precision bombing had been preserved, but he also must have felt apprehension about the end to which the incendiary tests might lead.[93]

Hansell had long been under pressure to use incendiaries and, by coincidence, the 22 December 1944 attack on Nagoya was an incendiary attack. It was, however, conducted in daylight and at high altitude. The bombs were dropped by radar because the cloud cover was 10/10. The 2.27 tons of M-76 incendiary bombs did little damage, and there was no loss of production at the Mitsubishi engine plant. On 27 December 1944 Hansell launched his last attack of the year on the Nakajima-Musashino complex outside Tokyo. The attack was a failure, with the bombs doing little damage to the target. The attack did inadvertently set fire to a hospital, thus giving the Japanese the excuse to accuse the American "devils" of intentionally targeting hospitals, schools, and private homes.[94]

By the end of December, Hansell was in his new headquarters on Guam. On 1 January 1945 Hansell received New Year's greetings from General Arnold, which read in part: "You have brought to a great many Japanese the realization of what this war holds for them. The year to come will provide you with many opportunities to drive that idea home."[95] Hansell's efforts had paid off. He had set up B-29 operations under incredibly difficult circumstances, and he had proven that his Superfortresses could range over Japan at high altitudes. With experience and better understanding of Japanese weather conditions would come more accurate bombing and fewer aborts. Soon his efforts to improve the supply situation would pay off and a permanent depot would at last be operating. At least two additional wings were scheduled to arrive at the beginning of the year, and reinforcements would allow him to put more pressure on Japanese industry. The capture of Iwo Jima, scheduled for early 1945, would provide an emergency landing field, fighter bases, and improved weather forecasts, and would end the attacks on his own airfields. Hansell had much to do, but with the support of General Arnold, the new year looked promising indeed.

Notes

1. Haywood S. Hansell Jr., *Strategic Air War against Japan* (Maxwell AFB, Ala.: Air War College, Airpower Research Institute, 1980) 45–46; and Barney Giles, interviewed by Murray Green, 12 May 1970, Murray Green Collection, US Air Force Academy Library, Colorado Springs, Colo.

2. Giles.

3. Thomas A. Coffey, *Hap: The Story of the U.S. Air Force and the Man Who Built It, General Henry "Hap" Arnold* (New York: Viking Press, 1982), 336, 354–55; and Haywood S. Hansell Jr., interviewed by Murray Green, 19 April 1967, Murray Green Collection, US Air Force Academy Library, Colorado Springs, Colo.

4. Col Emmett O'Donnell to Gen Henry Arnold, letter, 7 February 1944, Record Group 18, File 372.2, Box 17, National Archives, Washington, D.C.

5. History, 73d Bombardment Wing (very heavy), May–June 1944, Tactical Doctrine, AFHRA, Maxwell AFB, Ala.; and Hansell, *Strategic Air War against Japan*, 32.

6. Hansell, *Strategic Air War against Japan*, 33.

7. Haywood S. Hansell Jr., *Strategic Air War against Germany and Japan: A Memoir* (Washington, D.C.: Government Printing Office, 1986), 170–71; and Coffey, 355.

8. E. Bartlett Kerr, *Flames over Tokyo: The U.S. Army Air Forces' Incendiary Campaign against Japan, 1944–1945* (New York: Donald I. Fine, 1991), 90.

9. Haywood S. Hansell Jr., interviewed by Murray Green, 2 January 1970, US Air Force Academy, Colorado Springs, Colo.

10. *Washington Post,* September 1944.

11. Mrs. Haywood S. Hansell Jr., interviewed by author, 21 March 1992.

12. Ibid.

13. Hansell, *Strategic Air War against Japan,* 33; and Dennett Hansell, interviewed by author, 21 March 1992.

14. Hansell, *Strategic Air War against Japan,* 33; and Wilbur H. Morrison, *Point of No Return: The Story of the Twentieth Air Force* (New York: Times Books, 1979), 157.

15. Hansell, *Strategic Air War against Germany and Japan,* 173; and Hansell, *Strategic Air War against Japan,* 33–34.

16. Wesley Frank Craven and James Lea Cate, *The Army Air Forces in World War II,* vol. 5, *The Pacific: Matterhorn to Nagaski, June 1944 to August 1945* (1953; new imprint, Washington, D.C.: Office of Air Force History, 1983), 546.

17. Ibid., 546, 548; and "Target Hiroshima" from "The Twentieth Century with Walter Cronkite" (CBS), n.d.

18. Hansell, *Strategic Air War against Japan*, 34.

19. Ibid., 49; and Craven and Cate, 27, 547–48.

20. Hansell, *Strategic Air War against Germany and Japan*, 185, 187, 195.

21. Craven and Cate, 517; and Morrison, 158.

22. Craven and Cate, 515, 517; Hansell, *Strategic Air War against Japan*, 34; and Hansell, *Strategic Air War against Germany and Japan*, 174.

23. Craven and Cate, 536.

24. Ibid., 536, 543; Hansell, *Strategic Air War against Japan*, 34.

25. Hansell, *Strategic Air War against Germany and Japan*, 162–163; and Curtis E. LeMay and Bill Yenne, *Superfortress: The Story of the B-29 and American Air Power* (New York: Berkley Books, 1988), 98; and Haywood Hansell, taped interview by Bill Yenne, n.d., provided to the author by Bill Yenne.

26. Craven and Cate, 544.

27. Hansell, *Strategic Air War against Japan*, 43–44; and Conrad C. Crane, *Bombs, Cities, and Civilians: American Airpower Strategy in World War II* (Lawrence, Kans.: University Press of Kansas, 1993), 128.

28. Hansell, *Strategic Air War against Germany and Japan*, 171; and Crane, 128.

29. Hansell, *Strategic Air War against Japan*, 48; Hansell, *Strategic Air War against Germany and Japan*, 170; Crane, 67–68, 74, 128; Lauris Norstad to Haywood Hansell, letter, 7 October 1944, Box B-11, Curtis E. LeMay Papers, Library of Congress, Washington, D.C.; and Morrison, 159.

30. Hansell, *Strategic Air War against Japan*, 44; and Ronald Schaffer, *Wings of Judgment: American Bombing in World War II* (New York: Oxford University Press, 1985), 124.

31. Hansell, *Strategic Air War against Germany and Japan*, 197; and Hansell, *Strategic Air War against Japan*, 41.

32. Hansell, *Strategic Air War against Japan*, 42–43.

33. Craven and Cate, 507; and Hansell, *Strategic Air War against Japan*, 45–46.

34. Michael S. Sherry, *The Rise of American Air Power: The Creation of Armageddon* (New Haven: Yale University Press, 1987), 222–23.

35. Craven and Cate, 55.

36. Crane, 141.

37. Wesley Frank Craven and James Lea Cate, *The Army Air Forces in World War II*, vol. 6, *Men and Planes* (1953; new imprint, Washington, D.C.: Office of Air Force History, 1983), 55.

38. Hansell, *Strategic Air War against Japan*, 34–35, 50.

39. Schaffer, 121; Sherry, 229, 258; and Hansell, *Strategic Air War against Japan*, 51.

40. Hansell, *Strategic Air War against Japan*, 51.

41. Report of the Committee of Operations Analysts, 11 November 1944, Record Group 218, Box 65, National Archives, Washington, D.C.; Schaffer, 111; Sherry, 228; and Hansell, *Strategic Air War against Japan*, 51.

42. Schaffer, 107–98, 115; and Sherry, 228.

43. Sherry, 230.

44. Haywood Hansell to Henry Arnold, letter, 26 July 1944, Record Group 18, File 373.2, National Archives, Washington, D.C.

45. Hansell, *Strategic Air War against Japan*, 129.

46. Schaffer, 30.

47. Ibid., 164.

48. Robert T. Finney, *History of the Air Corps Tactical School, 1920–1940* (Washington, D.C.: Center for Air Force History, 1992), 40, 80, 82; Emmett O'Donnell, interviewed by Jack Loosbrock, 27 March 1970, Murray Green Collection, US Air Force Academy Library, Colorado Springs, Colo.; and Crane, 11.

49. Sherry, 179.

50. Schaffer, 182.

51. Hansell, *Strategic Air War against Japan*, 61.

52. Sherry, 228–29.

53. John B. Montgomery, interviewed by Murray Green, 8 August 1974, Murray Green Collection, US Air Force Academy Library, Colorado Springs, Colo.

54. Sherry, 184; and James M. Boyle, "The XXI Bomber Command: Primary Factor in the Defeat of Japan" (thesis, St. Louis University, 1964), 61.

55. Hansell, *Strategic Air War against Japan*, 42.

56. Craven and Cate, *Matterhorn to Nagaski*, 550.

57. Mission Folders, nos. 1, 2, 3, 4, and 6, Record Group 18, National Archives, Washington, D.C.

58. History, 298th Bomb Group, 1 October 1944–30 November 1944, AFHRA, Maxwell AFB, Ala.; Haywood Hansell to Lauris Norstad, letter, 1 November 1944, Record Group 18, File 201, National Archives, Washington, D.C.; Lauris Norstad to Haywood Hansell, letter, 13 November 1944, Record Group 18, File 201, National Archives, Washington, D.C.; Hansell, *Strategic Air War against Japan*, 36–37; and Sherry, 224.

59. Craven and Cate, *Matterhorn to Nagaski*, 550; Mission Folder, no. 5, Record Group 18, National Archives, Washington, D.C.

60. Hansell, *Strategic Air War against Japan*, 36; Craven and Cate, *Matterhorn to Nagaski*, 555; and Hansell, Yenne interview.

61. Craven and Cate, *Matterhorn to Nagaski*, 554, 556; Lee Kennett, *A History of Strategic Bombing* (New York: Charles Scribner's Sons, 1982), 169; and Mission Folder, no. 7, XXI Bomber Command, Record Group 18, National Archives, Washington, D.C.

62. Hansell, *Strategic Air War against Germany and Japan*, 183.

63. Hansell, *Strategic Air War against Japan*, 37; Hansell, Yenne interview; and LeMay and Yenne, 101.

64. Henry Arnold to Haywood Hansell, letter, 13 November 1944, Record Group 18, File 201, National Archives, Washington, D.C.

65. Hansell, *Strategic Air War against Japan*, 37–38.

66. Hansell, Yenne interview; and LeMay and Yenne, 103.

67. Hansell, *Strategic Air War against Japan*, 38.

68. Craven and Cate, *Matterhorn to Nagaski*, 558; and Hansell, *Strategic Air War against Japan*, 38.

69. Hansell, *Strategic Air War against Japan*, 39; Haywood Hansell to Henry Arnold, letter, 22 November 1944, Record Group 18, File 201, National Archives, Washington, D.C.; and Craven and Cate, *Matterhorn to Nagaski*, 558.

70. Hansell, *Strategic Air War against Japan*, 38; and Robert Morgan, telephone interview by author, 12 July 1994.

71. History, 497th Bomb Group, 1 November 1944–30 November 1944, AFHRA, Maxwell AFB, Ala.

72. Hansell, *Strategic Air War against Germany and Japan*, 189; Hansell, *Strategic Air War against Japan*, 39; Mission Folder, no. 7; and Craven and Cate, *Matterhorn to Nagaski*, 558–59.

73. Communiqué, 24 November 1944, Record Group 18, File 201, National Archives, Washington, D.C.

74. Henry Arnold to Haywood Hansell, letter, 24 November 1944, Record Group 18, File 201, National Archives, Washington, D.C.

75. *Atlanta Constitution*, 25 November 1944; *New York Times*, 25 November 1944; and Kerr, 102.

76. Battlefronts, *Time*, 4 December 1944, 29.

77. Hansell, *Strategic Air War against Japan*, 40.

78. Hansell, *Strategic Air War against Germany and Japan*, 191–92; Haywood Hansell to Lauris Norstad, 2 December 1944, Record Group 18, File 201, National Archives, Washington, D.C.

79. Hansell, *Strategic Air War against Germany and Japan*, 190; Hansell, *Strategic Air War against Japan*, 40; Mission Folder, no. 8, XXI Bomber Command, Record Group 18, National Archives, Washington, D.C.; Craven and Cate, *Matterhorn to Nagaski*, 560.

80. Mission Folders, nos. 9, 10, and 11, XXI Bomber Command, Record Group 18, National Archives, Washington, D.C.; Craven and Cate, *Matterhorn to Nagaski*, 561.

81. Hansell to Norstad, 2 December 1944.

82. Lauris Norstad to Haywood Hansell, 7 December 1944, Record Group 18, File 373.2, National Archives, Washington, D.C.

83. Ibid.

84. Ibid.

85. Lauris Norstad to Henry Arnold, letter, 29 November 1944, Record Group 18, File 373.2, National Archives, Washington, D.C.

86. Montgomery, Green interview.

87. Mission Folder, no. 12, XXI Bomber Command, Record Group 18, National Archives, Washington, D.C.; and Craven and Cate, *Matterhorn to Nagaski*, 563.

88. St. Clair McKelway, "A Reporter with the B-29s," *The New Yorker*, 9 June 1945, 34.

89. Hansell, *Strategic Air War against Japan*, 41.

90. Mission Folder, no. 13, XXI Bomber Command, Record Group 18, National Archives, Washington, D.C.; Craven and Cate, *Matterhorn to Nagaski*, 563; and memorandum, 14 December 1944, Record Group 18, File 201, National Archives, Washington, D.C.

91. Craven and Cate, *Matterhorn to Nagaski*, 564; Hansell, *Strategic Air War against Japan*, 51; and Sherry, 256–57.

92. Craven and Cate, *Matterhorn to Nagaski*, 564; Hansell, *Strategic Air War against Japan*, 51; and Sherry, 256–57.

93. Craven and Cate, *Matterhorn to Nagaski*, 564.

94. Mission Folders, nos. 14 and 16, XXI Bomber Command, Record Group 18, National Archives; and Craven and Cate, *Matterhorn to Nagaski*, 564–65.

95. Henry Arnold to Haywood Hansell, letter, 1 January 1945, Haywood S. Hansell Jr. Papers, microfilm edition, AFHRA, Maxwell AFB, Ala.

Chapter 7

Tragedy

Hansell began the year 1945 by launching the test incendiary attack Norstad had advocated. Fifty-seven B-29s attacked the city of Nagoya, while 19 attacked targets of last resort. Each aircraft was loaded with 14, 350-pound M-18 incendiary clusters, but the attack was made in daylight at an altitude of between 29,000 and 30,000 feet. The bombing ignited 75 fires in the city, but the disappointing results were far from what Norstad expected—a fact that probably pleased Hansell. Five B-29s were lost in the "test" action. Having satisfied Norstad's requirements, Hansell was ready to return to his practice of attacking selected industrial targets with high explosives.[1]

On 6 January 1945 Norstad arrived at Hansell's headquarters on Guam. This was not just the benign inspection visit that Norstad had implied in his letter of 7 December. Norstad informed a shocked Hansell that he had been relieved of command. This came as a total surprise to Hansell, who later characterized his emotions upon hearing the news: "I thought the earth had fallen in—I was completely crushed."[2] Maj Gen James E. Fechet, the retired former chief of the Army Air Corps, had volunteered to travel to Guam to lessen the blow to Hansell. He informed Hansell that Arnold was dissatisfied with the XXI Bomber Command's rate of operations and wanted to consolidate the two bomber commands and base them in the Marianas. LeMay would replace Hansell as soon as the transition could be made, but Hansell was offered a job as LeMay's deputy.[3]

Hansell rejected the offer of remaining as deputy commander "under the stress of surprise and emotion," but he always felt that he had made the proper decision. LeMay had been Hansell's subordinate in the 1st Bomb Wing in England and now, under the new command arrangement, would be his commander. Hansell knew that this new situation would not work: "I knew him [LeMay] well enough to know that he needed no second string to this bow. He did not need a second in command, and I would have been unhappy as a figurehead.

189

Furthermore, it is not a good thing to replace a commander and leave him in a subordinate position in his own outfit."[4] Even though Hansell could have had his choice of command assignments, he decided to return home. Hansell's strong sense of honor forbade him from staying on with the command he had built and loved, just as when he had been relieved as captain of cadets at Sewanee Military Academy and had rejected his West Point appointment.[5]

St. Clair McKelway, who was quartered very close to Hansell's tent and kept a close watch on his activities, approached Hansell to ask the reason for Norstad's visit. It was then he learned that Hansell had been relieved of command. When asked the reason, Hansell replied, "I don't *think*—'he emphasized and considered the word'—that they are dissatisfied with the way I've been running things. There is nothing to indicate that—I think what's happened is that the boss [Arnold] has decided LeMay is the best man to go on with this from here out."[6] Hansell would spend nearly the next half century pondering the reasons for his relief.

A number of factors were responsible for Hansell's downfall. One was his relationship with seniors and subordinates. The incident with Seventh Air Force Commander Gen Willis Hale over Isley Field was foremost in Hansell's mind in March 1945 when he wrote about the event in detail to General Harmon.[7] Hansell's chief of staff, Colonel Montgomery, also suspected that this and other incidents played a part in the decision: "Possum had gotten in some bad straits with people in the theater[.] General Hale, he crossed with him, and O'Donnell never liked Hansell. He was a close friend of Arnold's I'm sure. In fact, Rosie told me, he did what he could to encourage Hap to get rid of Possum. I always believed, I don't have any proof of this, but I always believed that Rosie was the prime factor in getting Possum out of there."[8] Hansell's difficulties with other commanders in the Marianas had indeed done him no good, but this alone was not the reason.

Hansell believed that Arnold had been under pressure from General Marshall or President Roosevelt to produce results. Norstad later recalled how Arnold was embarrassed about the delays in Hansell's first bombing mission. In fact, Arnold had a rule never to tell the president about a bombing mission until it was completed. In the case of San Antonio I, he had broken his own rule and was chagrined at the delays. He was, as Norstad reported, "embarrassed and mad at everybody, everybody. He was angry as hell—with me—with Hansell—with anybody who had anything to do with it."[9]

As we have seen, Hansell's correspondence with Arnold also disappointed "the Boss." Hansell was explaining in detail why his missions were not going as planned, and Arnold was comparing his letters to the terse missives of LeMay. Colonel Montgomery recalled Arnold's attitude: "LeMay was writing half-page reports telling Arnold what he did yesterday, and Hansell was writing a three-page report explaining why the mission aborted."[10] On 16 December 1944, Hansell had reported the fact that he was far from satisfied with the efficiency of his bomber operations and discussed the problem of weather and recent losses. He then explained that Dr. Edward L. Bowles, a civilian consultant on radar and electronic aids, had suggested stripping the B-29s of excess weight and launching night incendiary missions. Hansell saw the utility of such operations, but only when a new wing could be trained for night operations. He had no intention of devoting his current three wings to incendiary attacks. "I feel that our efforts can be directed against our primary target every time and that it will not be necessary to waste our bombs on large city areas as a secondary effort." Arnold did not even read the letter. At the top he scrawled, "Gen. Norstad[,] Summarize for me[.]"[11]

By the end of December, Hansell was well aware that Arnold was losing patience. Arnold reminded Hansell that they were watching him "with the greatest anticipation." He also reminded him of the obligation he had to "destroy our targets and then we must show the results so the public can judge for itself as to the effectiveness of our operations." He was willing to concede that Hansell had begun the job of destroying the Japanese aircraft industry, having just viewed the reconnaissance photos, but added, "I hope that you will send back an increasing number of pictures of increasingly interesting subjects." Finally, in his own hand, Arnold wrote at the bottom of the letter, "I am not satisfied with the 'abortives.' On that one day—21—is far too many—we must not let this continue. I want to hear from you about this."[12]

It is clear that by this time Arnold was not only displeased with Hansell's operations in the Marianas but with his handling of public relations as well. Hansell had taken his policy of being honest with the press too far for Arnold. On 27 December 1944, Norstad cautioned Hansell, "I believe the best thing we can do is to continue to report the facts only without any emphasis on the interpretation of those facts."[13] By January of 1945 Hansell had been quoted saying that he "had much to learn and many operational and technical difficulties to solve" concerning the B-29.[14] On 28 December 1944, the Honolulu *Advertiser* ran the headlines: "GENERAL GIVES SOBER REPORT ON BOMBER RESULTS OVER JAPAN."[15] In an interview given to *Time* after San Antonio II, Hansell admitted, "We haven't destroyed the plant—not by a damn sight." Norstad, in an attempt at damage control, was quoted, "Norstad judged the job better than he had seen in Europe." The article went on: "There was no more talk of burning Japan's paper-mache cities; some, like Nagoya or Osaka, never modernized (as Tokyo after the 1923 earthquake), might be fired by overs or shorts intended for factories on their outskirts. If so, it would be incidental."[16] Hansell had turned into a public relations problem for Arnold, and especially for Norstad who wanted to prepare the public to accept incendiary attacks. Hansell was clearly not going to follow Norstad's lead.

When Hansell was chief of staff of the Twentieth Air Force, Arnold depended upon him to bear the burden of coordinating the operations of the XX Bomber Command. When Hansell had demanded daylight precision attacks from Wolfe, Arnold had backed him up. Now Hansell was thousands of miles from Washington and Norstad was calling the shots. Norstad was very interested in incendiary attacks and sold the idea to Arnold as well. By mid-December when things were not going well for Hansell, it was apparent that Arnold was depending more and more on Norstad. Arnold never read the important 16 December letter from Hansell; Norstad summarized it at Arnold's request. It is apparent that Arnold's view of Hansell's operations came through Norstad. Hansell's rocky relationships with commanders in the theater, Arnold's disappointments in the rate and success of XXI Bomber Command operations, and Hansell's public relations problems all contributed to his downfall, but in the end it was Norstad who saw to it that Arnold fired Hansell.

Norstad realized that Hansell would not easily go along with firebombing Japan's cities and that his press releases were only confirming his commitment to daylight precision attacks and thus not preparing the public for the eventuality of urban area attacks. In Norstad's eyes, Hansell had to go. Years later Norstad was asked if he was only the "hatchet man" in the dismissal of Hansell. He revealed that he was much more: "I was more than a hatchet man. . . . I had to decide to take the action before we lost the goddamned war. That was part of it, because the Old Man really had to come to a point where he was torn between his great fondness for Hansell—very warm personal feeling—and what had developed. And surely there were . . . more circumstances in which Hansell had no control, and over those which he did have control, utter absolute complete and irreversible lack of competence."[17] Norstad and Hansell had been friends, so this judgment of Hansell's abilities was not prompted by personal animosity. Norstad had little appreciation of what Hansell had accomplished under very trying conditions, and he saw Hansell as an impediment to the proposed incendiary raids against Japanese cities. Hansell's belief in daylight precision bombing had cost him "the best job in the Air Force."

General Ramey flew back to China with LeMay to take over the XX Bomber Command. The two weeks remaining in Hansell's command were most unpleasant for him and those around him, but the daylight precision missions continued. On 9 January 1945 another attack on the Nakajima-Musashino aircraft complex near Tokyo was disappointing, with only 24 bombs landing in the plant site at a cost of six B-29s. On 14 January, 73 B-29s were launched against the Mitsubishi Aircraft Works at Nagoya. Forty Superfortresses bombed the plant, but only four bombs hit the works and four aircraft were lost.[18]

Hansell signed the last operational orders as commander of the XXI Bomber Command on 18 January 1945. The mission was code named Fruitcake I, and its target was the Kawasaki engine and airframe complex at Akashi, which accounted for 12 percent of combat engines and 17 percent of combat airframes built in Japan. On the morning of 19 January 1945, 78 B-29s lifted off for the target, with 62 actually bombing the primary. The bombers released 152.5 tons of bombs over the target in clear weather, and the bomb damage assessment (BDA) estimates recorded 129 hits on the engine and assembly plants. Thirty-nine percent of the roof area was destroyed at the airframe facility, and 58 percent of the roof area of the engine plant was destroyed. The B-29s suffered no losses.[19]

Hansell was undoubtedly pleased with this mission and saw its results as an indication that his efforts had not been in vain and, more importantly, as a vindication of his belief in selective bombing. Yet, the attack was far more successful than air force intelligence had determined. The United States Strategic Bombing Survey reported after the war: "The first attack on Akashi, on 19 January 1945 . . . was in large force. Every important building in the engine and air-frame branches was [sic] hit and production was cut 90 percent." Even though the machine tools suffered little damage, the plant itself was out of business. "Following this disastrous attack, the company moved 94 percent of all machine tools to dispersed locations. Therefore, when the Twentieth Air Force again bombed Akashi in small force on 26 June 1945 it was attacking what amounted to almost an empty plant, intended only for limited assembly operations."[20] The most successful daylight precision-bombing mission of Hansell's career came too late, but plainly demonstrated that under the right conditions, it could be done. LeMay took over the XXI Bomber Command on 20 January 1945.

Hansell's last days in Guam were spent winding up his responsibilities with the XXI Bomber Command and preparing for his new life in the States. On 8 January 1945, Hansell wrote Arnold in his usual gracious manner: "General Norstad arrived yesterday and informed me of your decision to relieve me of this command, and replace me with General LeMay. I was surprised, but I accept your decision." He had but one favor to ask, "I have a request to make. It is this: I should like to be protected against the well-meant efforts of my friends to find me a job that is 'commensurate with my varied experience' or one that will absorb my energies. I am being relieved of the best job in the Air Forces; my energies are, at least temporarily, spent. It has been my lot to prepare for and pioneer both the air offensive against Germany and that against Japan. I should like a job now which will afford me the time and opportunity to rehabilitate myself." Hansell's request was to command a training wing in the southwestern United States.[21]

On 14 January 1945, Hansell defended his actions as XXI Bomber Command commander in a 10-page letter to Arnold. He explained in detail the problems he faced in the Marianas. He told Arnold of the trials and tribulations of converting the 73d Bomb Wing from night radar bombing to daylight precision bombing. O'Donnell had been loyal enough, in Hansell's opinion, but the group commanders had been slower to "swing into line." He had considered relieving some of them and sending them back to the States for reassignment with the 315th Wing, which would be trained in night radar operations. Hansell's second problem was the deplorable lack of bombing accuracy, but he indicated to Arnold that bombing accuracy was "on its way to solution." He had insisted on more bombing practice and had instituted the Lead Crew School. His third problem was the "abortives" for the B-29. Here he reminded Arnold that the B-29 was a new airplane and that there were incomplete maintenance facilities and no supply depot. Only about 3 percent of the requests on the depot had been filled. Hansell also felt that he had made the "mistake of driving the force too hard," while attempting to fly as many missions as possible. Finally Hansell wrote of his efforts to improve air/sea rescue, listing the many safeguards he had put in place to save downed B-29 crews. In light of these difficulties, Hansell felt that he had not done badly at all.[22]

Hansell reminded Arnold that with the approaching capture of Iwo Jima the toughest part of "our air war" was nearing its end. The capture of that small island would provide better air/sea rescue, base defense, fighter cover for the B-29s, and much improved weather reports. "I have been dissatisfied with the effectiveness of our operations and have put extremely heavy pressure on the 73d Wing to correct this deficiency. Nevertheless, a glance at their accomplishments so far as compared with like operations of the 58th Wing doesn't look too bad." In terms of numbers of aircraft airborne on combat operations, aborts, total bomb tonnage dropped, casualties, and other considerations, the 73d Wing had compiled more favorable statistics on their first seven major missions than had the 58th. In conclusion, Hansell expressed his regrets that Arnold had not fully considered all the difficulties involved in launching B-29 strikes from the Marianas: "I feel, on reflection, that I have erred in not passing on to you my problems in more detail. I have felt that my first consideration should have been to solve my problems as best I could, rather than to send complaints to you. Perhaps I have overdone this conception." Arnold passed the letter on to General Norstad; it is doubtful if Arnold even read it.[23]

Hansell completed the difficult final two weeks in the Marianas with typical grace and style. Toward the end he visited the crew of the *Joltin' Josie* on Saipan. He had a special gift for the crew chief, Master Sergeant Hancock. Hansell presented the sergeant with a swagger stick with a stiletto inside, which had been a gift from a friend in the Royal Air Force. Major Catton and his crew choked back the tears as he walked away—they would remember him with affection. Hansell also received warm notes from his many friends. General Harmon offered him the use of his quarters in Hawaii as he passed through on his way home.[24]

When LeMay arrived back on Guam, he remained in the background until Hansell had departed. The two men held discussions concerning the problems LeMay would inherit. Even though LeMay and Hansell remained friends, the photographs of the two during those last days reveal the pain in Hansell's face. On his final evening in the Marianas, a dinner was held for Hansell. McKelway remembered the scene: "The strain showed on Hansell. Before dinner his final night on Guam he had two glasses of sherry instead of one, and sang, to guitar accompaniment, 'Old pilots never die, never die, they just fly-y-y away-y-y-y.'"[25]

On 20 January 1945, Hansell departed Guam for the United States. A brief ceremony was held in which Hansell received the Distinguished Service Medal. The citation spoke of his service as a member of the Joint Staff Planners, Chief of Staff of the Twentieth Air Force, and finally as commander of the XXI Bomber Command: "General Hansell personally followed his plan

Generals LeMay (left) and Hansell conferring in Saipan, January 1945

[for strategic bombing] by taking units of the Twentieth Air Force to the island of Saipan from which Japan's strategic targets could be reached and started operations that have clearly demonstrated the proficiency of this weapon in daylight bombing raids on these targets. These initial successes are testimony to the soundness of his judgment and a credit to the part he played in influencing a decision committing thousands of men of the Naval, Ground and Air Forces and millions of dollars worth of materiel."[26] Ironically, it fell to Maj Gen Willis Hale, as the ranking Air Forces general on Guam, to pin the medal on Hansell. Soon Hansell was on his way home.[27]

The name "LeMay" invoked magic among the aircrews. Those who had flown B-17s in the Eighth Air Force either knew him or were very familiar with his reputation. Maj Robert Morgan knew that LeMay was a man who was going to change things and make the XXI Bomber Command successful. LeMay had a poor opinion of the staff Hansell left behind, characterizing it as "practically worthless." In the end, however, he actually kept most of Hansell's senior staff, including Colonels Montgomery and Irvine. LeMay and Hansell had discussed the staff before the change of command; Hansell had pointed out the members of the staff he had found weak, and LeMay acted upon his recommendations. Hansell had been too loyal to his subordinates, but LeMay had no such fault. LeMay informed Norstad that he was going to replace two group commanders and that he should find a replacement for O'Donnell if the commander of the 73d Bomb Wing did not "pull his outfit out of the hole." LeMay also informed Norstad that he was going to get the 73d started on some "proper training," although he continued the Lead Crew School begun by Hansell.[28]

Between late January and early March, LeMay sent his crews on training missions to bomb Japanese-held islands (much as Hansell had) and then sent them to bomb daylight precision targets in the Japanese aircraft industry. The results from these attacks were much the same Hansell had experienced. The weather continued to be a problem that even the most determined daylight attack could not solve consistently. Norstad gave LeMay the "fullest latitude" in turning from "purely strategic targets" (i.e. daylight precision attacks). He first suggested incendiary attacks on Kobe. Then, on 12 February, he suggested a major incendiary attack on Nagoya, "to secure more planning data." Arnold was again getting impatient with the commander of the XXI Bomber Command.[29]

Historian Conrad Crane suggests that LeMay undertook the incendiary attacks "without real direction from Washington," but Hansell's fate was not lost on LeMay—Norstad had made it clear that LeMay had to act quickly.[30] On 3 March 1945, LeMay pondered the possibilities in a letter to Norstad: "Another out is night bombing. I don't believe it is an efficient method of operation but this is another case of a few bombs on the target being better than no bombs at all. . . . I am working on several very radical methods of employment of the force. As soon as I have run a few tests, I'll submit the plans for your comment."[31]

The field orders for the historic Tokyo raid of 9 and 10 March 1945 were not cut until 8 March. On that day General Norstad arrived at LeMay's headquarters on Guam. When he had been briefed on the mission, Norstad alerted the Twentieth Air Force's public relations officer in Washington to prepare for "what may be an outstanding show."[32] LeMay's tactics were indeed radical. The B-29s would be stripped down so they could carry six tons of incendiary bombs per plane. They flew at night at an altitude of between 5,000 and 10,000 feet. Since enemy fighters would not be a problem, the planes flew and bombed singly. Even though many crewmen were anxious about flying so low over Tokyo, the losses were acceptable at

14 B-29s or 4.4 percent. The Japanese suffered greatly in the firestorm, with 15.8 square miles of Tokyo burned out and an official death toll of 83,793. Over forty thousand were wounded. Even considering the atomic bomb attacks, this event stands as the world's single worst man-made disaster.[33]

Next came Nagoya, Kobe, and Osaka, all of which suffered low-level night incendiary attacks. These attacks got results that certainly were quantifiable and left no question as to their success. Photographs showed many square miles of burned-out urban areas. Norstad was pleased, writing on 3 April 1945 to LeMay: "Certainly your last month's operations have been the most impressive that I have seen in the field of bombardment." Finally Norstad had seen the air force make the most effective use of its available technology. If high-altitude, precision bombardment was a slow, agonizing process, the low-altitude, area bombing offered quick results in a strategy Norstad had advocated from the beginning of his tenure with the Twentieth Air Force. The news was no longer discouraging; Norstad characterized the results of the incendiary attacks as "tremendous."[34]

While Hansell struggled with daylight precision bombardment, his contemporaries had been carried away with what historian Michael Sherry called "technological fanaticism." The bad weather had rendered Hansell's method of bombing slow and seemingly unproductive; but, using the same technology, it was possible to visit a great deal of destruction upon the enemy through area attacks. Hansell simply considered area attacks a waste of bombs since in his view the destruction of a specific number of targets could bring an enemy to his knees. But, given the expectations associated with strategic bombing from the theories of Douhet to the firebombing of Hamburg, Germany, mass destruction seemed the logical conclusion to the use of such a weapon. The B-29 and the various types of incendiary bombs available gave the air force the means to destroy whole cities, and if the weather prohibited an effective selective bombing campaign, then another method was available. Those who directed the air war against Japan sought to attack Japan with any weapon at their disposal.[35]

Another factor in "technological fanaticism" is the powerful emotions that war invokes. Americans were reluctant to use area bombing against the Germans, but the Japanese were quite a different matter. After Pearl Harbor and the Bataan Death March, Americans were ready for revenge. The racial differences, as John Dower explains in his work *War Without Mercy,* helped many Americans view the Japanese as subhuman creatures worthy of being killed in mass. Hansell was also aware of this attitude and "recalled the widespread belief that the Japanese had placed themselves outside the human community by acts of barbarism and by flouting the customs of warfare."[36] The airmen who made the decision to follow the path of incendiary attacks were certainly not barbarians, but by the same token they were caught up in the same emotions that caused the public to accept such attacks.

Another important consideration in the decision to launch the incendiary attacks was the timetable for the invasion. Operation Olympic (the invasion of the Japanese home islands) was planned for the fall of 1945. This gave the Twentieth Air Force much less time to conclude a strategic air campaign than the Eighth Air Force had enjoyed. As Hansell pointed out, when Eaker convinced Churchill to continue the daylight precision-bombing campaign, Operation Overlord was still 17 months away. Hansell and LeMay were operating under a time constraint because all hopes had been pinned on an invasion that was to come within the year.[37]

General Arnold had no clear scheme for winning the war against Japan with bombers; he simply endorsed the planned invasion. As late as May 1945 he was still exploring new "wonder" technologies such as guided missiles, 50-ton bombs, nerve gases, lethal fogs, agents that destroyed lungs, special flammable gases, and bacteriological weapons. Likewise, there was no reason for LeMay to set down a strategic rationale for the incendiary bombing because if the raids worked, a rationale could be produced. Norstad was confident that he had found the war-winning strategy, even in the face of recent United States Strategic Bombing Survey data from Europe which found the bombing of selected transportation targets to be more damaging to the enemy war effort than urban area bombing.[38] In fact, Norstad and his staff sought to redefine precision bombing by stating that incendiary attacks would be referred to as precision attacks because the bombers were aiming at a specific target, even though they had to burn much of a city to destroy it.[39]

As we have seen, Norstad and many of his pragmatic fellow officers (graduates of the "short course" at ACTS) were ready to redefine precision bombing. In reference to the use of the atomic bomb on Hiroshima Norstad wrote: "It is understood that the Secretary of War in his press conference tomorrow will release a map or Photostat of Hiroshima showing the aiming point and the general area of greatest damage. . . . It is believed here that the accuracy with which the bomb was placed may counter a thought that the CENTERBOARD [A-bomb] Project involves wanton, indiscriminate bombing."[40] Nothing could better illustrate the lack of understanding of precision bombing or the belief that the destruction of Japanese cities was an effective precision-bombing objective.

To Hansell the reason for the incendiary attacks was painfully clear. It was easy to report the destruction of a single industrial facility, but it was difficult to evaluate what the destruction of the target meant in terms of economic impact on an enemy. "On the other hand, statistics of tons of bombs dropped and of sorties flown are easily compiled, seem factual and specific, and are impressive. Photographs of burned-out cities also speak for themselves."[41] Arnold and Norstad could show the public just how effective their strategic weapon was. In the race to defeat Japan before the invasion date and before the Soviets entered the war, the Army Air Forces had given the American people the added bonus of revenge against their mortal enemies. Hansell concluded, "The abandonment of [daylight precision bombardment] has produced surprisingly little debate. . . . Perhaps this is because the very success of the urban-area attacks against Japan simply engulfed any serious inquiries as to the wisdom of the decision, the manner in which the decision was reached, or its application to future air strategy."[42]

Even though Hansell later seemed to agree that the concept of area bombing was "decisively effective" and a "sound military decision," it is highly unlikely that he was totally genuine in his remarks.[43] Hansell's objection to area bombing was that it was wasteful. The killing of civilians was distasteful to him, but his main concern was to destroy selected economic objectives. He had initially accepted the idea of urban area attacks, but only as a means to drive an enemy on the verge of surrender over the brink. He conceded that the area bombings brought results, but he could not justify the destruction of 66 Japanese cities to achieve those results. At ACTS he had learned and later taught that area bombing against civilians was not acceptable, and in his opinion the firebombing had violated a principle that had been central to American bombing doctrine from the beginning.[44]

Hansell was more specific in his assessment of area bombing when he conceded that there was no alternative to it because there was no grand strategy. It was as if destruction in and of itself could win the war, without regard to what was being destroyed or why. The atomic bomb, the successor to the labor-intensive incendiary attacks, need not have been used, according to Hansell. He believed that the use of atomic weapons in 1945 was to demonstrate the new American firepower to the Soviets and to make the Army's planned invasion of Japan unnecessary. Hansell observed that, "nothing short of the atomic bombs would divert the single-minded determination of the US Army. It had to be the invasion or the [atomic] bomb."[45]

It has been assumed that the daylight precision-bombing campaign against Japan had been a failure, but was this assessment correct? In his postwar writings, Hansell constructed a scenario that he felt could have successfully ended the war with Japan before an invasion, without using area attacks or atomic weapons. Hansell believed that with more training and better use of radar, American airmen could have put Japan's electric power system, rail transportation system, and aircraft airframe and engine factories out of commission. In addition to this, aerial mining by B-29s could have sealed Japan's fate. He estimated that this could have been accomplished with 18,500 sorties; 7,900 sorties less than the number that the XXI Bomber Command actually flew from November 1944 to August 1945.[46]

Naturally Hansell was biased in his opinion, but Michael Sherry concludes that Hansell "constructed a powerful case."[47] But more importantly, the United States Strategic Bombing Survey tends to confirm the effectiveness of daylight precision bombing. The major miscalculation Hansell and his fellow planners made in AWPD-1 was the assumption that Germany had mobilized to the limit. This was clearly not the case, and the strategic bombing campaign in Europe did not cause the disruption to German industry as expected until toward the end of the war. Japan was mobilized to the limit, and Hansell's bombing attacks had much more impact than was believed at the time.[48] The *United States Strategic Bombing Survey Summary Report* states, "During this period [November 1944 to 9 March 1945], attacks were directed almost exclusively against aircraft, primarily aircraft engine, targets. The principal aircraft engine plants were hit sufficiently heavily and persistently to convince the Japanese that these plants would inevitably be destroyed. The Japanese were thereby forced into a wholesale and hasty dispersal program."[49] Along with the bombing, the effective naval blockade brought about severe shortages of special steels requiring cobalt, nickel, and chrome. These shortages contributed to the dramatic decline in Japanese aircraft production. Aircraft engine production was reduced by 75 percent and airframe production was reduced by 60 percent.[50] Hansell had been achieving his objective through daylight precision attacks after all.

Hansell was an air pioneer of the early barnstorming days when "Three Men on a Flying Trapeze" captured the imagination of a nation. As a student and instructor at the Air Corps Tactical School he was instrumental in developing and promoting the Army Air Corps's doctrine of daylight precision bombardment. He then made his mark in creating the air intelligence necessary to carry out strategic bombing. Hansell holds the distinction of authoring AWPD-1, AWPD-42, and the plan for the Combined Bomber Offensive—the remarkable air war plans that carried the United States Army Air Forces through World War II. He was also the guiding force in planning the air war plan for the strategic bombing of Japan, at least until he departed for the Pacific. As commander of the 1st Bombardment Wing, Hansell pioneered the use of B-17s in Europe at a time when the Eighth Air Force consisted of only four groups of B-17s and two of B-24s. He was the driving force behind the creation of the Twentieth Air Force, the world's first global bomber force and forerunner of the Strategic

Air Command. Finally, he pioneered the deployment of the B-29 against Japan, overcoming great odds just to begin operations and conducting a successful campaign in the face of opposition not only from the Japanese but also from Washington and his own subordinate commanders. In short, Hansell played a central and mostly unsung role in the ascendancy of American airpower before and during World War II.

Yet, Hansell's importance certainly transcends the fact that he served in important assignments during the war. Hansell was an innovator who helped create and give wing to an important and uniquely American air war doctrine. At ACTS Hansell had taught the principles of daylight precision bombing; the air war plans he wrote ensured that this doctrine was at the very center of the American strategic air war against Germany. As a general in command of B-17s and later B-29s, Hansell worked tirelessly to see his air war doctrine come to fruition. By early 1945 Hansell had become almost the lone champion of daylight precision bombing, and his dismissal as commander of the XXI Bomber Command marked a drastic change in American air war doctrine. Instead of practicing selective strategic bombing, the Army Air Forces resorted first to urban area bombing using incendiary weapons and then to the destructive power of nuclear weapons.

After Hansell's retirement in 1946 and the creation of the United States Air Force in 1947, American air doctrine depended more and more upon a Douhetian strategy using nuclear weapons. In 1948 the new Strategic Air Command selected aiming points with the primary objective of annihilating population centers. B-29s were deployed in the Korean War to bomb the North Korean capital of Pyongyang, but the resolve of the enemy was not broken. The concept of massive retaliation evolved from the incendiary and nuclear attacks on Japan and virtually held the world hostage for nearly half a century. In Vietnam, Rolling Thunder and Linebacker I and II were deployed against a simple economy and a resolute enemy; and if they yielded results, they did so at great cost.[51] Throughout this time Hansell continued to proclaim his selective bombing doctrine. In 1966 he wrote of the inadequacy of American nuclear weapons to respond to every contingency: "Strange as it sounds, we are back in our original argument. If we are going back to World War II tactics on the ground in order to achieve flexibility of response, I think we may have to go back to strategic bombing attacks against industrial targets using limited weapons. We can apply flexible response in air warfare if need be. We can go all the way from megaton 'H' bombs down to low-yield atomic bombs, and on down to conventional bombs."[52]

Hansell was also a strong advocate of the strategic defense initiative and the development of the B-2 bomber. He knew that the capabilities of a strategic bomber force were dictated by the existing technology. He therefore advocated advances in technology that would ultimately make selective bombing the most desirable and practical course for the United States Air Force to follow. During the Persian Gulf War, Hansell's precepts were fully realized: precision attacks by individual aircraft were highly effective against selected targets. According to Conrad Crane, "Traditional strategic bombing by mass raids of B-52s was not a factor in Coalition victory; instead, attacks by individual aircraft using precision tactics and technology

B-2 Bomber

B-52 Bomber

were highly effective against key targets in Baghdad, and a widespread recognition of the sincere and generally successful attempt to avoid civilian casualties in Iraqi cities demonstrated that American airmen had continued adherence to precision-bombing doctrine and had made significant progress toward achieving the ideal capabilities first envisioned at the Air Corps Tactical School almost sixty years earlier."[53]

Hansell had always known that airpower could destroy cities and kill thousands of people. His main contribution to air doctrine was the concept that through selective targeting and an ability to place the bombs on those targets, airpower could win wars by crippling an enemy's ability to supply his forces and without causing wanton death and destruction. Hansell's quest was indeed far from being quixotic because, with new aviation and weapons technology and the end of the cold war, his vision may well have become reality.

When Hansell returned to the United States toward the end of World War II he held a number of commands. In 1945 he commanded the 38th Training Wing at Williams Field, Arizona, where he trained B-29 crews for the Pacific. By June 1945 he had joined his old friend and mentor, Hal George, at Air Transport Command. He first commanded the Caribbean Wing of the Air Transport Command and then the North Atlantic Wing at Westover Field near Chicopee Falls, Massachusetts. Hansell retired from the United States Army Air Forces in 1946 at the rank of brigadier general after 19 years of service. His hearing had suffered since his days as a stunt flyer and, since he was taken off flying status, he used the disability to take early retirement.[54]

After leaving the Pacific, Hansell received letters from many people. On 1 February 1945, General Arnold wrote him a letter of encouragement. Generals Kuter and Ralph Cousins, commander of the Western Flying Training Command, congratulated Hansell on his performance as commander of the 38th Training Wing. Upon his retirement, he received a personal note of congratulations from General Spaatz. But the most revealing letter came from a Sgt Ben Sunday of the Headquarters Squadron of the Twentieth Air Force on Guam. The sergeant sent birthday greetings to the general and added, "Sir, off-the-record the enlisted men who were at Saipan always speak most highly of you and asked me to convey their very best wishes to you. . . . I would like to take the liberty to ask a personal favor. Sir, should you have an extra photo of yourself—I would be most appreciative if you would autograph it and forward to me as a reminder of the privilege of working with you and for you." If an enlisted man's view of a general is any measure of his greatness, Possum Hansell had achieved it. As Col Robert Morgan observed, "Above all, Hansell was a gentleman."[55]

Immediately after his retirement, Hansell and Hal George went into business operating Peruvian Air Lines. The Hansells moved to Lima, Peru, where Possum served as vice president of the airline. In 1949 the Peruvian government nationalized the airline; the Peruvians unceremoniously flew the Hansells back to Savannah, Georgia, in the back of a surplus C-47 transport. He then secured a position as vice president of the South Atlantic Gas Company from 1949 to 1952. During the Korean War Hansell was called back to active duty in Washington and promoted to major general. He served as chief of the Military Assistance Program and later as the Air Force's representative on the Weapons Systems Evaluation Group, working for the Office of the Assistant Secretary of Defense for Research and Development. In 1955 Hansell again retired, this time at the rank of major general.[56]

Hansell remained in the defense industry as an official of the General Electric Company in Europe. He and his wife lived in the Netherlands until his retirement in 1966. While in the Netherlands, Possum and Dotta made a decision that would hinder future historians; they burned all their personal correspondence. The Hansells moved to Hilton Head, South Carolina, where Possum enjoyed his retirement and reflected on his career and the role of airpower. He wrote three books and a number of articles during this period. He was also a member of the exclusive Madeira Club in Savannah. The club was begun in the early 1950s and was dedicated to Madeira wine, good food, and, most importantly, intellectual stimulation. The members would take turns preparing and delivering a

C-47 Transport Aircraft

scholarly paper, which was open to critique afterwards. Hansell gave his first paper in 1957 and picked up where he had left off when he returned in 1966, presenting his views on a variety of topics, including "The Need for and the Sources of Energy," "East of Eden: The Near East, Point of Crisis," "Military Posture and World Crisis," and "Ex-Comm," an analysis of the Cuban missile crisis.[57]

The postwar years did not see Hansell lose his sense of humor. In February 1951 he gave a speech before the Air War College, Maxwell AFB, Alabama, and opened his presentation with this anecdote:

> It is the story of an old Negro living on the outskirts of a small town in Mississippi. He had a reputation for insight and wisdom, and people came to him and sought his advice on all manner of things. One day a little delegation called upon him, and said: "You have a reputation in our community for unusual wisdom and we think you are quite an asset to our town. Tell us, to what do you owe this unusual gift?" And he replied: "Well, sir, wisdom come from good judgement, and good judgement come from experience, and experience come from po'r judgement." Although I make no claim to wisdom, I have at least had some experience, and I got it just that way.[58]

In spite of this self-deprecating humor, he held his views with confidence that he was right. When he received a call from the Air Force late in life, informing him that he was to be buried at the United States Air Force Academy, his very characteristic reply was, "I can't wait!"

Hansell was very active in airpower development in the 1970s and 1980s. He gave speeches at the Air Force Academy and Air War College and was preparing to deliver a speech in Canada when he passed away on 14 November 1988. He did not live to see the triumph of airpower in the Persian Gulf War, but one day during the conflict Mrs. Hansell received a phone call from a young Air Force colonel at the Pentagon. He said, "There are four of us sitting here having lunch and I'm sending the message for the others. We are all wishing that Possum Hansell could be here to see this."[59] It was not necessary for Possum to be present to witness the success of selective bombing—he had seen it all along.

Notes

1. Mission Folder, no. 17, XXI Bomber Command, Record Group 18, National Archives, Washington, D.C.; and Wesley Frank Craven and James Lea Cate, *The Army Air Forces in World War II*, vol. 5, *The Pacific: Matterhorn to Nagaski, June 1944 to August 1945* (1953; new imprint, Washington, D.C.: Office of Air Force History, 1983), 565.

2. Haywood S. Hansell Jr., interviewed by Murray Green, 2 January 1970, US Air Force Academy Library, Colorado Springs, Colo.

3. Lauris Norstad to Haywood Hansell, letter, 7 December 1944, Record Group 18, File 201, National Archives, Washington, D.C.; Hansell, Green interview; and Craven and Cate, 567.

4. Haywood S. Hansell Jr., *Strategic Air War against Japan* (Maxwell AFB, Ala.: Air War College, Airpower Research Institute, 1980), 49.

5. Barney Giles, interviewed by Murray Green, 12 May 1970, Murray Green Collection, US Air Force Academy Library, Colorado Springs, Colo.

6. St. Clair McKelway, "A Reporter with the B-29s," *The New Yorker*, 16 June 1945, 32.

7. Hansell, *Strategic Air War against Japan*, 140–43.

8. John B. Montgomery, interviewed by Murray Green, 8 August 1974, Murray Green Collection, US Air Force Academy Library, Colorado Springs, Colo.

9. Hansell, Green interview; Lauris Norstad, interviewed by Murray Green, 15 July 1969, Murray Green Collection, US Air Force Academy Library, Colorado Springs, Colo.

10. Montgomery interview.

11. Haywood Hansell to Henry Arnold, letter, 16 December 1944, Record Group 18, File 201, National Archives, Washington, D.C.

12. Henry Arnold to Haywood Hansell, letter, 27 December 1944, Record Group 18, File 201, National Archives, Washington, D.C.; for the letter with Arnold's addendum, see Haywood S. Hansell Jr. Papers, microfilm edition, AFHRA, Maxwell AFB, Ala.

13. Michael S. Sherry, *The Rise of American Air Power: The Creation of Armageddon* (New Haven: Yale University Press, 1987), 184.

14. Conrad C. Crane, *Bombs, Cities, and Civilians: American Airpower Strategy in World War II* (Lawrence, Kans.: University Press of Kansas, 1993), 129.

15. E. Bartlett Kerr, *Flames over Tokyo: The U.S. Army Air Forces' Incendiary Campaign against Japan, 1944–1945* (New York: Donald I. Fine, 1991), 119.

16. "Battle of the Pacific," *Time*, 8 January 1945, 24.

17. Norstad, Green interview.

18. McKelway, 32; Mission Folders, nos. 18 and 19, XXI Bomber Command, Record Group 18, National Archives, Washington, D.C.; and Craven and Cate, 565.

19. Mission Folder, no. 20, XXI Bomber Command, Record Group 18, National Archives; Hansell, *Strategic Air War against Japan*, 52, 58; and Craven and Cate, 565–66.

20. United States Strategic Bombing Survey Report No. 19, "Kawasaki Aircraft Industries Company, Inc.: Corporation Report No. IV. Aircraft Division," May 1947, 46.

21. Haywood Hansell to Henry Arnold, letter, 8 January 1945, Hansell Papers, microfilm edition, AFHRA, Maxwell AFB, Ala.

22. Haywood Hansell to Henry Arnold, letter, 14 January 1945, Record Group 18, File 201, National Archives, Washington, D.C.

23. Ibid.

24. Wilbur H. Morrison, *Point of No Return: The Story of the Twentieth Air Force* (New York: Times Books, 1979), 177–78; and Millard Harmon to Haywood Hansell, letter, 14 January 1945, Hansell Papers, microfilm edition, AFHRA, Maxwell AFB, Ala.

25. Haywood S. Hansell Jr., *Strategic Air War against Germany and Japan: A Memoir* (Washington, D.C.: Government Printing Office, 1986), 230; McKelway, 34; and Steve Birdsall, *Saga of the Superfortress: The Dramatic History of the B-29 and the Twentieth Air Force* (Garden City, N.Y.: Doubleday & Co., 1980), 144.

26. "Commendation for the Distinguished Service Medal," 18 December 1944, Record Group 18, File 201, National Archives, Washington, D.C.

27. McKelway, 36.

28. Curtis LeMay to Lauris Norstad, letter, 31 January 1945, Curtis E. LeMay Papers, Box B-11, Library of Congress, Washington, D.C.; Curtis LeMay to Lauris Norstad, letter, 1 February 1945, LeMay Papers, Box B-11, Library of Congress, Washington, D.C.; Hansell, *Strategic Air War against Japan*, 60; and Robert Morgan, interviewed by author, 12 July 1994.

29. Craven and Cate, 568, 571–72.

30. Crane, 7.

31. Curtis LeMay to Lauris Norstad, 3 March 1945, LeMay Papers, Box B-11, Library of Congress, Washington, D.C.

32. Craven and Cate, 614.

33. Ibid., 614–17.

34. Lauris Norstad to Curtis LeMay, letter, 3 April 1945, LeMay Papers, Box B-11, Library of Congress, Washington, D.C.

35. Sherry, 251–52, 254.

36. John W. Dower, *War Without Mercy: Race and Power in the Pacific War* (New York: Pantheon Books, 1986), passim; and Ronald Schaffer, *Wings of Judgment: American Bombing in World War II* (New York: Oxford University Press, 1985), 175.

37. Hansell, *Strategic Air War against Japan*, 75–76, 91, 93.

38. Sherry, 292; and Schaffer, 183.

39. Lt Col Hartzel Spence to Lauris Norstad, 22 May 1945, Record Group 18, File 322.01, National Archives, Washington, D.C.

40. Crane, 142.

41. Hansell, *Strategic Air War against Japan*, 48.

42. Ibid., 74.

43. Crane, 141.

44. Hansell, *Strategic Air War against Germany and Japan*, 13; and Schaffer, 30.

45. Hansell, *Strategic Air War against Japan*, 91, 93.

46. Ibid., 49, 90.

47. Sherry, 309.

48. Ibid., 267.

49. *United States Strategic Bombing Survey Summary Report (Pacific War)* (Washington, D.C.: Government Printing Office, 1 July 1946), 16.

50. Ibid., 18.

51. Sherry, 175–76; Schaffer, 190–91; and Crane, 148, 152–53.

52. Haywood S. Hansell Jr., "Strategic Air Warfare," *Aerospace Historian*, Winter 1966, 160.

53. Crane, 157.

54. Haywood Hansell, interviewed by Edgar F. Puryear, 25 February 1979.

55. Henry Arnold to Haywood Hansell, 1 February 1945, Hansell Papers, microfilm edition, AFHRA, Maxwell AFB, Ala.; Maj Gen Ralph Cousins to Haywood Hansell, letter, 25 June 1945, Hansell Papers, microfilm edition, AFHRA, Maxwell AFB, Ala.; Gen Carl Spaatz to Haywood Hansell, letter, 9 January 1947, Hansell Papers, microfilm edition, AFHRA; and Sgt Ben Sunday to Haywood Hansell, letter, 21 September 1945, Hansell Papers, microfilm edition, AFHRA, Maxwell AFB, Ala.

56. Haywood Hansell III, interviewed by author, 16 February 1992; and Mrs. Haywood S. Hansell Jr., interviewed by author, 21 March 1992.

57. Haywood Hansell III; and Mrs. Hansell.

58. "Development of the United States Concept of Bombardment Operations," 16 February 1951, Air War College, K 239.716251–75, AFHRA, Maxwell AFB, Ala.

59. Mrs. Hansell.

Bibliography

Manuscript Sources

Air Force Historical Research Agency. Maxwell AFB, Ala. Air Corps Tactical School Files. Army Air Forces Planning and Operational Records. Haywood S. Hansell Jr. Papers (microfilm).

Library of Congress, Manuscript Division, Washington, D.C. Henry H. Arnold Papers. Ira C. Eaker Papers. Curtis E. LeMay Papers. Carl Spaatz Papers.

National Archives, Washington, D.C. Headquarters Twentieth Air Force, Record Group 18.

———. Report of the Committee of Operations Analysts. Record Group 218.

US Air Force Academy Library, Special Collections, Colorado Springs, Colo. Murray Green Collection.

Books

Ambrose, Stephen E. *Rise to Globalism: American Foreign Policy, 1938–1976.* New York: Penguin Books, 1976.

Arnold, Henry H. *Global Mission.* New York: Harper & Brothers, 1949.

Bailey, Ronald H. *The Air War in Europe.* Alexandria, Va.: Time-Life Books, 1981.

Birdsall, Steve. *B-29 Superfortress.* Carrollton, Tex.: Squadron/Signal Publications, 1977.

———. *Saga of the Superfortress: The Dramatic History of the B-29 and the Twentieth Air Force.* Garden City, N.Y.: Doubleday & Co., 1980.

Bowman, Martin W. *Castles in the Air: The Story of the B-17 Flying Fortress Crews of the U.S. Eighth Air Force.* Cambridge, England: P. Stephens, 1984.

Buell, Thomas B. *Master of Sea Power: A Biography of Fleet Admiral Ernest J. King.* Boston: Little, Brown and Co., 1980.

Burns, James MacGregor. *Roosevelt: The Soldier of Freedom.* New York: Harcourt Brace Jovanovich, 1970.

Butcher, Harry C. *My Three Years with Eisenhower: The Personal Diary of Captain Henry C. Butcher, USNR, Naval Aide to General Eisenhower, 1942–1945.* New York: Simon and Schuster, 1946.

Byrd, Martha. *Chennault: Giving Wings to the Tiger.* Tuscaloosa, Ala.: University of Alabama Press, 1987.

Carrington, Charles. *Soldier at Bomber Command.* London: Leo Cooper, 1987.

Chandler, Alfred D. Jr., ed. *The Papers of Dwight David Eisenhower.* Baltimore: Johns Hopkins Press, 1970.

Clausewitz, Carl von. *On War.* Edited by Anatol Rapoport. New York: Penguin Books, 1982.

Coffey, Thomas M. *Decision over Schweinfurt: The U.S. Eighth Air Force Battle for Daylight Bombing.* New York: D. McKay Co., 1977.

———. *Hap: The Story of the U. S. Air Force and the Man Who Built It, General Henry "Hap" Arnold.* New York: Viking Press, 1982.

———. *Iron Eagle: The Turbulent Life of General Curtis LeMay.* New York: Avon Books, 1986.

Copp, DeWitt S. *A Few Great Captains: The Men and Events that Shaped the Development of U.S. Airpower.* Garden City, N.Y.: Doubleday & Co., 1980.

———. *Forged in Fire: Strategy and Decisions in the Air War over Europe, 1940–1945.* Garden City, N.Y.: Doubleday & Co., 1982.

Comer, John. *Combat Crew: A True Story of Flying and Fighting in World War II.* New York: William Morrow & Co., 1988.

Crane, Conrad C. *Bombs, Cities, and Civilians: American Airpower Strategy in World War II.* Lawrence, Kans.: University Press of Kansas, 1993.

Craven, Wesley Frank, and James Lea Cate, eds. *The Army Air Forces in World War II.* 7 vols. *1948–1958.* New imprint, Washington, D.C.: Office of Air Force History, 1983.

Davis, Burke. *The Billy Mitchell Affair.* New York: Random House, 1967.

Divine, Robert A. *The Reluctant Belligerent: American Entry Into World War II.* New York: John Wiley & Sons, 1968.

———. *Roosevelt and World War II.* New York: Penguin Books, 1981.

Doolittle, Gen James H. "Jimmy," with Carroll V. Glines. *I Could Never Be So Lucky Again.* New York: Bantam Books, 1991.

Douhet, Giulio. *The Command of the Air.* Washington, D.C.: Office of Air Force History, 1942.

Dower, John W. *War Without Mercy: Race and Power in the Pacific War.* New York: Pantheon Books, 1986.

Duerksen, Menno. *The Memphis Belle: Home at Last.* Memphis: Castle Books, 1987.

Eisenhower, David. *Eisenhower at War, 1943–1945.* New York: Random House, 1986.

Finney, Robert T. *History of the Air Corps Tactical School, 1920–1940.* Washington, D.C.: Center for Air Force History, 1992. Originally published at Maxwell AFB, Air University Press, 1955.

Frankland, Noble. *The Bombing Offensive against Germany: Outlines and Perspectives.* London: Faber & Faber, 1965.

Freeman, Roger. *The Mighty Eighth.* Garden City, N.Y.: Doubleday & Co., 1970.

Frisbee, John L., ed. *Makers of the United States Air Force.* Washington, D.C.: Office of Air Force History, 1989.

Futrell, Robert Frank. *Ideas, Concepts, Doctrine: A History of Basic Thinking in the United States Air Force, 1907–1964.* Maxwell AFB, Ala.: Aerospace Studies Institute, 1971.

Galland, Adolf. *The First and the Last: The Rise and Fall of the German Fighter Forces, 1938–1945.* Translated by Mervyn Savill. New York: Bantam Books, 1954.

Gaston, James C. *Planning the American Air War: Four Men and Nine Days in 1941.* Washington, D.C.: National Defense University Press, 1982.

Getz, C. W. "Bill," ed. *The Wild Blue Yonder: Songs of the Air Force.* 2 vols. San Mateo, Calif.: Redwood Press, 1981.

Greenfield, Kent Roberts. *American Strategy in World War II: A Reconsideration.* Baltimore: Johns Hopkins Press, 1963.

Greer, Thomas H. *The Development of Air Doctrine in the Army Air Arm, 1917–1941.* Washington, D.C.: Office of Air Force History, 1985.

Hansell, Haywood S. Jr. *The Air Plan that Defeated Hitler.* Atlanta: Higgins-McArthur/Longino and Porter, 1972.

———. *Strategic Air War against Germany and Japan: A Memoir.* Washington, D.C.: Government Printing Office, 1986.

———. *Strategic Air War against Japan.* Maxwell AFB, Ala.: Air War College, Airpower Research Institute, 1980.

———. "The Military in American Society Today: The Questions an Old-Timer Might Raise." In *The Military and Society: The Proceedings of the Fifth Military History Symposium.* Edited by David MacIsaac.

Hastings, Max. *Bomber Command.* New York: Simon and Schuster, 1979.

Hayes, Grace Person. *The History of the Joint Chiefs of Staff in World War II: The War against Japan.* Annapolis: Naval Institute Press, 1982.

Holley, I. B. *Buying Aircraft: Materiel Procurement for the Army Air Forces.* Washington, D.C.: Office of the Chief of Military History, 1964.

Ienaga, Saburo. *The Pacific War, 1931–1945: A Critical Perspective on Japan's Role in World War II.* New York: Pantheon, 1978.

Infield, Glenn. *Big Week: The Classic Story of the Crucial Air Battle of WW II.* Los Angles: Pinnacle Books, 1974.

Jackson, Robert. *Storm from the Skies: The Strategic Bombing Offensive 1943–1945.* London: Arthur Barker Ltd., 1974.

James, D. Clayton. *The Years of MacArthur.* Vol. 2, *1941–1945.* Boston: Houghton Mifflin Co., 1975.

Kennett, Lee. *The First Air War, 1914–1918.* New York: Free Press, 1991.

———. *A History of Strategic Bombing.* New York: Charles Scribner's Sons, 1982.

Kenney, George C. *General Kenney Reports: A Personal History of the Pacific War.* New York: Duell, Sloan and Pearce, 1949.

Kerr, E. Bartlett. *Flames over Tokyo: The U.S. Army Air Forces' Incendiary Campaign against Japan, 1944–1945.* New York: Donald I. Fine, 1991.

Larrabee, Eric. *Commander in Chief: Franklin Delano Roosevelt, His Lieutenants, and Their War.* New York: Harper & Row, 1987.

LeMay, Curtis E., and Bill Yenne: *Superfortress: The Story of the B-29 and American Air Power.* New York: Berkley Books, 1988.

LeMay, Curtis E., with MacKinlay Kantor. *Mission with LeMay: My Story.* Garden City, N.Y.: Doubleday, 1965.

Levine, Alan J. *The Strategic Bombing of Germany, 1940–1945.* Westport, Conn.: Praeger Publishers, 1992.

Lowe, James Trapier. *A Philosophy of Air Power.* Lanham, Md.: University Press of America, 1984.

MacCloskey, Monro. *Torch and the Twelfth Air Force.* New York: Richard Rosen Press, 1971.

MacIsaac, David. *Strategic Bombing in World War II: The Story of the United States Strategic Bombing Survey.* New York: Garland, 1976.

McArthur, Charles W. *Operations Analysis in the U.S. Army Eighth Air Force in World War II.* Providence: American Mathematical Society, 1990.

McFarland, Stephen L. and Wesley P. Newton. *To Command the Sky: The Battle for Air Superiority over Germany, 1942–1944.* Washington, D.C.: Smithsonian Institution Press, 1991.

Meilinger, Phillip S. *Hoyt S. Vandenberg: The Life of a General.* Bloomington, Ind.: Indiana University Press, 1989.

Mets, David R. *Master of Airpower: General Carl A. Spaatz.* Novato, Calif.: Presidio Press, 1988.

Middlebrook, Martin. *The Schweinfurt-Regensburg Mission.* New York: Penguin Books, 1983.

Milward, Alan S. *War, Economy and Society, 1939–1945.* Los Angeles: University of California Press, 1979.

Morrison, Wilbur H. *Fortress Without a Roof: The Allied Bombing of the Third Reich.* New York: St. Martin Press, 1982.

———. *The Incredible 305th: The "Can Do" Bombers of World War II.* New York: E. P. Dutton, 1962.

————. *Point of No Return: The Story of the Twentieth Air Force.* New York: Times Books, 1979.

O'Connell, Robert L. *Of Arms and Men: A History of War, Weapons, and Aggression.* New York: Oxford University Press, 1989.

Paret, Peter, ed. *Makers of Modern Strategy: From Machiavelli to the Nuclear Age.* Princeton, N.J.: Princeton University Press, 1986.

Parton, James. *"Air Force Spoken Here": General Ira Eaker and the Command of the Air.* Bethesda, Md.: Adler & Adler, 1986.

————, ed. *Impact: The Army Air Forces' Confidential Picture History of World War II.* 10 vols. Harrisburg, Pa.: National Historical Society, 1989.

Perret, Geoffrey. *There's a War to be Won: The United States Army in World War II.* New York: Random House, 1991.

————. *Winged Victory: The Army Air Forces in World War II.* New York: Random House, 1993.

Pogue, Forrest C. *George C. Marshall.* Vol. 3, *Organizer of Victory, 1943–1945.* New York: Viking Press, 1973.

Potter, E. B. *Nimitz.* Annapolis: Naval Institute Press, 1976.

Price, Alfred. *Battle over the Reich.* New York: Charles Schribner's Sons, 1973.

Schaffer, Ronald. *Wings of Judgment: American Bombing in World War II.* New York: Oxford University Press, 1985.

Seversky, Alexander P. de. *Victory Through Air Power.* New York: Simon and Schuster, 1942.

Sherry, Michael S. *The Rise of American Air Power: The Creation of Armageddon.* New Haven: Yale University Press, 1987.

Shiner, John F. *Foulois and the U.S. Army Air Corps, 1931–1935.* Washington, D.C.: Office of Air Force History, 1983.

Sigal, Leon V. *Fighting to a Finish: The Politics of War Termination in the United States and Japan, 1945.* Ithaca, N.Y.: Cornell University Press, 1988.

Spector, Ronald H. *Eagle against the Sun: The American War with Japan.* New York: Free Press, 1985.

Speer, Albert. *Inside the Third Reich: Memoirs.* New York: Macmillan, 1970.

Time-Life Books, eds. *Japan at War.* Alexandria, Va.: Time-Life Books, 1980.

Underwood, Jeffery S. *The Wings of Democracy: The Influence of Air Power on the Roosevelt Administration, 1933–1941.* College Station, Tex.: Texas A&M University Press, 1991.

United States Army Air Forces. *The Official Guide to the Army Air Forces.* New York: Simon & Schuster, 1944.

US Government. *United States Strategic Bombing Survey: Overall Report (European War).* Washington, D.C.: Government Printing Office, 30 September 1945.

———. *United States Strategic Bombing Survey: Summary Report (Pacific War).* Washington, D.C.: Government Printing Office, 1 July 1946.

Van Creveld, Martin L. *Technology and War: From 2000 B.C. to the Present.* New York: Free Press, 1989.

Verrier, Anthony. *The Bomber Offensive.* London: Batsford, 1968.

Walser, Michael. *Just and Unjust Wars.* New York: Basic Books, 1979.

Warden, John A., III. *The Air Campaign: Planning for Combat.* Washington, D.C.: National Defense University Press, 1988.

Watts, Barry D. *The Foundations of U.S. Air Doctrine: The Problem of Friction in War.* Maxwell AFB, Ala.: Air University Press, 1984.

Weigley, Russell. *The American Way of War: A History of United States Military Strategy and Policy.* Bloomington, Ind.: Indiana University Press, 1981.

Wheeler, Burton K., and Paul F. Healy. *Yankee from the West.* Garden City, N.Y.: Doubleday & Co., 1962.

Wheeler, Keith. *Bombers over Japan.* Alexandria, Va.: Time-Life Books, 1982.

———. *The Fall of Japan.* Alexandria, Va.: Time-Life Books, 1983.

Dissertations

Boyle, James M. "The XXI Bomber Command: Primary Factor in the Defeat of Japan." Thesis, St. Louis University, 1964.

Crane, Conrad C. "The Evolution of American Strategic Bombing of Urban Areas." PhD diss., Stanford University, 1990.

Fabyanic, Thomas A. "A Critique of United States Air War Planning, 1941–1945." PhD diss., St. Louis University, 1973.

Articles

Battlefronts. *Time,* 4 December 1944, 24.

Crane, Conrad C. "Evolution of U.S. Strategic Bombing of Urban Areas." *Historian* 50 (1987–1988).

Frisbee, John L. "The Loneliness of Command." *Air Force Magazine,* July 1983.

Hansell, Haywood S., Jr. "General Laurence S. Kuter, 1905–1979." *Aerospace Historian,* June 1980.

———. "Strategic Air Warfare." *Aerospace Historian,* Winter 1966.

Hopkins, George F. "Bombing and American Conscience During World War II." *Historian* 28 (May 1966).

Keegan, John. "We Wanted Beady-Eyed Guys Just Absolutely Holding the Course." *Smithsonian* 14 (August 1983).

McKelway, St. Clair. "A Reporter with the B-29s." *The New Yorker,* 9 June 1945; 16 June 1945.

Schaffer, Ronald. "American Military Ethics in World War II." *Journal of American History* 67 (September 1980).

Shalett, Sydney. "This Possum Is Jap Poison." *Saturday Evening Post,* 25 November 1944.

Sherry, Michael. "The Slide to Total War." *New Republic* 185 (16 December 1981).

Werrell, Kenneth. "The Strategic Bombing of Germany in World War II: Costs and Accomplishments." *Journal of American History* 73 (1986–1987).

Other Sources

Cronkite, Walter. "Target Hiroshima." *The Twentieth Century with Walter Cronkite.* CBS.

Hansell family private collection.

Snyder, William P. "Developing Air Power Doctrine: An Assessment of the Air Corps Tactical School Experience." Paper presented to the Annual Conference at the Society for Military History. Fredericksburg, Va., 10 April 1992.

United States Strategic Bombing Survey Report No. 19. "Kawasaki Aircraft Industries Company, Inc. Corporation Report No. IV. Aircraft Division." 14 May 1947.

Yenne, Bill. Taped interview with Haywood Hansell and Curtis LeMay. n.d., n.p.

Newspapers

Atlanta Constitution, 6 June 1943.
Atlanta Journal, 6 June 1943–25 November 1944.
Chicago Daily Tribune, 4 December 1941.
New York Times, 25 November–4 December 1944.
Washington Post, 11 December 1941.

Index

223

Vandenberg, Hoyt S.: 43, 47, 91
Vietnam: 204

Walker, Kenneth N.: 41, 44, 67–68, 79,
   83, 95, 151, 170
War Department: 39–40, 48, 63, 67
West Point: 28, 30
Wiener-Neustadt, Austria: 130

Williamson, Luke: 36, 46, 138, 147–51,
   166, 192
Wolfe, Kenneth: 46, 138, 147–51, 166,
   192

Yawata: 149–50
YB-40: 110

Zeppelin: 6–7